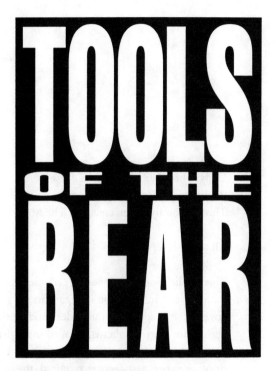

TOOLS OF THE BEAR

HOW ANY INVESTOR CAN MAKE MONEY WHEN STOCKS GO DOWN

CHARLES J. CAES

MARKETPLACE BOOKS
Columbia, Maryland

ISBN 1-883272-20-3

Printed in the United States of America.

1 2 3 4 5 6 7 8 9 0

Table of Contents

List of Tables

Preface

The stock market is an exciting theater where there are many roles and scripts. Sometimes it is a casino where contracts on the performance of stocks making up an index are sold, where stocks or stock options are sold before they are owned, where you can play a stock or option so you can win if it goes up or down in price. Few investors know all the games.

This book makes no attempt to show all the ways to play the market. Instead, it concentrates on three: short-selling, puts, and calls. There is no pretense that these subjects have not been written about extensively. There are books the size of this text just dealing with covered calls, with short-selling or with stock options. Nor is there any pretense that this book goes beyond all the others in finding new ways to make money or utilize the investment tools at hand.

This book has as its goal the education and instruction of the reader in three tools of the bear, tools of those speculators who know how to make money when the stock market is heading south. The book's technique is to simplify a generally complicated group of subjects, and to present working examples and explanations that leave the reader with no misconceptions.

Misconceptions plague all investors. In fact, if there is anything that has motivated the author into writing this and other books on the math and madness of investing, it is the general misconceptions he finds in neophyte and intermediate investors alike.

When asked the following list of questions in the classroom or in general discussions about the stock and options markets, even the more experienced independent investors were unable to answer half of them successfully. Their replies showed evidence of a lack of perspective and an inability to understand some fundamental concepts.

- Is it better to play the stock market to go down or up?

- Is it true that only stocks on the major exchanges can be sold short?

- Is low trading volume in a stock indication that the stock will go down?

- Are stocks reaching new lows poor candidates for short selling?

- Are stocks with high P/E ratios good candidates for short selling?

- Is hedging stock positions with puts or calls too expensive to be worthwhile?

- Are in-the-money options always the best bet?

- Must you either be a buyer or a seller of a put or call?

- Is it true that if an option that was out-of-the-money goes into-the-money, the owner of the contract will always make money?

- Is it true that when calls on an underlying stock go down in price, the puts on that same underlying stock go up in price?

- Is it true that an out-of-the-money call sold short always means a loss for the writer holding it when it goes into the money?

- In the case of stock splits, is the exercise value of an option affected?

These are just some of the very important questions to which this book responds in what intends to be a clear and precise method. Knowing the answers will not make you an expert; being an expert comes with well-guided and extensive experience. But knowing the answers will keep you from making some serious mistakes.

In searching these pages for the directions and answers you need to start investing more wisely, bear in mind that this book is by a scholar and researcher of investment and business math, and not by an investment counselor or broker who can prosper from selling a particular perspective. Keeping this in mind, expect that some of the advice goes against the norm. For instance, particularly expect to learn that it is very difficult to make money in the stock and options markets, and that spreading the risk is not a particularly good philosophy unless you are a man or woman of means.

Above all, this book is a text on the important rules, tools and arithmetic of playing for profit when the stock market goes down.

Charles J. Caes

Introduction

Many men and women—we will not call them "investors" because this term denotes a level of patient professionalism that is highly goal oriented, and we will not call them "speculators" because they do not have the special timing and knowledge to "play" the market—invest in the stock market because they feel their chances of making more, or even becoming rich, are much greater than if they invested in the money markets or left their money in the bank.

The truth is that it is very hard to make money in the stock market and almost impossible to make a lot of money, unless you have a great deal of money to play with in the first place—a great, great deal of money. Stocks are not only expensive but they also fluctuate in price. It takes a careful, experienced investor to always buy at the right price and sell at the right price. Additionally, many people hold on to losers for much too long a period and the opportunity cost becomes so great that even if the stock turns profitable, their return on investment is far less than they would have received if they simply purchased a certificate of deposit.

There are other difficulties in making money in the market for the small investor. He is told to spread his risk, so he distributes $10,000 or $20,000 over five or ten stocks. Some will go up and some will go down, and he'll be no better off than he would have been with some humble savings account at the local Credit Union—and his broker will make more money on the buy and sell transactions than he does on his investments. If he wanted to spread his risk, he should have purchased a couple of mutual funds. Regardless of all the advice on spreading risk (and the income it means to brokers), the rule should be to stay out of the market unless you are going to go after the big bucks. Don't play the law of averages; study hard, select a couple of good stocks, hedge your positions, and go for the money. If things change and your positions no longer look good, take your losses pell mell and try again on a couple of more stocks you have carefully researched. Just make sure you are playing with no more than 20% of your savings.

Going for the money means using all the tools that are available to you. You wouldn't bowl with a tennis ball or play tennis with a racquetball racket, so don't go into the market unless you are equipped to play the game properly.

What This Book Is About

There are many, many tools the investor needs. Among them are those he needs to make money when the market is going down or remaining stagnant. These are tools of the bear, and they are what this book is about.

The book is divided into five parts. Part 1 is an overview of the basics; Part 2 discusses short-selling; Part 3, puts; Part 4, calls; and Part 5 gives an overview of the marketplace.

These topics can be very confusing to the neophyte and some knowledge of each tool is required to fully comprehend each—which presents an instructional dilemma. Part 1, therefore, starts off with a holistic approach to the subject matter, spiraling around the topics of short-selling, puts and calls to prepare you for the detail that comes in the following parts. The objective is to give you some history of experience in the subject matter so you can better digest the definitions, explanations and examples which will eventually follow. Chapters 2 and 3 give account information, explaining what the requirements are for setting up and maintaining an account which allows you to sell stocks short or to deal in puts and calls.

School starts with Part 2, which looks specifically at short-selling stocks. The types of short-selling are reviewed in Chapter 4. These include short-selling of a purely speculative nature, hedging, shorting-against-the-box and arbitraging. It tells you the reasons you might want to sell stocks short.

Once you understand the reasons why you might want to sell stocks short, you need to know something about investment perspectives, particularly those of the bear. This is where you learn how to change your positions for profit, how it takes money to make money, and how to respond to market indicators.

Chapter 6 tells you exactly how to play the game of short-selling. Here you will be given specific examples of winning and losing transactions and how to utilize your margin account. You will learn how to determine the equity in your account, how to determine your short-selling power, and how to play some tricks—like taking dual positions.

No one enters any discipline without some misconceptions. This is fully expected in this case, too; so, Chapter 7 covers some common misconceptions that first-time and even intermediate investors have about the market. And Chapter 8 provides some guidelines to keep you from falling on your face—or, rather, having your money fall into someone else's hands.

Part 3 looks at buying puts long. Chapters 9 and 10 introduce some basic definitions and concepts about options in general, and Chapter 11 covers some basic strategies, such as types of orders and types of hedges. How to specify an order is very important to options traders and they should know the advantages and disadvantages of such strategies as fill-or-kill and contingent orders. The remaining chapters in Part 3 cover common misconceptions that new put traders have, what guidelines they should follow, and some of the special risks inherent in options trading.

Part 4 discusses calls—how you can make money or lose a lot of money. Like the writing of puts, the writing of calls means "dangerous turn ahead." You've got to be careful here, for options writers can lose a lot of money; on the other hand, they can earn quick income and give a great deal of flexibility to their portfolios. Chapter 14, therefore, looks at the special perspective of the call writer, how he can write for income or play for capital gains as he would in short-selling a stock. Chapters 17 and 18 cover some misconceptions that can lead call writers into a life of debt, and offer guidelines on how not to make a fool of oneself.

Part 5 deals with backgrounds and workings of both the stock and put and call markets.

Limitations and Capabilities

Every student must always be aware of his or her limitations and capabilities. Anyone opening this book is a student, because they are here to learn.

A book, however, can only serve as an introduction, a means of understanding basic concepts and philosophies and learning the methodology. Books do not make anyone an expert.

You can pick up a book on racquetball and it will tell you the rules of the game and a lot about history and technique. When you finish the author's words of wisdom you know the rules of the game, how to keep score, how to serve, how to volley, maybe even how to hold the racket. But that book is not going to make you a winner.

Neither is this book going to make you a winner. It will tell you the rules of the game, how to keep score, what the tools are and how they can be used. But get something straight: it takes awhile to be a winner. Proceed with caution. Solicit but weigh all advice. When in doubt, don't. And hedge!

Part
1
The Basics

1

The Three Ways

The most common approach to investing in the stock market is to first buy and then sell. This is called taking a long position, being bullish. The symbolic representation for this strategy is a full-grown black bull, hoofs well-formed to stomp and trample, horns fully developed and very sharp, ready to charge, slash and stab. Like the bull, those who buy long are chargers.

A second approach to investing in the stock market is to first sell and then buy. This is called taking a short position, being bearish. The symbolic representation for this strategy is a full grown, brown bear, fangs long and sharp, claws ready to cut away. Like the bear, those who sell short want to see their stocks cut away from the marketplace, hurt by lagging investor interest, and falling swiftly in price.

Stock Market Games

The great auction markets we collectively refer to as the stock market are actually great financial casinos where many investment games can be played.

After all,

■ You do not have to own a stock to sell it.

■   You do not have to sell a stock to make a profit.

■   You do not have to own stocks to profit by their price fluctuations.

■   You can let a dollar do the work of a hundred dollars.

■   You can profit when stocks go down in price as well as up.

Selling short is a way of selling a stock you do not own and profiting when stocks go down in price. Writing covered calls against a stock you own is one way to make a profit from the stock without having to sell the stock. Dealing in put and call options and thereby profiting (or losing) by price fluctuations in the underlying stock is a way to profit by stocks without owning them. Using margin and dealing in low-priced options is a way to make a dollar do the work of tens or hundreds of dollars.

Stock and Options Market

The games can be greatly profitable for astute investors. You already know the ones that enable you to profit when stocks go up, so let's look at the ways to profit when everyone else is losing.

These three ways are selling stocks short, buying puts, and selling calls—very risky games but ones that can also mean brand new success in the marketplace. They are not guaranteed to bring success but the risk inherent in each strategy can be greatly reduced by using combinations of strategies.

Selling Stocks Short

When you sell a stock short, you are actually selling a stock you do not own.

How in heaven's name can you do this?

Quite easily, actually. It is all very automatic. All you have to do is tell your broker you want to sell, say, 100 shares of IBM stock *short*. Your broker does the rest. He borrows the stock from another account—maybe his own—under the express condition that he will return it to the original owner on demand—and lets you sell it.

But why would you want to sell a stock before you own it?

The reason is that you are anticipating a decline in the price of the stock. Your plan is to sell it now at the higher price and buy it back at the lower price.

If your broker has borrowed the stock from one of his customers, it is relatively inexpensive for him to cover your short sale. He simply shuffles some records around. But if he has to borrow the stock from another broker because neither he nor any of his customers own enough IBM stock, then he must deposit with the other broker an amount of money equal to the current market value of the IBM shares being sold short.

This deposit gives the lending broker cash to use at will and to cover himself in case there is any default. As the IBM shares increase in value, or decrease, either broker may demand an increase or decrease in the funds used to "insure" the transaction.

You must also provide cash to cover your short position. As all short selling is done in margin accounts, you will not necessarily be required to put up an amount of money equal to the proceeds from the "sale." If the 100 shares of IBM cost $10,000, you would only have to pay enough money to cover whatever the current margin regulations may require. (The formula for margin requirements on short sales is discussed in Chapter 2.)

"But how long can I maintain my short position?" you may ask. This is a rather important question considering that the stock on which you have based your transaction has been borrowed from another account and may be called back by the owner on a few days notice.

In the case of a widely held stock like IBM, you have little worry about unexpected calls. Your broker will run interference for you by borrowing from other accounts. From a technical standpoint, as long as the broker can arrange to borrow stock, you can stay short. As trading is done today, you can stay short for as long as you would ordinarily stay long on a stock. (Long refers to the traditional transaction in which you buy first, then sell.)

Short sellers, however, have less interest in maintaining their positions for the long term. They are, by nature, speculators. They will want to take their profits or cut their losses after a reasonable time. For instance, if the shares of IBM decrease from $100 to $85 per share in a few months time, it would be wise to buy back the shares and realize the $15 per share profit unless further decline is a certainty.

Sold 100 sh. IBM at $100 per =	$10,000	
Bought 100 sh. IBM at $ 85 per =	8,500	
Profit	$ 1,500	

On the other hand, if IBM shares increase in value to $115, it would be wise to buy them back before they increase too much in value.

Sold 100 sh. IBM at $100 per =	$10,000	
Bought 100 sh. IBM at $115 per =	11,500	
Loss	$ 1,500	

There are guidelines for when to take profits or cut losses, and these will be discussed in Part Two. When to sell, when to buy—tough decisions, with the latter one the tougher for the short seller.

By now it may have dawned on you just what the major risk is in selling any stock short. Losses mount when the stock goes up and how far a stock can go up is, theoretically, limitless. But a stock can only go down to zero. In short selling, then, the amount that can be lost is always far greater than the amount that can be won.

This is to say that if you purchased IBM long at $100 per share, you know that the most you can lose is $100 per share plus commissions.

However, if you had sold IBM short at $100 per share, it could go up to $500 or $600 per share and even more before you could or were smart enough to bail out. That means you could lose five or six times what the value of the stock was when you sold short. There are safeguards to prevent such losses, of course, and these include stop-loss orders and stock-option combinations. Stop loss orders are orders to a broker to sell your stock as soon as it reaches or falls to a certain price; stock-option combinations you will learn more about later.

Buying Put Contracts

If you have the concept of short selling fixed in your mind, as well as the related risk, you can now consider a way of profiting when a stock goes down that reduces the risk of extraordinary losses, though it represents a bit more of a gamble.

This way is by buying put options.

By buying put options, you are actually dealing, not in stock, but rather in a contract giving you the right to sell shares of a given stock within a certain amount of time. Usually, each put represents 100 shares of stock.

For instance, let us consider again IBM stock currently selling at $100 per share.

Suppose you fully expect IBM will be worth only $85 per share within the next three months. This might entice you to sell short the 100 shares except for two reasons. The first is that you are afraid the stock could possibly stampede north if certain events take place; and in this case you might lose your entire investment. The second is that you only have a few hundred dollars to play with.

So, you decide to purchase a put option.

What the put does is give you the right to sell IBM at $100 per share by a certain date. And for this right you might pay $500, or whatever the market value of the put happens to be.

If IBM stock drops to $85 per share, you can buy it and IMMEDIATELY sell it for $100 per share. Why can you sell it for $100 per share? Because you have a put option giving you the right to do this. Your profit is $1,000 before commissions.

Bought 100 sh. IBM at $ 85 per	= $ 8,500
Sold 100 sh. IBM at $100 per	+ $10,000
Result	$ 1,500
Less Cost of Option	500
Profit	$ 1,000

The purchase of the put limits your risk. If IBM stock were to go up instead of down, you would lose no more than your investment in the option. As a short seller of the stock, however, you can lose much more than what the option would have cost you.

A major disadvantage is that the put contract will have a time limit. The put can expire worthless if you do not sell it before its expiration date.

Exercising rights is not very common in options trading. Most traders prefer to deal only in the options.

For instance, if you did purchase a put, in most cases (but not all—and this will be explained in Part 3) it would increase in value as the stock decreased. You can therefore sell the put at a higher price and profit it from it just as you would profit by selling a stock at a higher price than you paid for it.

Bought 1 IBM put:	$500
Sold 1 IBM put:	$750
Profit	$250

But, of course, you can also lose when the put decreases in value (as the stock goes up). Put movement in relation to stock movement is a bit complex, and this will be discussed in Part 3.

Never forget about that expiration date. If you do not exercise your option in time, it expires worthless. All puts do not expire on the same date, so you must always keep in mind the particular expiration date for your option.

Once upon a time, put trading could only be done in the OTC (over-the-counter) market by dealers who functioned specifically as market makers. But the way the OTC was set up at that time, options trading became so cumbrous that it was extremely nerve racking and difficult to close out a put contract before the expiration date.

To remedy the situation, the Chicago Board Options Exchange (CBOE), launched in 1973 to standardize call option trading, began handling put contracts in the mid-70s. The CBOE standardized expiration dates and execution prices, and in so doing brought such stability to both the put and call markets that these contracts could be traded as easily as shares of stock.

Now, it is possible for anyone to be either a buyer or seller of puts; but as the goal of this book is to show how you can benefit when stocks go down, emphasis will be placed on buying rather than selling.

Selling a Call Contract

Bearing in mind that the short seller's profits increase as the price of a stock falls, and that the put buyer's profits *can* increase when the underlying stock drops in price, notice now how the writer of calls profits. Remember that the writer of a call is the *seller of the call*.

The seller of a call is also gambling that the underlying stock will go down in price—or will at least stay at about the same price. But the call seller (writer) will not see his profits *increase* as the underlying stock goes down in price. Writing (selling) calls is an *income* play usually, and the writer will never receive more than the premium he gets when the call is written.

Puts, calls and short-selling—the differences can get confusing—let's review them once more.

The *put* is a contract giving the holder of the put the right to *sell* (usually) 100 shares of stock at a certain price within a certain time period.

The *call* is the opposite—it gives the holder the right to *buy* (usually) 100 shares of stock at a certain price within a certain time. (See Table 1-1.)

While the owner of a *put* might benefit as a *stock decreases* in price, the owner of a *call* might benefit as a *stock increases* in price. ("Might" is an important quali-

---

Table 1-1
Important Definitions

Short Sale

Selling a stock you do not actually own in anticipation of a decline in the value of the stock. The goal is to buy it back later at a lower price, but it may also be to insure paper profits in a long position. In the latter case, the strategy is called "selling short against the box." For instance, you may have a substantial profit in a stock such as Coca Cola but it is not to your advantage to take the profits in the current year. Therefore, you shell short the same number of shares that you own and then close out the long and short trades when it is to your advantage. While you have both long and short positions in the stock, you will not be affected by any price movements one way or another.

Put

A contract giving the owner the right to sell the underlying stock at a specific price during a specified period of time. It is a type of stock option contract and is the opposite of a call. The buyer and seller of the put are never dealing directly in the underlying stock but only in options on the stock.

Call

A contract giving the owner the right to buy stock at a specific price during a period of time. Calls, like puts, are used as a means for entering into the game of making money on stocks with a lower investment than would be required if one were to actually buy the underlying stocks on which options are written. Calls are also purchased as a type of insurance on short positions in the underlying stock.

---

fier here because the value of an option contract is affected by a number of variables which will be discussed in following chapters.)

But now we are speaking of "buyers." When it comes to calls, *you* want to be the seller (writer). And it stands to reason that if the buyer of a call expects to profit when the underlying stock goes up in price, you—as the writer of the call—would expect to benefit if it did not go up in price.

Let's look at some examples of call option trading, leaving in mind that each call usually represents 100 shares of the underlying stock.

> *Example #1. You sell one call contract for 100 shares of IBM stock, giving the owner of the contract the right to buy the stock at $100 per share by January 20. You receive $500 for the call you wrote. (You do not own the stock and you do not own the call.) The stock never goes beyond $100 per share by January 20. The contract expires worthless. You make $500.*

You do not have to first buy a call before you sell it. When you sell a call, all you are doing is "writing" a contract on an underlying stock. And, as the example stresses, you do not have to own the underlying stock. But if the owner of the call option does exercise his option, you will be required to deliver the shares of IBM stock to him. And there lies the danger. You see, writing calls is easy money *unless* the stock goes up in price beyond the agreed upon contract price, which is more commonly called the *strike price*.

> *Example #2. You sell one call contract for 100 shares of IBM stock, giving the owner of the contract the right to buy the stock at $100 per share by January 20. You receive $500 for the call you wrote. The stock goes to $120 per share and the buyer of your call decides to exercise his option. You will have to buy the stock at $120 per share and sell it to owner of the call at $100 per share. You lose $20 per share on the stock trade, or $2,000. You've wiped out the income from writing the call contract and lost another $1,500.*

This is risky business. But call writers try to circumvent the risk by selecting stocks for their writing that have little or no upside potential, or writing calls with *striking* prices that seem to be well beyond probability. In the previous examples, to play it safe, you might have written a call on IBM that had a striking price of $120 per share instead of $100. But the further from the market price the striking price is, the less money you will receive for writing the call. There are always tradeoffs in option and stock trading between safety and profit potential.

One safety feature in writing calls (or puts) is that you can always bail out of your contracts by buying them back.

> *Example #3. You have written a call on Pepsi Cola stock. The striking price is $40, the current market price of the stock is $36. Before the expiration date, you learn there is a good chance the stock will increase markedly in value. So, you decide to cancel your position. You call your broker and tell him you want to buy that call on Pepsi and that "this is a closing transaction." The broker executes the order and you are out of the ball game.*

You may or may not be able to buy the option back at the same price. This will depend upon the current market price of the stock, in relation to the striking price, and the time remaining until the expiration date of the contract. You may, in fact, be able to buy the option back for less than you paid for it, thereby profiting from the writing, then buying, of the same option.

As is the case for puts, call option holders rarely decide to exercise their options but rather buy and sell them much as they buy and sell stocks.

We'll look at options trading in further detail in coming chapters. For now, you may want to review Table 1-2 to clearly distinguish the disadvantages and advantages of bear strategies and Table 1-3 to review important terms.

Risk and Reward

You have now had a brief introduction to the three ways of benefiting from declining stocks with which this book is conceived. Each has its risks and its advantages. But even when you buy long in a stock, you are taking chances. There are no guarantees in the stock and options markets—or in most financial markets, actually. There are national and international economic forces always at work and these can greatly influence your investments; you have no control over these. In addition, there are the personal financial considerations that may force you prematurely out of an investment before you can realize a profit.

Let's briefly summarize the risks inherent in the three ways of going into the marketplace to make money on falling prices.

A bear, as you well know by now, is someone who anticipates falling prices in a particular stock or in the market as a whole, and will try to benefit from these expectations if possible.

In selling short, the bear runs the risk of losing much more than the cost of his original investment. This is because stocks can only depreciate 100 percent but can increase hundreds of percent.

This same risk is inherent in selling calls. If a bear sells a call (or calls) for the income it will produce, and it should happen to increase in value, he or she may be required to deliver the underlying stock, or else close out the call contract, at a loss.

In each case, losses can be drastic. The bear might have to deliver the underlying stock at a price far below what he must buy it for, or will have to buy back the call at a much higher price than it cost. When you write (sell) a call, the most you can make is the premium (amount of money) you receive—but your losses can be much more than that premium!

In the case of buying puts, the risk is relatively low compared with that of selling a stock short or selling calls on that stock. When you buy a put, you are taking a long position in the option. You are hoping to sell it later at a higher price. That price will be higher if the underlying stock on which the put was written falls in price. The risk here is the time frame within which you must make

Table 1-2
Disadvantages and Advantages of Bear Strategies

Strategy	Major Disadvantages	Major Advantages
Selling Short	Losses can far outweigh profits, as a stock can only fall to zero but can theoretically climb in price forever.	When stocks tumble, it is usually with great force. No interest charges from broker on margin trading.
Buying Puts	Expiration dates can leave your option worthless. Too many variables affect put movement and profits are unpredictable even when the underlying stock falls in price.	You cannot lose more than your initial investment. A few of your dollars can do the work of many. You can get rich pretty quick if you pick the right underlying stocks and put options.
Selling Calls	Picking the wrong underlying stock can result in tremendous losses. The initial amount received for selling the call is the maximum amount of money you can earn.	You can greatly increase your income and risk can be reduced or alleviated by selecting high striking prices and owning the underlying stock.

Chapter 1

Table 1-3
Comparing Terms

Terms	Explanations
Bull, Bear	A bull is anyone who has a generally optimistic attitude toward a stock or the market in general. A bear is anyone who is pessimistic about a stock or the market but nonetheless optimistic about her chances of profiting from declines in market prices.
Long, Short	Being long in a stock means you have purchased it with the intention of later selling it at a higher price. Being short in a stock means you have sold it with the intention of buying it back later at a lower price.
Sell, Write	These words are synonyms in options trading. A seller of an options contract is also known as the writer.
Striking Price, Strike Price, Exercise Price, Contract Price	These terms all refer to the same thing: the price at which the buyer of an option can exercise his rights.

your profit. Once the contract expires, the put becomes worthless. But on the positive side, you cannot lose any more than your initial investment. That is, if you purchase a put on Capital Cities for $1,000 and the stock increases 300 percent in value (putting downside pressure on the value of the put), or the contract expires, you can never lose more than the $1,000 plus broker commission.

It is important to keep in mind that in the investment community, potential risk and potential reward share the same bench seat on a ferris wheel. As the seat goes higher and higher, so go the potential risk and potential reward. High risk, high reward; little risk, little reward.

risk ↑   reward ↑
risk ↓   reward ↓

How much can you afford to risk? If you are the average small investor, the true answer is nothing at all. Even after considering the opportunity costs provided by a simple savings account, every $1 you lose today would have been $2 twelve years from now. If you lose $10,000 this year, you'd have at least $20,000 if you stashed it elsewhere over the next decade or so.

Never mind that all-too-familiar excuse "I'll win it back." You never will. Even if you make $10,000 tomorrow on another stock or options play, you would be $20,000 ahead instead of $10,000 had your first gamble paid off.

You cannot afford to lose. Remember that. Keep telling yourself that. And you will find yourself weighing every investment before you try it on. Remember that if something can go wrong, it probably will. That is an old adage that every successful investor keeps repeating before she invests any of her savings.

In approaching every opportunity—whether it be in stocks, corporate bonds, stock options, commodities, or other investment vehicles—the pro always takes full measure of what she is about and never overestimates her abilities. To begin with, that pro will have taken the time to research her target, or will have had someone do it for her. Once an investment opportunity shows fundamental and technical promise, she will look at what can be expected. How much can she possibly make? How much can she possibly lose? Is the potential reward worth the risk? Can she do better with her money elsewhere?

Some independent investors have an incredible record of right picks. Yet a closer examination of their trading records reveals they would have done just as well or better by investing in CDs, treasury bills, or even savings bonds. We all hear of the investors who just doubled their money on a stock. But how long did they have to hold it before it doubled? Had they lost money on it previously? And how much have they lost before they found this winner? Sometimes investors put a lot of money at risk for returns they can get with a lot less sweat.

Why risk your money if you do not have to? The answer, of course, is greed, or just plain entrepreneurship. It is either the challenge of having a lot, lot more, or the pride in making it yourself—or both.

2

Account Prerequisites

For the three types of trading discussed in this book, you will open a margin account. This allows you to trade with money borrowed from your broker, or it means you are required to have a certain amount of collateral. The definition of margin changes depending on whether you are trading stock, or are the buyer or writer of an option. The margin requirements for selling short differ qualitatively and quantitatively from those required for trading options. In turn, the margin requirements for writing calls and selling puts also differ.

Most of you come to this book after having had some experience in traditional stock trading and may be familiar with margin buying; but many small investors buy mainly in cash and have no experience with these types of accounts.

Margin for stock trading refers to a brokerage account that allows you to automatically borrow money from your broker to do additional trading, to trade more shares than you would be able to do on a cash basis.

Margin for Long and Short Positions

Margin accounts are of extreme importance to speculators who are constantly trying to find ways to make each and every investment dollar do the work of two or more. They also want to be able to take a position in a stock at almost any time, whether or not they have all the cash on hand to play their game.

Margin on stock trades works like this:

You have roughly $10,000 to invest in Walt Disney stock, which we will assume is selling for $100 per share. But you feel that the 100 shares you can purchase for this amount of money necessitate too much of a movement in the stock before you will reach your break-even point. Remember that there will be buy and sell commissions on your trades and these can total roughly $200. Given this, the stock will have to move two points before you are in the black.

If you could purchase at least 200 shares and take advantage of the lower commissions that come with larger investments, and thereby gain $200 with each one-point movement in the stock, you could reduce your break-even point.

Well, you can purchase those 200 shares with only $10,000 if you have a margin account with your broker. Given that buy and sell commissions for 200 shares might only come to $300, your break-even point will be only 1½ points above the purchase price. But lowering the break-even point is only one reason you would like to purchase twice as many shares. You are thinking about making twice as much money with each 1/8th of a point the stock moves up.

Suppose that you expect a 10 percent increase in the price of Disney stock in the next three to six months. Wouldn't you rather be making $200 with each $1 advance in price beyond that break-even point than $100?

You can. Here's how it works.

When you place the order, you simply tell your broker, "I want to purchase 200 shares of Disney on margin." The broker bills you for half the cost of the trade and puts up the rest of the money, charging you the current rate of interest for the use of his money.

Assume now that Disney stock does indeed increase 10 percent to $110 per share and you sell it. Before commissions are considered, you will actually have realized a 20 percent gain.

Think about it. The stock has increased 10 percent but your profits have increased 20 percent!

Let's look at how this was accomplished.

1. You had $10,000 to invest in Disney stock selling at $100 per share.

2. You purchased the stock on margin so that with the $10,000 you could purchase 200 shares.

3. Disney stock jumped to $110 per share, and you sold it—all 200 shares. The amount you received from the sale was $22,000, $10,000 of which the broker will deduct, because it belongs to him. (To simplify this example, brokerage fees are not considered.)

4. Your account, therefore, is credited with $12,000.

5. $12,000 is 20 percent more than you started out with.

That's the bright side! If the stock had depreciated 10 percent, the margin would work against you and you would lose 20 percent on your investment.

Bearing in mind the example above in which you have taken a long position in Disney, consider how margin figures into *short selling.*

Assume that instead of an upside swing in price, you expect Disney to tumble in price. Versatile investor that you are, you decide to try to profit if and when this happens, so you sell the stock short.

Again you have $10,000 to invest in Disney, currently selling at $100 per share. Using margin to its full advantage, you short 200 shares of the stock. The stock decreases 10 percent to $90 per share, at which time you put in an order to cover your short position. The result is a 10 percent depreciation in the price of the stock but a 20 percent gain for you.

Let's look again at how this little miracle happened.

1. You had $10,000 with which to sell short Disney stock.

2. Using margin, you were able to short $20,000 worth of stock, enabling you to sell short 200 shares instead of 100.

3. Disney stock *decreased* in price to $90 per share and you called your broker and told him you wanted to cover your short position.

4. The broker immediately deducted the $10,000 you owed him and credited your account with $12,000.

5. $12,000 is 20 percent more than the $10,000 you started out with.

You can easily see that margin works to the same advantage (or disadvantage) for both long and short players. Margin gives that extra leverage an investor needs to make (or lose) more. Everything is done quite simply, for once you have established a margin account with your broker you only have to inform him that you are trading on margin and the broker automatically does the rest.

In the preceding example, it was assumed that the trader needed to put up 50 percent of the money required for the transaction, but how much he will actually have to put up for initial trades will depend on current Federal Reserve requirements. The Federal Reserve's control of margin is part of overall economic strategy, and changes periodically. In the past, the Federal Reserve has required as little as 25 percent and as much as 100 percent.

In reality, margin requirements specified by the Federal Reserve do not necessitate cash percentages, but rather equity ratios. Thus, other securities in your account may serve as collateral. (A history of Federal Reserve margin requirements is given in Table 2-1 and the margin regulation is given in Table 2-2.)

Additionally, stock exchanges require a minimum deposit, or minimum collateral, on account before any margin trades will be allowed. This is usually $2,000.

Beyond this minimum deposit and the margin requirements of the Federal Reserve, exchanges and brokers have additional requirements which they strictly enforce. These have to do with what is referred to as *maintenance margin.* Federal

Table 2-1
Federal Reserve Margin Requirements
for Stock Purchases and Short Sales

From	To	Stock Purchases	Short Sales
Oct 1, 1934	Mar 31, 1936	25%–55%, depending on present price to lowest price ratio for each security.	Determined by broker.
Apr 1, 1936	Oct 31, 1937	55%	Determined by broker.
Nov 1, 1937	Feb 4, 1945	40%	50%
Feb 5, 1945	Jul 4, 1945	50%	50%
Jul 5, 1945	Jan 20, 1946	75%	75%
Jan 21, 1946	Jan 31, 1947	100%	100%
Feb 1, 1947	Mar 29, 1949	75%	75%
Mar 30, 1949	Jan 16, 1951	50%	50%
Jan 17, 1951	Feb 20, 1953	75%	75%
Feb 20, 1953	Jan 4 , 1955	50%	50%
Jan 4, 1955	Apr 22, 1955	50%	60%
Apr 23, 1955	Jan 15, 1958	70%	70%
Jan 16, 1958	Aug 4, 1958	50%	50%
Aug 5, 1958	Oct 15, 1958	70%	70%
Oct 16, 1958	Jul 27, 1960	90%	90%
Jul 28, 1960	Jul 9, 1962	70%	70%
Jul 10, 1962	Nov 5, 1963	50%	50%
Nov 6, 1963	Mar 10, 1968	70%	70%
Mar 11, 1968	Jun 7, 1968	70%	70%
Jun 8, 1968	May 5, 1970	80%	80%
May 6, 1970	Dec 3, 1971	65%	65%
Dec 6, 1971	Nov 22, 1972	55%	55%
Nov 24, 1972	Jan 2, 1974	65%	65%
Jan 3, 1974		50%	50%

Table 2-2
Selected Margin Requirements Set by the Board of Governors of the Federal Reserve System

Regulation	Summary
G	Governs the extension of credit by persons other than brokers, dealers, or banks for the purchase of registered equity securities.
T	*Directly affects shortsellers.* It governs the extension and maintenance of credit by national securities exchange members as well as the extension of credit for trading in over-the-counter stocks.
U	Controls the loans made by any bank for the direct or indirect purchase of stocks registered on the national securities exchanges.
X	Governs loans by U.S. borrowers and the foreign borrowers governed by them.

Reserve regulations do not inhibit exchanges and brokers from imposing whatever maintenance margin requirements they feel necessary.

Some exchanges leave maintenance margin requirements entirely up to member brokers; others like the New York Stock Exchange require member brokers to meet the exchange's guidelines.

Generally, for short *selling,* the maintenance margin requirements on stocks under $5 is 100 percent. On stocks with a market value of $5 or more, it is usually 30 percent to 50 percent of the market value. On stock *purchases,* the maintenance requirements are a bit easier, with some stocks under $5 qualified for purchase on credit and, generally, a margin requirement of 25 percent of all long positions in the account.

How does this all translate for the short seller?

Before you can trade on margin, you must have a minimum of $2,000 in your account, or put up a minimum of $2,000 on your first purchase.

For example, suppose you want to sell short $2,100 worth of Disney stock on margin. You must deposit in your account $2,000.

If you want to sell short $3,000 worth of Disney stock, you still only have to put up $2,000.

Now, what if you want to sell short $10,000 worth of Disney stock? How much must you put up? It depends upon the current margin requirement. If it is 50 percent, then you must put up $5,000. But under no circumstances can you make any margin purchase or short sale if you have less than $2,000 in your account unless you will put up the money within five trading days. An exception to this rule occurs when you sell short and buy back on the same day.

What about the maintenance margin set by your broker? Generally, it is 50 percent for one-position accounts, 35 percent for two-position accounts, and sometimes 30 percent for three-or-more-position accounts. These percentages vary among brokers.

What happens if the stock sold short goes up, putting you in the red? The Federal Reserve only requires that your account be restricted. However, it allows exchanges or brokers to require you to deposit in your account additional cash or securities to change the ratio between your equity and the market value of the securities you have purchased.

Your broker has your account activity computerized. As soon as your percentage margin falls to a certain point, he will notify you that additional cash or securities must be deposited, or he has the right to sell some of your holdings to meet maintenance requirements.

These percentage margins are figured in the following way.

1. Take the net proceeds from the short sale and subtract commissions and other costs.

2. Add the result to the initial margin requirement.

3. Divide the sum arrived at in #2 and subtract 1 (one) from it.

4. The result is the percentage margin.

Putting this into formula, we can illustrate how the percentage margin relates to maintenance calls.

> *Example #1. You sell short 100 shares of Disney at $100 per share; this results in a net of $10,000. Assuming the margin requirement is 50 percent, you must have in your account cash or equity totalling $5,000, or you must deposit cash or securities in this amount within five business days. The percentage margin was figured on the following basis:*
>
> $$\frac{\text{Net from short sale} + \text{Margin}}{\text{Value of Stock}} - 1 = \text{Percentage Margin}$$
>
> *or*
>
> $$\frac{\$10,000 + \$5,000}{\$10,000} - 1 = 50 \text{ percent}$$

Example #2. Disney stock shoots up in price, meaning paper losses for you as a short seller. Its new market value is $120 per share. You will receive a margin call from your broker requiring you to put up additional collateral. Why? Because your percentage margin is now only 25 percent. How much collateral you will be required to put up will depend on how many positions you have in your account.

$$\frac{\$10,000 + \$5,000}{\$12,000} - 1 = 25 \text{ percent}$$

Risky Business

Margin can be risky business, whether you are long or short on a stock. Consider the following.

1. You want to sell short $20,000 worth of IBM stock.

2. Adhering to margin requirements, you put up $10,000.

3. The stock increases 50 percent in price. If you are forced to sell because of a maintenance margin call, the amount you would receive is $10,000. But you'll never get it.

4. You owe the broker $10,000, and he will deduct that amount from the proceeds.

The stock went up 50 percent and you lost 100 percent of your money! Thus, don't even consider trading on margin unless you have backup cash or securities to cover maintenance calls. Otherwise you will be forced to sell your stock to cover the debt you owe your broker and have to borrow from your broker to pay the remainder of the debt. In short, you lose everything and save your broker.

Generally, unless the stock tumbles suddenly, your broker will have sent you a margin call as soon as your percentage margin brought your equity down to about 35 percent. The call will contain words similar to this: "The market value of the securities on hand as collateral for your indebtedness is not sufficient to meet margin requirements. Please forward the necessary securities or the necessary cash to meet the margin requirements." The call will let you know just how much money or collateral is required.

Keep in mind that if you send securities instead of cash to meet your maintenance call, only 50 percent of the market value of those securities will count toward your indebtedness. If the margin is not sent immediately or is insufficient, the broker has the right, as specified in the margin agreement that you signed when you opened the account, to sell the subject securites pledged in order to satisfy the outstanding debt and interest due.

If the broker's maintenance margin requirements are set higher than those of the exchange on which the stock is traded, there is room for some negotiation. In any event, respond to the maintenance call as soon as possible. Call your broker and let him know the money is on the way, or why you may need a delay. Do not fall into the habit of liquidating your holdings to satisfy margin requirements; otherwise you will be restricted from trading on margin in the future.

Remember that maintenance calls are not required by the Federal Reserve. If the equity percentage in an account drops below the board's initial margin requirement, the board only requires that trading in the account be restricted. It requires no deposit of funds. The necessity of meeting margin calls by depositing cash or securities are broker and exchange regulations, not the Federal Reserve's.

Restriction does not necessarily mean that trading cannot take place in the account. As long as there is no resulting change in the percentage margin as a result of stock substitutions made on the same day, trading is permitted. But any withdrawal of cash or securities from the account, or new short or long positions, will not be allowed.

Just how risky trading on margin can be is amply illustrated by a bizarre case that occurred during the 1987 market crash. The subject of the story was not a short seller but nonetheless a speculator who used margin too indiscriminantly for his own good.

The man was Arthur Kane, a disbarred lawyer who became so obsessed with the stock market that he was a habitual tape watcher and constant trader. For a short time, he had as much as $4 million in the market.

He was a short seller's magic man. That is, he was picking so many losers that if you knew what his next stock pick would be, you would want to sell short the same stock.

Kane was after big profits. As a man of means, he was not going to be interested in the kind of return on investment that would impress you or me. Besides, he liked the game, the challenge of it, the excitement of it. Just before the stock market crash, he had built his portfolio up to more than $10 million worth of stocks. But the money wasn't all his. More than half that amount was margin debt.

You don't have to be a mathematical genius to realize the danger of Kane's position. As highly leveraged as he was, he would be losing a great deal of money with each one-eighth of a point that his portfolio dropped. And his portfolio continued to depreciate, for he was gambling mainly on takeover candidates, the kind of stocks on which the bottom could fall out if the probability of takeover turned sour. Kane became more and more depressed as time passed. And to add to his depression were the margin calls from his broker. Merrill Lynch was turning on the pressure for him to cover some of his losses.

Kane had now become so dizzy with despair that he was contemplating suicide. He had lost millions in the market in a short time, and had lost it so quickly because he had let himself become very highly leveraged through margin. Then came the stock market crash of 1987. Kane was devastated. Out of his mind now with despair and resentment, he went to his broker's office, pulled out a gun and killed the office manager and wounded his account representative. Then he took the gun and pointed it at his right temple. Without hesitation, he squeezed the trigger. His life was over.

Margin for Buying Puts and Selling Calls

Stock options are highly volatile investments. Though their price movement is tied to the movement of the underlying stocks on which they are based, some options will move almost point for point with the underlying stock, while others may not move at all; there are many factors affecting the price movement of stock options. Though it is possible for the underlying stock to change in price and the related option not to change, a 10 percent gain in the underlying security *might* mean a 100 percent gain in the related call, and a 10 percent drop in price in the underlying security can mean a 100 percent gain in the related put. This is because of the extremely low prices of puts and calls relative to the underlying common. For instance, though IBM stock may be selling for over $100 per share, it is possible to play the stock by investing no more than a few hundred dollars in puts or calls.

Remember that as a trader who wants to benefit from declining prices, *you* only want to *buy puts* and *sell calls*. The selling of puts and the buying of calls you will gladly leave to the bulls. After all, you are a bear.

Options transactions are cash transactions. So, margin has a very different meaning here.

If you buy a put on IBM that is currently listed at $1.50, then you must have $150+ in your account to cover the cost of the option and the buy commission. If you do not have the $150+ in your account, you must have sufficient collateral in your margin account so the broker can deduct the necessary cash for the transaction. This is tricky. You cannot buy the put on margin but you can use the loan value in your brokerage margin account to get the money to pay for the option.

If you are going to write a call (or put), then you will be required to pay up even more than your purchase price plus commission. In the case of writing (selling) options, the word margin takes on an even different meaning. Rather than referring to the fraction of every dollar you must pay for each one-dollar trade, the word margin now refers to the additional money you must put up to assure your broker your account has some insurance against the kind of volatility that may leave him holding an empty cash bag.

Assume you write a call selling at $1 on IBM stock when the stock is at $100 per share. The expiration date on the contract is March 17. You receive $100 for writing the call (as the published price is for each share and each option represents 100 shares of the underlying stock). If the stock decreases significantly in value, you have little to worry about. But let's suppose that the call you have written gives the owner the right to buy IBM at $110 per share and the stock jumps to $120 per share. That call you wrote is now worth, possibly, $10.

Your losses to date are $900. Why? Figure it out. Each call is for 100 shares of stock, and the market value of the call is now $10, or $1,000. You originally shorted the call for $100. $1,000 less $100 is $900. If you have to purchase back the calls to avoid delivering the stock when required (as it will be more expensive for you to deliver the stock because of buy and sell commissions), you may find yourself unable to meet your commitment. That leaves the broker in a rather precarious situation.

Thus, when you write a call, your broker will have required you to have on account or deliver the same day:

Cash for the premium (value of the option)
plus 5 percent to 15 percent of the value of the stock.

Before you wrote that $1 call on IBM then, your broker would have required you to put up $100 to cover the premium, $40 to cover the commission, and up to $1,500 of the stock's value.

The only way you can get around the margin requirement is to own the underlying stock, in which case you would be dealing with a *covered call*. But we're not interested in covered calls because of the cost to own the underlying stock. We are interested in uncovered, or naked, calls. These are not as safe an investment as covered calls but offer greater leverage. And greater leverage means greater profit—or greater loss.

Margin, then, has different meanings in the investment community. What it means to the three types of bear plays discussed in this and following chapters is summarized in Table 2-3.

Table 2-3
Margin Requirements for the Three Ways

Strategy	Requirement
1. Short selling	There must be a minimum deposit of $2,000 in cash or equivalent securities. If stock sales are $4,000 or more, then investor must put up 50 or more percent of all money over $4,000.
2. Put buying	Full payment must be made on all trades, but securities in a cash or margin account may serve as collateral for the purchase of the option.
3. Naked call writing (investor does not own the underlying stock)	Payment cannot be less than the premium for the option *plus* the commission *plus* 5 percent to 15 percent of the value of the stock.
Covered call writing (investor owns the underlying stock)	All margin requirements are satisfied through ownership of the underlying stock. Brokers require the stock to be on deposit with their firm.

3

Order Information

Both the stock and options markets allow investors to use a number of different orders to obtain additional advantage and flexibility in their pursuit of profits. Every trader should be aware of the different types of buy and sell orders available. They can mean the difference between profit and loss, can cut losses or add to profits. Stock traders like yourself cannot afford to sit in front of a computer all day watching market movements. Investing is a part time job for you. You need to include special order strategies in your buying and selling program.

Orders for Stock Trades

Major types of orders on stock trades are:

- Market orders
- Limit orders
- Discretionary orders
- Day orders and other time orders
- Open orders
- Stop orders
- Cancellation orders
- All or none

Market orders are generally given when the trader is not interested in getting the stock at a specific price, or selling the stock at a specific price. Generally, the market order is not for the trader who wants to turn a profit on a point or fraction of a point movement in a stock. For instance, suppose you want to buy 100 shares of AT&T for dividend income and long-term capital gain, or possibly for covered call income. It matters little to you if you get the stock at $42 or $42½. You simply want to buy the stock as soon as possible. In this case you call your broker and order him "to buy 100 shares of AT&T *at market*." This means your broker is committed to buying the shares as soon as possible at the best prevailing price. Sometimes market orders work to the advantage of the trader. The stock may have opened at $42 but be at $41¼ when the broker executes the trade. Of course, it may also be at $42½—but that's the chance you must take with a market order. Short sellers will also use market orders, except when they plan to play a stock for a small decline.

Limit orders are placed when a trader has a technical feel for a particular stock and some very specific goals. For instance, you may be interested in selling short Digitial Equipment at $75 with the anticipation of buying it back at $70 in a couple of weeks. In this case, you will order your broker "to sell short X shares of Digital at $75 or better." This means your broker is committed to selling the shares at no less than $75. Later when you decide to buy back the shares you have sold short, you will order your broker "to cover the short position by buying Digital at $70." Now, your broker is committed to buying back the shares at $70 or less.

Discretionary orders put the trade entirely in the hands of the broker. The broker picks the stock, the quantity of shares, the long or short position, the price. Most brokers shy away from discretionary orders because of the tremendous liability they may incur if their customers become dissatisfied with overall performance of their portfolios. Thus, discretionary orders are generally only allowed under very specific conditions.

Day orders are placed when the trader wants the stock purchased on the day the order is placed. All orders are accepted as day orders unless the trader specifies otherwise. However, many brokers severely limit the kinds of time orders they will accept. Some brokers will also accept one week or one month orders; others will accept only one month orders, and some will accept no time orders beyond one day.

Open orders are also known as "good 'til cancelled" orders. They generally have no time limit, except that brokers will request confirmation of these orders periodically. Suppose you want to sell short Citicorp at $25 per share when it is below this market price. Your feeling is that the way the stock has been swinging in price, it will probably rise to $25 per share or slightly above, and then fall back to $20 per share or less. As you want to play the stock for about a 25 percent return in one year's time, the sale at $25 and the buyback at $20 fits your program. Thus, you place your order in the following way: "I'd like to sell short 200 shares of

Citicorp at $25 per share—good 'til cancelled." Either immediately or at some time in the future, you would place the buyback order in the following way: "I'd like to cover my short position on Citicorp at $20 per share—good 'til cancelled." Your broker will execute your orders at, or better than, the prices you requested. One short note here: Open buy orders are automatically adjusted downward on ex-dividend dates.

Stop orders are extremely helpful to traders. The stop order specifies a price at which the trader wants to get out of his position. For example, assume you have sold short Citicorp at $15 per share. You feel that if it reaches $18 per share it will pick up momentum and continue to rise. So you tell your broker you want to put in a stop order at $18. Should Citicorp stock reach $18, your order to the broker immediately becomes a market order and will be executed as soon as possible at the best possible price.

Cancellation orders come in three types. These are straight cancellations, replacements, and "fill or kills." The straight cancellation is self-explanatory; the broker is simply ordered to ignore the order. The replacement order changes one order for another: "Change my order to sell short 200 shares of General Motors at $28 to 300 shares at $26." The "fill or kill" order is to be executed immediately; if the broker cannot do so, he will cancel it. This last type of order might be given by a trader who feels that because of published news stories the day before, or news of an impending buyout, he wants the stock at the very current price or not at all.

An all or none order is very frequently used in stock orders. It is an order specifying that the purchase or sale of shares must be in the quantity specified, or the order is not to be executed. Many times orders given for a trade at a specific price cannot be completed in full, so the broker purchases or sells as many as he can. It comes as a surprise to traders when they give an order to short 200 shares of a stock at a certain price, that actually only 150 are shorted. This can easily occur if "all or none" is not specified when the order is given. This author learned this lesson the hard way. He once put in an order for 10 out-of-the-money calls on Warner Communication, when it was a listed stock, only to be notified that the broker was able to purchase only one call at the specified price, and did so. Outlandish, of course! But this is what happened. Considering the commission to the broker, that one low price call was expensive and there was no way it could be profitable. The author changed brokers immediately afterward.

Orders for Options Trades

The same types of orders are available on options trades, but as their impact on the options trader is somewhat different, it is well to look at them from this new perspective.

Market orders, which are executed as soon as they reach the trading floor, are dangerous for the options trader, and it is recommended that you do not use them. Put and Call prices can swing in large percents. You may tell your broker to purchase five puts on IBM at $5 each *at market* only to find that by the time the order can be executed the put is at $6. That means the order will cost you $3,000 instead of $2,500 (as each option is for 100 shares of the underlying stock and the price quoted is *per share*).

Limit orders, which establish a specific price at which the order should be executed, are, on the other hand, indispensible to the options trader. They assure that you pay no more, or receive no less than expected for a put or call transaction.

Discretionary orders, which take the trading completely out of the hands of the investor, are done under special agreement with the brokerage house. For new options traders, discretionary orders may make a lot of sense. It is a good way for them to learn the game in the way that an experienced broker plays it. It is imperative, however, that you have given discretionary privileges to an account executive at the brokerage house who has a reputation for ethical account management.

Day orders, which specify that if the order is not executed the same day, it should be canceled, are always the standard. Every order is assumed to be a day order unless the broker is informed otherwise. Day orders make sense for options traders. Each day brings new opportunities and a need for changes in strategy. Placing other time limits that go beyond a day is for the very lazy, and no one makes money by being lazy. This clearly means that "good 'til cancelled" orders are not recommended for options traders.

Fill-or-kill orders, which must be executed as soon as possible, are also advantageous to the options trader. As "all or none" instructions are inherent in "fill or kill" orders, these orders are of primary importance to traders who have very complex strategies, or require immediate action to meet their special goals.

Options traders must always be careful about their instructions to a broker. Because of the low-price nature of options a mere one-eighth of a point saving on a purchase or one-eighth of an advantage on a sale can mean a 100% gain. Every fraction of a point counts heavily in most options trades.

This last is best demonstrated by a put buyer who places a day order for 10 Dow Jones puts listed at $1/4. Options plus commission cost him $290. The put advances to $3/8, at which price he sells and receives $337 after commission. His profit is $47. Now he goes after Citicorp puts selling at $1/4. But this time he forgets to specify "all or none." As it turns out, the broker buys at the first opportunity, the first time only one put, the second time three puts, the third time six puts. Because all transactions are made on the same day, the broker does discount some of the trades, but still the total commissions come to $95. Total cost to him for the puts, then, is $345. When the puts climb to $3/8, he sells, but again forgets to specify "all or none." This time the puts are sold in lots of five, and commissions of $75 are charged. His proceeds are $300, or $45 less than he paid to take his initial position. The Dow Jones puts and the Citicorp puts were bought and sold at the same prices but only when "all or none" orders were placed was there a profit.

Part 2

Short Sales

4

Types and Restrictions

When you sell a stock short, you are actually selling something that you do not yet own, something your broker has borrowed from someone else and has lent to you with the understanding that you will return the stock on demand. Transactions such as this are possible because, when you get right down to it, the financial markets have really become gaming environments.

But short selling is nothing new. It must be thousands of years old. Farmers, for one, have always sought to sell their crop before it was harvested, mercenaries to sell their services before they fought their battles, explorers to sell their success before they made their discoveries.

Basic Strategies

Strategies used in short selling may be broken down into four basic types:

- Speculating
- Hedging
- Shorting against the box
- Arbitraging

Speculating

The speculative type of short sale is one in which the trader seeks to maximize his profit by selling short a stock he does not own. His game plan is simply to sell first at a high price, then buy back later at a lower price. His interest is only in a capital gain. There is no income potential for the short seller. That is, he does not receive dividends.

The speculator is motivated by some general facts about stocks and the stock market. The first is that most stocks will generally decline in price during some period in the short to intermediate term. The second is that when stocks with poor fundamentals do fall, the tumble is usually exaggerated. The third is that there are enough bear phases, even in a bull market, to make the marketplace a happy hunting ground for the short seller.

This does not mean, however, that the short seller can just throw a dart at a board of stock listings and sell short whatever stock the dart selects. There are inherent dangers in short selling. Low-priced stocks can sometimes jump so quickly that losses will far outweigh whatever the possible gains could have been. Even stocks with poor fundamentals and poor press can wind up being takeover candidates, in which case their market prices will skyrocket and the shortseller's losses will rupture his bank account. This is, again, because there is no limit on how high a stock can go, but there are limits on how low it can go. Rarely does a stock go below zero. But stocks can triple in price.

(How can a stock go below zero? Actually, the market price of the stock cannot go below zero but the shareholder's investment in the stock can depreciate more than 100 percent. This happens when stockholders acquire their shares at less than par value; if the company goes belly-up, the shareholders are liable for the difference to par for each share of stock. For this reason, corporations usually fix the par value of their common at an extremely low value, or give it no par value at all. Par value on common stocks these days is a contrived value anyway. It is used simply to facilitate bookkeeping efforts. But this does not hold true for preferred stocks, because the preferreds contain some of the provisions of a debt instrument and therefore their par value is an important base when the stock is being recalled, and when the dividend rate is determined.)

Because a short seller is such a hard and fast bear in the marketplace, it does not mean she cannot also take long positions in other stocks. But generally when she does do this, her positions are independent of each other and have been taken solely to play *the underlying* stocks or options in the best possible way; the long and short positions are not meant as a hedge. In the stocks that she is long, she will always have the added advantages that come with being the recipient of regular and special dividends and with being an owner of the company; but in the stocks that she is short, the dividends do not belong to her and she has no ownership in the corporations.

Dividends are an important concern to the short seller. Short sellers should stay away from stocks with good dividend histories and payouts. These are generally strong companies popular with investors and are more likely to remain stable in price or move upward rather than to depreciate in market value. But this is not always true. Sometimes a corporation will declare dividends even when it is hurting in order to impress the marketplace with its faith in its own future, or to impress stockholders and would-be investors with the corporation"s commitment to an uninterrupted schedule of dividends.

Dividends are generally accepted to be an appropriation of accumulated earnings or of current earnings. In this case, they indicate strong performance by the corporation and a signal to the short seller to go hunting elsewhere. But sometimes a dividend is a return on invested capital. In this case, the shortseller *might* have a possible target.

Because a stockholder really gets nothing *additional* from a dividend, the effect on the market value of the stock should be minimal. But in the market, rarely are things the way they should be. The accountant will tell you that dividends reduce the value of each share of stock because they are basically distributions from the net earnings of the corporation. But in reality, stock investors are excited by dividends and often bid up the value of the stock in which they are being declared. Declaration of a stock dividend can drive the market value of a stock too far up for the short seller's economic and mental health.

Theoretically, if the short seller is short on a stock for which a stock dividend has just been declared, he should be no worse off after the distribution. This is because a stock dividend is just another bookkeeping game, as illustrated in Table 4-1. The stock dividend, in effect, revises the capital structure of the corporation by reducing the earnings surplus to the same degree that the capital stock has been increased. The stockholder has actually received nothing additional. But here's the threat to the short seller: The stock dividend is not treated by the IRS as ordinary income but as a capital gain, and if tax law should allow dividends and capital gains to be treated differently, there may be tax advantages for the stockholders. This might put upward pressure on the stock. Additionally, if cash dividends are maintained for each share even if there are more shares now, or if they are increased for each share at a future date, the investment community starts seeing dollar signs and the price of the stock will be bid up. And when stocks go up, the short seller's losses go up.

The stock split is another bookkeeping game (Table 4-2). But it differs substantially from the stock dividend. When a *stock dividend* is made, the par value of the shares is not reduced. But when there is a *stock split*, the par value *is* reduced.

If you were originally short 1,000 shares at a $1 par value before a two for one stock split, after the split you would be short 2,000 shares each now with a par value of 50 cents. From an accounting perspective the total value of the shares has not changed. But as a short seller, you are probably in harm's way anyway. This is because a company splits its stock to reduce the price in order to excite higher trading activity. Higher trading activity usually means greater demand, and greater demand generally means higher prices. If the stock does go up after the split, the short seller is losing twice the amount of money he would have before

Table 4-1
Effects of Stock Dividends

Dividend Payment	Capital Account Before Dividend	Retained Earnings	Capital Account After Dividend	Retained Earnings	Book Value per Share Before	Book Value per Share After
50% Stock	100,000 sh., $5 ea.	$500,000	150,000 sh., $5 ea.	$250,000	$10	$6.67
20% Stock	100,000 sh., $5 ea.	$500,000	120,000 sh., $5 ea.	$400,000	$10	$8.33
10% Stock	100,000 sh., $5 ea	$500,000	110,000 sh., $5 ea.	$450,000	$10	$9.09

The stock dividend has reduced the earnings surplus by the same percent that the capital stock has been increased. Stockholders now own a greater number of shares, but the book value of each share is reduced. The formula for determining the book value is to take the Capital Stock + Retained Earnings ÷ Number of Shares. The capital stock value is determined by multiplying the number of shares times the dollar value of each share.

Table 4-2
Effects of Stock Splits

Stock Split	Shares Owned Before	After	Par Value per Share Before	After	Total Market Value Before	After	Dividend per Share Before	After
3 for 1	1,000	3,000	$.03	$.01	$10,000	$10,000	$.60	$.20
2 for 1	1,000	2,000	$.03	$.015	$10,000	$10,000	$.60	$.30
1½ for 1	1,000	1,500	$.03	$.02	$10,000	$10,000	$.60	$.40

The stock split does not change the proportionate ownership of the stockholder. Note how, although more shares were owned after each split, the value of the stock remained the same. Par value and dividends were reduced proportionately. Sometimes, stock dividends are not reduced or are reduced in a different ratio than the split.

the split because he now has twice as many shares. However, if the stock goes down after the split, the short seller would be making twice as much money. But as stock splits are specifically designed to put upward pressure on the price of a stock, the short seller must be aware of their inherent danger to his investment strategy.

Reverse splits, however, may signal eventual opportunities for the short seller. In a reverse split, each shareholder receives less stock than he had before, though the par value of each share will be raised accordingly. As with the stock split, there is no change in proportionate ownership for each shareholder. Why would a company want to declare a reverse split? For the same reason that Storage Technology did in the late '80s. The price of the stock was so low the directors of the company feared investors might think it too risky a situation. So they declared a 10 for one reverse split. It was a play on investor psychology and it worked—the stock climbed impressively. But the strategy could have backfired, for reverse splits can often signal financial difficulty, in which case there will be opportunities for the short seller.

The short seller, as speculator, must keep a wary eye on the marketplace at all times. There are always those little "flags" that signal trouble, and he must be aware of them.

Hedging

In hedging her positions in the market, the short seller may go long in stocks in the same or different industries or purchase low-priced calls on the stocks she has shorted.

Since the mid-1970s when the Chicago Board Options Exchange (CBOE) instilled new life in the options markets, it has become much more popular to use stock and stock option or, with the advent of index options, stock and index option combinations. The pros today are more often than not long on stock and long with puts on some index options, or short on stocks *and* long on calls on one of the Indexes.

These stock indexes are compiled and published by a number of different sources, and are designed to be representative of total stock market activity on a particular exchange such as the New York Stock Exchange, of a broad market sector such as industrials, or of a selected industry such as computer technology.

But index options are not a tool for new players like yourself. *You* will only want to be interested in hedging stock positions with stock options.

Shorting Against the Box

This is a means of putting up the red flag and, in effect, saying, "Hold it. I don't want my stock going up or down until I decide whether to bail out, hold it, or buy more."

Can this actually be done? Yes, in a way. It is called "selling short against the box."

Suppose you own 100 shares of Citicorp selling at $30 per share. For some reason you want to assure that you will in no way be affected by any rise or decrease in the market value of the stock. So you sell short 100 shares. Now if the stock drops to $20 per share, though you lose $10 per share on your long position, you gain $10 per share on your short position. You cannot be affected by any market turns, although you will have to pay some extra brokerage commissions.

Example #1. You are showing a $10,000 paper profit from your holdings in Digital Equipment stock which you bought some time ago. But you do not want to take your profits in this tax year. You would rather wait until next year, but that's a two and one-half month wait. In this time, Digital stock can drop in market value and wipe out your gains. So, you sell short against the box. You have your broker borrow other shares of the same stock so you can sell them. Now, if Digital goes down in price, it makes no difference, for your short position will gain penny for penny what your long position loses. When the first trading day of the new year arrives, you simply sell the stock you have long and buy back the stock which you have sold short. You have turned your paper profit into cash profit in the tax year you prefer.

If Digital gained another five, 10, or 20 points in those two and one-half months, you'd be banging your head against the wall for hedging the way you did, but safety counts for a lot, and you did indeed play it safe.

Example #2. You own 200 shares of Grumman which you keep in a safe deposit box in your hometown bank in Illinois. You are currently vacationing in Hilton Head. Vacation or no, you like to check the stock listings every morning to see how your stock is doing. You note on the third day of your vacation that Grumman has jumped to $26.25 per share. You want to sell the stock immediately but know you cannot deliver it to your broker in the time allowed. Your vacation is not over for another three and one-half weeks. So, you sell short against the box to halt any losses that may be incurred from the long position. Later, when you are back in Illinois, you can retrieve those shares by calling your broker to close out both the long and short positions in that same stock.

Arbitraging

Arbitrage is the buying or selling of securities in one market while simultaneously buying or selling them in another. The arbitrager is able to do this because many stocks are dually listed. For instance, if you were to check *Investor's Daily* for Pacific and Boston stock exchange listings, you would see certain stocks that are not only trading on both exchanges but which will have closed at different prices on each exchange. During the course of the day, the actual price variances from one exchange to another can be a point or two, or more. The arbitrager seeks to take advantage of these price spreads by taking the necessary short or long positions. This type of trading is not for readers of this book. Arbitrage short sales require a great deal of sophistication and excellent timing. This is a game for the Big Money guys who can buy in quantity.

Price Restriction Rule

The stock markets went into a panic on October 19, 1987. By the close of the trading day, the Dow Jones Industrials had plummeted 508 points. One trading day earlier, they had plummeted almost 13 percent, or about 108 points. The bulls were scrapping to get out of their positions, cover themselves with puts, or just praying. All the indexes which measured market muscle went the way of the Industrials. The New York Stock Exchange Index was down 30½ points, Standard & Poor's 500-Stock Index was down 58 points, the American Stock Exchange Index was down 41 points, and the NASDAQ composite of OTC stocks was down 46 points. The marketplace was clearly in disarray. Independent traders could not even reach their brokers. The chairman of the New York Stock Exchange was quoted in the *Wall Street Journal* as saying that this was the worst market he had ever seen. Banks were thinking twice about extending credit to hurting brokers, and called in some brokerage loans. Large investment firms were shouting for the New York Stock Exchange to ring the closing bell early and not to open until reason would once again prevail. On that exchange alone, more than 600 million shares were traded.

One would think that this was a great time for the short sellers. But there is a price restriction rule which prevented many from reaping the benefits of a bearish strategy. The rule is the SEC's and it states that short sales on any security cannot be made below the price at which the last regular way sale was made or unless the price "is above the next preceding different price at which a sale of such security ... was effected."

Specifically, this means that the relationship between the current price of a stock and its previous transaction prices determines whether or not a short sale can be made.

To understand this rule, it is necessary to also understand what, in stock trading, is known as a tick. *A tick generally represents a one-eighth of a point movement in stock price.*

There are four categories of ticks: plus ticks, zero plus ticks, minus ticks, and zero minus ticks. (These are summarized in Table 4-3.)

Table 4-3
Short Sale Price Restrictions

Price Transactions	Last Price Description	Short Sale
10, 9, 9⅛	Plus Tick, because it is higher than the preceding price.	ALLOWED
10, 9, 9⅛, 9⅛	Zero Plus Tick, because it is not different from the immediately preceding price but it is up from the last price that was different.	ALLOWED
10, 10⅛, <u>10</u>	Minus Tick, because it is less than the last price that was different.	PROHIBITED
10, 10⅛, 10, <u>10</u>	Zero Minus Tick, because it is less than the last price that was different.	PROHIBITED

Short sales may be executed on *plus ticks* and *zero plus ticks*.

Example #1. The Plus Tick. Successive transactions in Citicorp stock are made at $25, $24, and $24⅛. As the last price is above the previous, it is considered an uptick and a short sale cannot have been executed at that price.

Example #2. The Zero Plus Tick. Successive transactions in Citicorp stock are made at $25, $24, $24¼, $24¼. The third price cannot have been a short sale because it is above the previous although below the first. However, the fourth price can have been a short sale because, although it is the same as the previous price, it is above the $24 price.

Example #3. The Minus Tick. Successive transactions in Citicorp stock are $25, $25, $25⅛ and $25. The last price cannot have been a short sale because it is below the previous price, and therefore represents a minus tick.

Example #4. The Zero Minus Tick. Successive transactions in Citicorp stock are $25, $25⅛, $25, $25. The last price cannot have been a short sale because it is still less than the preceding different price of $25⅛.

Exceptions to Price Restrictions

The price restriction rule, if applied to all trading, would wreak havoc in many instances, or make impossible certain trading activities upon which professionals depend. Thus, the SEC allows many exceptions to the rule.

Regular-way trades are, of course, excepted and so are any odd-lot sales (sales of less than 100 shares). Additionally, arbitrage transactions between different markets or with different securities are exempted.

The Controversy

Why the restrictions on short sale prices? Precisely to prevent bear raids on stocks. Often, in times past, bear raids were preceded by false rumors which undermined not only the target stock but market integrity as well. As spooked investors bailed out of their positions, short sales were executed by those in the know and stock prices were forced to panic levels.

Short selling has always been a controversial subject.

There are those who argue that it undermines the investment community by advertising that the stock market is a place for profiteers who care little about supporting the market as a place for serious long term investment. On the other hand, short sellers have been with us since ancient times, and the practice prevails in all areas of our lives.

More specifically, short selling has been suspect because of the way it adds to market declines; thus the restrictions by the SEC on when short sales can or cannot be made. Still, even with the tick rules, short selling still has a tremendous impact on market direction.

The one very positive aspect of short selling is that the short seller must eventually cover his short position. This helps halt downslides. But, on the other hand, short sellers closing out their positions during a rising market will put unusual upward pressure on stock prices, driving the market to unsustainable highs. This means great fluctuations in prices—an ideal situation for speculators but not an ideal situation for long-term investors or for market integrity.

Short sellers will argue, however, that in both bear and bull phases, short selling can provide a safety net on market activity; it can counterbalance any extraordinary movement one way or another in stock prices.

There will always be arguments about the value or necessity of short selling. The important thing is that it is very legal, sometimes very profitable, and is part of the game of trading in stocks and other securities. (Short selling is not allowed on many foreign stock exchanges.)

5

Market Views

The bear's view of the marketplace must, understandably, be different from that of the "usual way," or bullish, investor. This means, specifically, that what the usual way investor might interpret as opportunity, the bear sees as risk. And what everyone else sees as risk, the bear sees as opportunity.

Before looking at the way the short seller will interpret fundamental and technical signals, however, it is well to look at one perspective that both the long and short positioner should have in common: finding the right method to reap profits. Table 5-1 gives the risk inherent in different strategies.

Money Makes Money

It takes big money to make big money in the stock market, but the average investor does not have a lot of money. Whether he is selling short or buying long, he most likely is not going to get rich in the stock market. If he is an especially astute investor who pays attention to his portfolio, to the business and financial markets, and to the advice of *some* of the pros, he will possibly do better than he would if he just banked his money. But the market offers no guarantees.

Opportunities for tremendously high returns on investment are possible from the buying of calls, the buying of puts, and investing in commodities, but these are highly speculative investments that require a great knowledge of the markets,

Table 5-1
Money Making Money

Strategy	Relative Risk	Leverage
Buying stock cash	Medium to high	None
Buying stock on margin	High	Medium
Buying puts	High	High
Buying calls	High	High
Selling puts	Dangerously high	Medium
Selling uncovered calls	Very high	Medium
Selling covered calls	None*	None

*Risk is minimal if you sell out-of-the-monies and none at all if the call is far enough out-of-the-money to assure profit on the stock even after all commissions are paid.

It takes a lot of money to make money unless you can find methods or investments which provide a high amount of leverage. Leverage is basically the opportunity to have each invested dollar do the work of more than one dollar. But the greater the leverage, the greater the risk.

of the underlying stock in particular, and of *when* to take your profits. In the case of commodities trading, this is an especially high-risk game.

Why the small chance of getting rich in the stock market? Suppose you are lucky enough to have $25,000 to invest. Also suppose you are lucky enough to pick a couple of stocks over a three-year period that allow you to triple your money. After three years, you have $75,000. This is a lot of gain for some people; but even if it could be made, it can very well be lost or diminished on your next trade.

But let's face it: the odds are you will not triple your money in three years. The odds are you will not double it in three years.

To do so not only takes special investment skill and knowledge but also *luck*. You are not going to pick winner after winner after winner. Nobody does, not even the pros. Additionally, chances are high that sooner or later you are going to have cash needs—for that new house, car, vacation, college tuition, or medical bills—and you will have to bail out of your positions before they reach their full potential, or when they are showing losses.

Big Money can afford to play a very different game than you can. First of all, it can afford to spread the risk by taking large positions in many different stocks. Secondly, it can afford to be patient, very patient. Stocks in Big Money portfolios do not have to take off in a year or two or even three; Big Money can wait and wait and wait. Thirdly, Big Money means back-up money to reverse positions, or buy into a stock or option again at more advantageous prices.

What is meant by "reverse position"? Well, consider you have purchased 1,000 shares of Rigg & Cotter stock when it was selling at $10 per share. Now, it is selling at $5 per share and you have a $5,000 paper loss. You have some decisions to make.

1. **You can just hold on to the stock and hope it regains lost ground.** This you would only chance if bullish signs prevail. But if you do this, you are stuck with a paper loss of $5,000, and paper losses are not tax deductable.

2. **You could sell the stock, take the cash loss and then buy the stock back.** In this way, you can write off the loss and if you are in, say, the 28 percent tax bracket, that write off means a $1,400 tax savings. *But* the IRS says you must wait 31 days before you can buy the stock back, and while you are waiting for those 31 days to pass, the stock could climb to new highs.

3. **You can reverse your position by buying another 1,000 shares and selling the first 1,000 after 31 days.** Now, if the stock goes up in those 31 days, you come out an even bigger winner because you profit on both the new shares purchased, and on the old shares.

4. **You can buy more shares at the lower price, thereby lowering your break-even point, and sell all shares as soon as the break-even point has been reached.**

The last two strategies require additional money, either through direct payment, or margin. This is why it always pays to have back-up money. But number 3 and number 4 also present additional risk: the stock can continue to go down, and you can lose twice as much money. In this case, you have the choice of going in again to change positions, or lower your break-even point; or you can buy calls instead of the stock. The lower price of the calls limits your loss if the downslide continues, but gives you opportunity to profit handsomely on upticks.

The short seller can play these same games. When the stock which is supposed to go down in price goes up instead, the short seller can short more stock and take advantage of the 31 day rule. He may also buy puts on this same stock.

As may now be clear, the more money someone has with which to play the stock market, the safer he can make stock investing. But it cannot be said enough times that even the pros can lose, and that there are no guarantees in the stock market except for premium income from the writing of out-of-the-money covered calls.

Then why play the market, you may ask?

People play the market because the *chance* to make more money than they can in the money markets is always present.

Market Indicators

Because of the precarious nature of stock investing, brokers have compiled some ingenius indicators which they use to gauge market direction, relative perform-ance, and stock group dynamics. With the advent of the home computer, even the independent investor can call up all sorts of graphs and charts to help confuse him even further about where the market is going and what stocks are worth taking long or short positions in. Compared to what the home computer can call up, the computer terminals in the major brokerage firms have a jungle of charts, graphics and statistics from which to draw.

Yet with all this information at hand, the stock market is still a gamble. There are always losers as well as winners.

The major indicators (Table 5-2) on which the investment community depends can all be found in the large city daily newspapers, like the *New York Times*, and in the financial papers such as *Investor's Daily*. The *Daily* seems to know that investors are just as eager for statistics on individual stocks and the market in general as sports fans are eager for game and player statistics. So, the editors fill a large percentage of the paper with stock and market data and help point to new dynamics in stock and options trading for the small investor.

The Dow Jones averages are probably the most frequently quoted indicators. Three stock groups make up these averages: 30 industrials, 20 transportation, and 15 utilities. The stocks that make up these averages are listed in Tables 5-3 through 5-5, but by the time this book gets into your hands, some of the stocks which make up the averages will have changed. The ever-changing nature of the stock market necessitates that the lists be updated periodically. Eventually new stocks become more representative of market activity in general than some stocks already included in the listings; thus the need for revision.

The true value of the Dow Jones averages, however, is a subject of continuing debate in the investment community. Many feel the number of stocks that may be traded on all the major exchanges leave it improbable that the activity of 65 stocks can be indicative of overall market performance. Thus, it is not unusual to find some who favor other indicators over the Dow Jones averages, indicators such as those listed in Table 5-6.[1]

On radio and television, it is very popular to gauge market activity by citing the Dow Jones Industrial Average along with the number of advancing, declin-ing, and unchanging stocks on the New York and American stock exchanges.

Very often, radio or television reporters will say "the market is up," or "the market is down," but what they actually mean is that the Dow Jones Industrial Average is up or down. The stocks in which you may be short or long may very

Table 5-2
Major Indicators

Dow Jones Averages
  30 Industrials
  20 Transportation
  15 Utilities
  65 Composite
  Equity Mkt.

New York Stock Exchange
  Composite
  Industrials
  Transportation
  Utilities
  Financial

Standard & Poor
  500 Index
  Industrials
  Transportation
  Utilities
  Financial

NASDAQ
  OTC Composite
  Industrials
  Insurance
  Banks
  NMS Composite
  NMS Industrials

Russell
  Russell 1000
  Russell 2000
  Russell 3000

AMEX

Value Line Geometric

Wilshire 5000

well be going in the wrong direction regardless of the overall market's direction. Actually, the industrials alone were never meant to be an indication of future market performance. According to the theory developed by Charles H. Dow, the founder of the *Wall Street Journal*, all three Dow Jones averages must be compared before any predictions can be made, and no single day's activity is a sign of anything. The way the theory goes is that if the industrials, utilities, and transportations reach new highs for consecutive periods, then a bull market is expected. If they all reach new lows, then a bear market is in the making. Thus, to the short seller, if the Dow Jones averages are UP, and have been reaching new highs over the past weeks, it may be time to cover positions.

The new high and new low lists (Table 5-7) in your daily paper will also be of some help in deciding whether or not to go long or short. According to market

Table 5-3
The Dow Jones Industrials

Stock	Ticker Symbol	Principal Business
Allied Signal	ALD	Aerospace, automotive
ALCOA	AA	Aluminum producer
American Express	AXP	Travel, banking, insurance
American Tel. & Tel.	T	Telecommunications
Bethlehem Steel	BS	Steel
Boeing Co.	BA	Jet planes, missiles
Caterpillar	CAT	Earthmoving equipment, diesel engr.
Chevron Corp.	CHV	Oil
Coca-Cola	HO	Syrups, juices, film
Du Pont	DD	Chemicals, gas, oil
Eastman Kodak	EK	Cameras, photo equip, chemicals
Exxon	XON	Oil
General Electric	GE	Broadcasting, consumer & industrial goods
General Motors	GM	Automobile manufacturing
Goodyear Tire	GT	Tires and rubber
IBM	IBM	Business machine manufacturing
International Paper	IP	Paper production
McDonald's	MCD	Restaurant franchiser
Merck & Co.	MRX	Pharmaceuticals
Minnesota M&M	MMM	Adhesive tapes, coated abrasives
Morgan (JP)	JPM	Commercial and wholesale banking
Philip Morris	MO	Tobacco, brewing
Procter & Gamble	PG	Household items, food products
Sears	S	Department stores, insurance
Texaco	TX	Oil
Union Carbide	UK	Chemicals, plastics
United Technologies	UTX	Aerospace
Westinghouse Elec.	WX	Electric equipment, nuclear power
Woolworth	Z	Department stores

The stocks that make up the Dow Jones 30 industrials will change from time to time.

Table 5-4
The Dow Jones Transportation Stocks

Stock	Ticker Symbol	Principal Business
AMR	AMR	Holding company (American Airlines)
Airborn Freight	ABF	Air freight
Alaska Air Group	ALK	Scheduled and chartered airlines
American President	APS	Container ships operator
Burlington Northern	BNI	Railroads, pipelines
CSX Corp.	CSX	Railroad holding company, coal carrier; pipelines
Carolina Freight	CAO	Holding company (general freight)
Consolidated Freightways	CNF	Trucking, air freight
Consolidated Rail	CRR	Rail freight system
Delta Air Lines	DAL	Airline company
Federal Express	FDX	Air and land package delivery
Norfolk Southern	NSC	Railroad holding company
Roadway	ROAD	Holding motor freight carrier
Ryder System	R	Equipment leasing and transporation services
Santa Fe Pacific	SFX	Railroad holding company
Southwest Airlines	LUV	Texas airline
UAL Corp.	UAL	Holding company (United Airlines)
USAir Group	U	Airline holding company
Union Pacific	UNP	Rail and truck transportation; oil and gas; mining
Xtra Corp.	XTR	Transportation equipment leasing

The stocks which make up the DJ transportation average will change from time to time.

Table 5-5
The Dow Jones Utility Stocks

Stock	Ticker Symbol	Principal Business
American Electric Pwr.	AEP	Utility holding company
Arkla Inc.	ALG	Natural gas utility
Centerior Energy	CX	Holding co. for Cleveland Electric, Toledo Edison
Columbia Gas System	CG	Utility holding company
Commonwealth Edison	CWE	Utility service in IL
Consolidated Edison	ED	Electric, gas, steam utility
Detroit Edison	DTE	Electric and steam utility
Houston Industries	HOU	Texas electric utility holding company
Niagara Mohawk Power	NMK	New York electric, gas utility
Pacific Gas & Elec.	PCG	California electric and gas utility
Panhandle Eastern	PEL	Natural gas line operator
Peoples Energy	PGL	Chicago gas utility
Philadelphia Electric	PE	Electric and gas utility
Public Service Enterp.	PEG	Holding company for Public Service Electric & Gas
SCEcorp	SCE	Holding company for S. Cal. Edison

The stocks which make up the DJ utility average will change from time to time.

watchers, if the number of stocks reaching new highs is greater than those reaching new lows over a marked period of time, then the possibilities of a general market upswing are in the making. Be careful about selling short under these conditions unless you feel as certain as possible that your target stock is too fundamentally and technically weak to run with the herd. On the other hand, if the number of stocks setting new lows is greater than those setting new highs, then the marketplace is weakening, and is game for short sellers.

A popular indicator for many professional traders is the short interest on the New York Stock Exchange (Big Board) and the American Stock Exchange. This list simply gives the number of shares sold short for specific stocks. If the number of shares sold short is relatively high, this reflects the sentiment that a stock is in for a decline. (But keep in mind that sentiment can be wrong.) The problem with

Table 5-6
Relative Directions of Major Indicators
on a Typical Trading Day

Index	Annual High	Annual Low	% Chng
Dow Jones Averages			
30 Industrials	2810.15	2382.88	+14.92
20 Transportation	1532.01	1031.83	+3.91
15 Utilities	236.23	191.68	+10.88
65 Composite	1115.15	911.72	+10.90
Equity Market Index	337.63	288.39	+10.95
New York Stock Exchange			
Composite	199.34	171.71	+9.57
Industrials	237.76	207.56	+11.10
Utilities	102.92	81.93	+12.89
Transportation	212.37	161.32	+4.03
Finance	173.29	134.60	− 2.09
Standard & Poor's Indexes			
500 Index	359.80	306.95	+12.01
Industrials	411.20	353.48	+13.22
Transportation	331.07	251.57	+6.87
Utilities	157.86	124.18	+14.76
Financials	35.24	26.59	− 0.85
NASDAQ			
Composite	485.73	410.72	+ 0.60
Industrials	472.42	410.71	+7.02
Insurance	561.34	472.31	+ 1.83
Banks	491.16	346.08	− 24.15
National Market Composite	212.43	179.53	+0.99
National Market Industrials	185.12	161.31	+7.91
Others			
Amex	397.03	342.64	+0.95
Value Line	278.98	232.04	− 6.52
Russell 2000	180.78	152.62	− 2.64
Wilshire 5000	3523.47	3037.25	+ 8.16

This table compares ranges and changes in the major indexes for a selected 12-month period to show their general relationship to each other. These major indexes are used to measure stock market performance. One group of indexes is rarely sufficient for a balanced market picture. Here you will notice that the rates of change vary, but the direction of change is consistent in most cases.

Table 5-7
New Highs/New Lows

NEW HIGHS — 129

ACM Mgd	Elcor	LaPac s	SaraLee
ALLTEL Cp	EnglhrdCp	MFS IntInc	ScieAtl
AmStores	EnronOG	MGMG rt	ScudNwEur
Amer T&T	EuroFd	Mesalnc n	Seagul
Amsco	EuroWtFd	MinnMng	Singer
Arvin	FedRlty	Motorola	SmthBck s
BarclyBk pfC	FtCmwFC n	Mylan s	SmthBc eqt s
BarB pfD	FishrPrce s	NewGermny	Snyder pf
Bemis s	FtDearbn S	NICOR Inc	SwAirl s
BroadInc pfP	FostrWhlr	NorStaPw	Standex
BuckeyePar	FounH s	NSPw 4.56pf	StatMut Sec
CBS	France	OfcDepot s	SunbmOstr n
CPC s	FundAmer	OffshP pf	SwissHelv
CapstdMtg	FutureGer	OhPw 7.6pfC	Tadrian n
CatalnMkt n	GRC Intl	OrionCap	TempGlGv
Chrysler	GenCinema	OrionCa pf	TexasInst
Circus s	GenInst n	OrionCa pf	TexInst pf
ColgP	GenMotE prC	PHH Cp	ThomBett
ConEd 5pfA	GtechHld n	PacA IncSh	Trchmk s
Constr s	HlthCP s	PepBoys	ToysRUs
CoprTr s	HomeDepot s	PitnyBw s	20CentInd s
CwnCrk s	IllPw 4.70pf	Polaroid s	UnEI 4.50pf
CyprusMn	IndiM 8.68pf	PolicyMgt n	UnEI 6.40pf
CypresMn pf	IntGame	Potash g	UtdHlthCre
DPL wi	IntpbGb s	PromusCo	UHltCr wi
DQE	K mrt pf	PubSvc Col	UtdKingdom
DeltaAir pf	KCSou s	PutnDvInc	Varity pf
Dexter	Kellogg s	QuestValCap	WinnDixie
Donlley s	LGE s	ReadrDig	Winnebago
DuffPhUtil	LeeEnt	RdrDg B n	WiscPubSv
EdisonBro	LincN pfA	Riverwdln n	Wrigley
ElPasoNG n	Loral	SPS Tran n	Wrigley wi
		SFER pf	

NEW LOWS — 14

AydinCp	FstFed s	LeslieFay	UnoRest
BritPtr wt	FrkInQst n	NuvSTFl3 n	vlValeyIn
EngChina	Hartmarx	OMI Corp	Wstpc ADS rt
EnvElem	ImperChem		

s-Split or stock dividend of 25 per cent or more in the past 52 weeks. High-low range is adjusted from old stock. n-New issue in past 52 weeks and does not cover the entire 52 week period.

This new highs/new lows listing, taken from the *Wall Street Journal*, simply gives the names of the stocks reaching new peaks and valleys on the previous day's trading. Bear in mind that the stocks making new highs can still go higher, and the stocks making new lows can still go lower. Thus, these lists are never to be used as the only criteria for taking short or long positions. They are generally used only to determine whether the market in general is trending. If the number of stocks setting new highs is continually greater than those setting new lows, a bull market is in the making.

the short interest numbers is that they may be interpreted in completely opposite ways because when a short seller makes his closing trade, he actually buys back the stock he originally borrowed so he could sell short. Many feel this pending buy-back actually sets up a bullish trend for the market. Yet others will insist that the short interest data reflects the kind of bearish sentiment that usually drives stock prices down. (Short interest in certain stocks, it should be noted, may be the result of arbitraging.)

Then again, there is still another way of interpreting this data. It has to do with the "contrarian" philosophy which states that an investor should always go against the tide. When the majority is bearish, be bullish; when the majority is bullish, be bearish. In this case, if the short interest is relatively high, it is time to go long; and if it is relatively low, it is time to go short.

The widely followed put-call ratio is usually used in parallel with short interest figures. This is a tricky little indicator that looks at the put-call trading on underlying stocks that comprise Standard and Poor's 100 Index (S&P 100), as well as the Chicago Board Options Exchange (CBOE) equity ratio. Theory has it that if the ratio of puts to calls is 70/100 on the S&P 100 and 65/100 on the CBOE equity ratio, then stocks are probably going to climb in price. However, if the put/call ratio on either index is 40/100 or less, then stocks are probably going to decline in price. (See Table 5-8 for further clarification.)

Again, what we have here is a contrarian interpretation of the ratio. The contrarians are always guided by the rule that the majority of investors, particularly individual investors, are usually wrong. Because the contrarian approach to the market generally holds up fairly well (though not consistently), you will often find the pros going opposite the short interest indications, especially when the put/call ratio verifies the trend.

Table 5-8
CBOE Put-Call Ratio

Index	Trades		Ratio
	Puts	Calls	
S&P 100	500,000	600,000	83/100
CBOE Equity	300,000	500,000	60/100

If the ratio of puts to calls on the S&P 100 is 70/100 and is 65/100 on the CBOE Equity, then stocks will probably climb in price. If the ratio on either index, however, is 40/100 or less, then stocks may decline in price.

But professional analysts, brokers, investors, and speculators will often emphasize that stock investing is hardly a science, and that the market is almost always contradictory. The same data often yields opposite recommendations from stock pickers, whether they are all fundamentalists or all technicians. But regardless of their past success and their awareness of market contradictions, the professionals are still hung up on statistics, indexes, and indicators as though they were signs from some oracle who would show the way to profit.

Market watchers are also particularly fond of the advance/decline indicator. This one makes a lot of sense, and is listed in almost all newspapers providing stock listings as well as in the financial dailies and weeklies. This indicator gives the number of stocks that have advanced, declined, or remained unchanged in their closing prices from the day before. Theoretically, if the Dow Jones averages are down and the advance/decline indicator is showing more declines, and this has been the case on most days over a couple of weeks, then the signs are bearish. If, however, the Dow Jones averages are up and the advance/decline indicator is showing a greater number of advances, then the signs are very bullish and the market may not be the place for the short seller unless, again, he has a stock so technically and fundamentally weak that it will fall in price regardless of the way the market goes. But bear in mind that a few days of coincidence between the averages and this indicator mean little.

Some investors prefer to develop their own indexes. They may have their own 20 to 50 stocks that they like to watch and have learned over the years that their performance is more indicative of things to come than any of the professionally developed indicators. However, it is important to realize that no indicator can help you call market movements to the dollar, or within any clearly defined time span.

Table 5-9 indicates typical bear signals, but the truth of the matter is that there is no one who can tell you *when* the market is going to do anything. In fact, bull or bear markets are rarely recognized until the market is halfway through them. The indicators that market predictors develop or depend upon only serve as general guidelines. Pay attention to them, but do not take them as gospel. If you read enough of the financial newspapers and magazines, you will find the pros making completely opposite predictions as the result of studying the same data. Generally, this is a sign to stay away from the market, or just play covered calls.

On the other hand, there are always those contrarians who believe that when everyone has lost faith in the market, things can only get better; and when everyone is enthusiastic about the market, things can only get worse, and take their positions accordingly.

Knowing general market direction, of course, does not help you zero in on a specific stock or stock group. After all, most of the market may go in one direction, but certain stocks or stock groups will go in another. Finding the right stock to short is going to mean a great deal of research, or faith in your broker's recommendations.

Table 5-9
Bear Signals

- Interest rates are going UP

- The number of stocks setting new lows is continually greater than those setting new highs

- The put-call ratio on the S&P 100 as well as the CBOE Equity Index is 40 puts or less to each 100 calls.

- Short interest is relatively high

- Volume is on a steady decline on the major exchanges

- The major indicators are showing declining averages

- The number of stocks declining each day almost continuously outnumbers the stocks advancing

- The investment community is highly bullish and has been so for some time

These are just some of the major signals that indicate it may be a short seller's market. But the short seller has got to know his target stock. Not all stocks go the way of the market.

Still, you should have little interest in shorting any stock in general market indicators are heavily bullish. Why take the chance?

But suppose the Dow Jones average and the other major indicators, as well as the advance/decline indicator, are showing signs of a major market downturn. Suppose also that the general feeling about the market is positive. Considering the *contrarian theory* as well as these indexes and indicators, what else might you want to know about general market direction before you zero in on the stock or stocks you wish to short?

If you are a particularly astute investor, you might also want to look at the Short Term Trading Index to find out where most of the action in the stock markets has been. This index is also known as the Arms Index. It is computed separately for the New York and American stock exchanges and for NASDAQ, the computerized trading program of the National Association of Securities Dealers which makes the market for over-the-counter stocks. (Listing in the NASDAQ

Table 5-10
Arms Index

Market	Mon.	Tue.	Wed.	Thur.	Fri.
NYSE	.83	1.30	.50	.72	1.20
AMEX	.81	.95	.98	.62	.80
NASDAQ	.87	1.00	.52	.75	.80

The Arms Index, also known as the Short-Term Trading Index, is used to locate market action. If an index reading is less than 1, then most of the action has been in rising stocks.

system requires not only the meeting of financial requirements set by the National Association of Securities Dealers, but also certain marketing requirements. Still, stocks will not be listed in the NASDAQ system if the issuing corporations do not give their okay.)

The Arms Index (Table 5-10) is computed by taking the average volume of declining issues and dividing it by the average volume of advancing issues. If the result is less than one, then most of the action has been in rising stocks.

Now, you have a general idea of market direction and where most of the action is in terms of rising and declining issues. But what about activity on the particular exchange on which the stock you might select is trading? Is that exchange showing strength or weakness?

To answer this last question, you would refer to the Closing Tick Indicator (Table 5-11), which your broker will gladly quote for you. This indicator gives the relative strength of the selected markets as well as the Dow Jones Industrial Average. When the figures are positive, the market is showing strength. When they are negative, the market is showing weakness.

Now, you are ready to pick the stock you want to short: Indexes and indicators say there may be a downturn, that most of the trading activity has been in high-priced issues and the New York Stock Exchange has been showing weakness.

Stock Selection

There are two major methods for selecting stocks. One is based on financial, marketing and management data and the other is based on stock activity alone. The first is referred to as fundamentals analysis and the second as technical analysis. But, in reality, investors have their own hybrid or unique methods, and

Table 5-11
Closing Tick Indicator

Market	Mon.	Tue.	Wed.	Thur.	Fri.
NYSE	-240	-220	+300	+256	+312
AMEX	-38	-88	+86	-12	+100
DJIA	-10	-11	+20	-10	+19

The closing tick indicator gives the relative strength of selected markets near the close of the day. If the closing tick figures are positive, then the related market is showing strength. If they are negative, then the selected market is showing weakness. The figures are derived by subtracting the number of stocks in which the last change was downward from the number of stocks in which the last change was upward.

even the pros sometimes ignore the basic rules and go with gut feelings or follow-the-leader strategies.

It is not unusual that people ignore the textbooks and go with their own instincts and methods. People have a natural tendency to attempt things in their own unique way. While in most cases this attitude results in nothing more than spinning one's wheels, in other cases this experimentation brings new ideas and sophistication to the marketplace.

Some of the methods which investors use to flag potential candidates for short or long positioning are meritorious, though the methods have dangerous downsides. "So what?" some reply, when their stock selection methods are challenged. They point out that in reality all methods of stock selection have their failings, that none can be guaranteed, so why not go with one's own methods if they have worked in the past? Additionally, they argue, selecting stocks on very strict financial principles can be even less rewarding than the dart board approach. Strong companies may not have their stocks take off for years; and accounting is an art, not a science, which means values assigned to a balance sheet can be a source for great argument.

Some investors subscribe to one or two investment newsletters and make their selections from their recommendations. They feel it is impossible to do the research themselves, and that their overall average of success from playing the newsletters will certainly be better than their own picks. This is good thinking, as long as it takes into account three counter-arguments.

The first is that many newsletters take a shotgun approach to stock picks, knowing well that in a bull market most of their picks will be correct. So while the newsletter's average turns out to be impressive, the investor may be stuck with a couple of very bad losers. The second argument is that every newsletter has its own perspective and personality, and that the investor should study one for awhile until he learns just when he can trust its recommendations. The third argument is that the more popular letters create a short term market in the stocks they pick, so there is generally a run-up in price in these stocks around the time of publication. Very often the investor cannot get the stock at the recommended price because of this unusual demand created by others trying to beat everyone else into the stock.

There are those who let the "New Highs, New Lows" lists be their flag. For instance, a short seller will watch the daily listings of stocks reaching new highs. When he notices one stock on the list "x" number of times in "x" number of days or weeks, he sells it short after double-checking that there is not a takeover or special dividend in the works. (Times and days will be determined by whatever values he feels are valid.) The danger here is that stocks can always go higher, just as they can go lower, so neither the list of new highs nor the list of new lows can be completely depended upon. However, they are a good flag for potential stocks in which to invest, and should not be overlooked.

Some short sellers like to look for stocks which have just declared hefty stock splits. Now, ordinarily, one would think there would be strong bullish tendencies for a stock on which there has recently been declared a two for one, or better, split. And generally there is—but early on. What astute bears will do is wait until about the time of the split and take their positions, either selling short the stock, buying puts, or selling short the stock and buying calls in case the stock continues to go up. Generally, a stock will begin its upward climb before the split occurs— news always leaks out. Then, after the news is reported in the press, there is a run on the stock, adding a few more points to the price. But, as there are often weeks or even months from the time of the declaration until the actual split, the stock usually drifts for awhile and then turns south for a short time after the date of the split. This is the period when the short sellers and put buyers try to make their speculative gains. This strategy is certainly not for the neophyte, but can work well with speculators who are familiar with both the technical and fundamental aspects of the target security. The danger, of course, is that sometimes the stock continues to increase in price even after the record date of the split. This is why it pays to play the stock both ways by either shorting the stock and buying calls, or buying both calls and puts.

Contrarians like to wait for good or bad news to make the business headlines, then they take the appropriate position in the subject stock. For instance, if a major bank has its debt downgraded, by the time the news makes the headlines, bullish speculators will be getting ready to take their long positions. On the other hand, if the headlines read that this same bank has just made record profits, the shortsellers will be getting ready to take their positions on the belief that by the time the news hits, the stock price will already be reflecting overbought conditions. This is the contrarian's game, going against the news, going against the herd. But there is a danger to responding only to news items. Dirty tricks are being played very frequently by both bears and bulls. Sometimes these dirty tricks only result in rumors, but often the rumors are deliberately fed to the press and lead to published "news."

This might appear to the reader to be a dangerous accusation and one that undermines the marketplace. But everyone knows about these "dirty tricks," and in particular about how the marketplace will respond to rumors. Have you ever noticed how a listless stock will suddenly jump in price the week that its options come due so that call buyers can reap a nice gain, or the stock suddenly plummets in price that week so that put buyers might profit?

Some of the false rumors that can send a stock into a downward spin might relate to the illness of the company's chief executive officer, or to the use of drugs at the executive level. Those that can send a stock upward might have to do with possible takeovers, stock buybacks, or magic products—magic in the sense that they are the first in what will be a thriving market.

The *Wall Street Journal* has reported on some of these dirty tricks. In one "Heard on the Street," a *Journal* column by John R. Dorfman, some more sophisticated tricks were discussed. One of these includes forcing a short seller to cover his positions by buying back his stock. It is called a "buy-in." What happens is that someone who has lent stock to a short seller calls it back. Aware of the buy-in, which just may have been deliberately planned, speculators load up on the stock. As they do so they force the price of the stock up and up, until the short seller panics to cover his positon. The point here is that there are always those who would undermine market integrity for their own gain.

Technical Analysis

Of the two major schools of investment, the one that has been getting the most interest lately is the technical school. Those who adhere to it are called technicians. Pay special note to the fact, however, that technical analysis is an art, not a science; it can let you down as surely as every other approach to making money in the market can.

Technical analysis was developed because it has always been apparent that market movement has a lot to do with mass psychology and, therefore, also with mass communications. What creates interest in a stock? What causes individuals to be interested in the stock market as a source of profit?

Everything affects investor interest, perspective, and attitude—including economic, political, and psychological forces. Technicians try to ascertain what the investment public is thinking, mainly through an analysis of price and volume movement. But as price and volume movement by themselves are relatively undependable, the technician becomes mainly interested in comparisons or moving averages. He wants to know what the 12-month or 50-day moving price average has been for Citicorp or A. H. Belo, for instance. He wants to know how the stock is moving in relation to some index such as the S&P 500 or the Dow Jones

Industrials: He wants to know how the daily, weekly, or monthly volume in a specific stock compares with other stocks in its group.

For the technician, it comes down to the law of supply and demand. The greater the demand for a given stock, the higher the price the stock can command. The less the demand, the lower the price will go. When the technician finds a stock with an upward trend in price and an increasing trading volume compared to other stocks in its industry group, he feels he's got a winner; and he is going to tell everybody. When he does tell everybody, he further increases the demand for the stock. The stock then feeds on its own good press until its price becomes so high that investors begin to shy away. As they shy away, volume decreases and the short sellers go on standby.

Trends, however, are very unpredictable. Sometimes they are discovered too late for anyone to take any truly profitable position. There is a lot of Monday-morning quarterbacking in the investment world. One help in identifying trends before it is too late to take advantage of them is something called the "moving average." This is actually a mean average which constantly changes (and, therefore, "moves") because each day, or at some predefined interval, a new item of information is added as the very first item is deleted. Then, a new sum is taken and the new average figured.

As an example, consider the case where we may be constructing a five-day moving average for IBM. Suppose the closing price of the stock 51 days ago was $95.25 per share and yesterday it was $120.00 per share. If today the stock closes at $118.50, to update the average, we delete the $95.25 of 51 days ago and add today's closing price. Next we add up the closing prices for the last 50 days, divide by 50, and have the new average.

Technical analysts will now study the moving averages for IBM, and chart the closing daily prices against the moving average. When the closing price crosses either above or below the line representing the moving average, they usually assume this indicates a trend reversal. But they do not stop here. They try to double-check themselves by noting if the moving average reverses direction. When it does, they compare the data to see if there is strong confirmation of a trend.

The technical analyst is a chartist. He is always charting the movements of a stock's price and its trading volume, as well as doing the same for stock groups and for the market in general. Many analysts have their own very complex formulas to help them determine the results of their charting. Their final decisions on what to buy, sell, or stay away from are based on a lot more than just the way a couple of lines on a chart intersect. In the final analysis, however, much depends upon the individual's interpretation of the data at hand, and two technicians will not necessarily interpret the same data in the same way. Technicians are necessarily also historians. Their data means little if it is not placed in some historical context. History only repeats itself when all the variables are the same, and they rarely are. What is really going to happen to a stock today or tomorrow is not only contingent upon volume and price movements, but also on any number of unpredictable events from legal suits to Chapter 11 filings, from new product developments to closing markets, from new competition to monopolized markets, from boom times to economic crashes.

Many investment advisors and investment newsletters today use moving averages to recommend stocks to their subscribers, either for the purpose of selling short or buying long. Never get in the habit of depending on any recommendation based solely on some "moving average."

For example, consider the following true story. An independent investor was interested in buying stock in Harcourt Brace. Because he was planning on making a substantial investment, he sought out the opinions of a number of professionals, including his broker. Among the professionals he queried was the publisher of a financial news and phone service who used a 50-day moving average as the basis for his recommendations. Harcourt Brace, then listed on the New York Stock Exchange, was recommended for purchase. Currently at $8.00, its upside resistance was put at $12.00 and its downside resistance at $6.50.[2] Because he was getting negative signals from his broker, the investor decided to hold off. But when the stock dropped to $5.00, he decided it was time to take a position. But first he called the investment service. The computer replied that it was mildly bullish on the stock, with a downside potential of $5.75 and an upside resistance of $8.00.

Now, the investor was confused. The stock was at $5.00 but the investment service was saying that the downside resistance was at $5.75. He decided the service had not updated its information so he called the publisher and explained the problem. "No, nothing is wrong," he was told. "We use a 50-day moving average and based on this the downside resistance is at $5.75."

"But the stock is at $5.00," the investor replied. "How can the downside resistance be $5.75? What are you telling me? Shouldn't you adjust those figures?"

"Well, we would be fraudulent if we did so," came the explanation. "We use a formula based on a 50-day moving average. Harcourt recently plummeted on bad press, and when this happens the moving average is undependable."

"But then so must be your recommendations. I mean, how can I trust them? Here is a stock at $5.00 that you are saying should not have gone below $5.75. What is my downside risk if I do buy this stock? How can I know?"

"Well," came the explanation, "assume that Harcourt is oversold and should bounce back."

In frustration, the investor decided to stay away from the stock. Good thing, too, because before long it sunk to $2.75. It bounced back up briefly to around $6.00, then eventually declined to less than a dollar. (Harcourt eventually sank to below $1.00 per share and was taken over.)

Now, many other recommendations by this same investment service were on the mark, and its track record has indicated that it is a relatively well-respected service. But in this case, its reliance on a 50-day moving average was absurd and left one investor not only confused about whether or not to take a position in the stock, but also terribly disenchanted with the service to which he had subscribed.

Moving averages, then, are not the last word in technical analysis, and very few try to sell them as such. Technicians, by the way, also try to measure the actual rate of change taking place in price and volume movements. To do so, they have developed momentum indicators which help them pinpoint overbought and oversold situations.

Because the short seller is basically a speculator, and because successful speculation depends on good timing, technical analysis should play an important part in the short seller's decision making. But being a chartist not only takes special skills, it takes a great deal of time. Thus, it is not something the independent investor should take on himself. He should find a dependable investment service offering stock recommendations based on moving price averages. Then, when they say sell short in a stock which he has already determined to be weak in its fundamentals, he can take his position with some assurance.

Fundamental Analysis

The data necessary for a fundamental analysis of any stock on the major exchanges is usually available from your full-service broker, from your local library, or from your investment counselor.

Just exactly what constitutes a stock's fundamentals, though, is up for debate. Some analysts look at only four or five business and financial items and consider these the fundamentals for any investment decision. Others have as many as 20 or 25. For all practical purposes, you, as an independent investor without sophisticated computer programs to use in your decision making and research, would be best to confine yourself to the following six fundamentals:

1. Current assets and liabilities

2. Projected assets and liabilities

3. Projected earnings

4. Historical and projected price-to-earnings ratio (P/E ratio)

5. Management

6. Labor relations

Current assets and liabilities

The current strength of any company is measured by what it has and what it owes. One of the ways you can determine the soundness of a company is to look at certain tell-tale ratios. One of these is the *current ratio* which is found by totalling the current assets and dividing that total by the current liabilities. If a company has current assets of $50 million and current liabilities of $25 million, the current ratio is two to one, meaning the company is quite capable of meeting its short-term obligations and is too solid to consider for any short selling.[3] Another is the *quick ratio,* calculated in the same way as the current ratio except that inventory is not included in the current assets. This is because inventory may include items that cannot actually be sold and, therefore, give an unreal value to current assets. (See Table 5-12 for other formulas and ratios.)

Projected assets and liabilities

Future projects as well as general business and economic events can greatly alter a company's current and quick ratios so you will want to keep tuned to the financial news and in frequent touch with your broker. No one has a crystal ball, but companies that are taking on new debt to pay off old debts are usually well-known, and excellent prospects for some shortselling profits. Additionally, pending labor problems, product failures or marketing problems are indications that a company's stock will soon be heading south, so you will always want to keep your eyes and ears open for these opportunities.

Earnings

Investors do not buy stocks because they performed well in the past or are performing well today. They buy them because of what they will do in the future. If projected earnings are relatively impressive, the demand for the stock will be just as impressive and no opportunity for the short seller. However, if projected earnings look disappointing and the price of the stock has not yet retreated to reflect the disappointing future, then it's time to consider taking a short position. The problem facing any investor here, however, is that earnings forecasts do not always influence share prices. This is because the current price of the stock may already reflect future performance. How do investors usually determine the relationship between price and performance? They look at current and projected P/E ratios.

P/E Ratio

The price-to-earnings ratio is calculated by dividing the current price of a stock by its earnings. If a stock is selling for $50 per share and earning $2 per share, then its P/E ratio is 25. Most stock tables found in daily newspapers publish the P/E ratios for listed stocks; and financial dailies and weeklies like the *Wall Street Journal, Investor's Daily* and *Barron's* definitely include the P/E ratio in their tables.

But knowing the current P/E ratio is of little use to any investor; that is, it is of little use to him unless he has researched what that P/E ratio has been in the past and has some idea of what future earnings will be. Historical P/E's can be gotten from your broker or, again, from the library. Future earnings projections can be gotten from your investment advisor or broker.

How do you use the P/E ratio and projected earnings data?

Table 5-12
Important Formulas

Name	Description	Formula
Current Ratio	Measures liquidity. Generally, a current ratio of 2 (assets) to 1 (liabilities) is considered sound.	$\dfrac{\text{Current Assets}}{\text{Current Liabilities}}$
Quick Ratio	Measures how quickly a company can come up with cash to cover debts. Assets to liabilities should be in at least a 1.25 to 1 ratio.	$\dfrac{\text{Current Assets} - \text{Inventory}}{\text{Current Liabilities}}$
Working Capital	Measures how much a company has to not only meet its obligations, but also to compete and expand.	Current Assets − Current Liabilities
Debt to Equity Ratio	Measures the amount of leverage (debt) a company is depending upon.	$\dfrac{\text{Total Liabilities}}{\text{Total Liabilities} + \text{Shareholders' Equity}}$
Return on shareholders equity	Also referred to as the ROI (Return on Investment), it indicates whether or not the return from owning stock may be competitive with other investment or savings instruments.	$\dfrac{\text{Net Income}}{\text{Shareholders' Equity}}$

Suppose that a stock we will call Radion traditionally sells between $10 and $20 and its P/E ratio has traditionally fluctuated between 4:1 and 2:1. This means the stock has traditionally traded between two and four times earnings.

Suppose also the latest predictions are the stock will earn $5 per share next year. If so, what price range would you expect the stock to be trading at next year? The answer is "about the same range," as multiplying $5 by both 2 and 4 would indicate. Now, suppose the predictions are that the stock will earn only $2 per share next year and the current price of the stock is $20. What price range would you expect it to be trading at next year? Why, between $4 and $8. Should you sell short? Most definitely.

Bear in mind, however, that P/E ratios can be conflicting signals. Sometimes just a comparison of historical and current levels can flag a worthwhile candidate for selling short or buying long; at other times they are of little or no value unless they are included with an extensive list of technical and fundamental data. For instance, if a P/E ratio is relatively high (historically for the stock and currently for that stock's industry), one might assume that any future advances are already reflected in the price of the stock, or that the investment community simply has a lot of faith in the stock. If the ratio is relatively low, one might assume that the investment community has lost interest, or that there is a bargain here no one else has yet discovered.

There is no strict guideline for what should be a stock or stock group's P/E ratio. Growth stocks will generally trade at high ratios and utility stocks at low ratios. So, if you are contemplating selling a stock short just because its P/E ratio is high—look again, and look deeper. Look at past P/Es for this stock and how it compares with other stocks in the same group. And, are you looking at a cyclical or non-cyclical stock, because their P/Es have different meanings? The point is that as a short seller you may use a high P/E ratio to help you flag a stock for further research, but do not use it as the deciding factor. Look at all the stock's fundamentals; get a technical analysis.

Management

Taking a good, hard look at who is running a company is just as important as looking at balance sheets and income statements. In the final analysis, it is the people in an organization who make it great, not just the product or the company's size. If the men and women at the top of an organization have a history of experience in the marketplace and product lines, and have been with their company long enough to fully understand its complexity, weaknesses and strengths, that corporation is going to do well.

Those at the executive levels need not know the detail of each and every operation or department, but they must understand how individuals, groups, and divisions mesh. They must be astute in basic business and economics, and understand how international events can affect their companies. Too often in the United States movement to the top of an organization is the result of political or promotional maneuvering rather than the kind of sound management that has taken care to groom future candidates for the executive suites over extended periods of time.

Today many CEO's come and go every few years; this is mainly because they were brought in to the top spot instead of being groomed from the inside. Brilliant executives that they may be, rarely do they fully understand the companies they are brought in to run. Few people know a corporation the way the founders did, the men or women who put it together and grew with it. If the management is strong, regardless of the current financial negatives, the stock is no candidate for short sellers

Labor relations

A corporation with union problems which have been persisting for some time should always be on a short seller's list. Few things can change the color of an accountant's ink quicker than labor problems.

The Cost of Money

The cost of money generally has a heavy impact on most stocks, so when short sellers are anticipating increasing interest rates they are generally more comfortable about shorting their target stocks. The cost of money is what interest rates are all about. When interest rates are too high, corporations cannot afford to borrow to expand; and so the economy eventually suffers. When interest rates decline to what corporations feel are acceptable levels, they borrow to expand or increase production, and so the economy eventually gains.

On the other side of the economic scene, when interest rates are high, consumers are going to hoard their money in savings and money market accounts. Thus, the money that would otherwise be invested in corporate America has been diverted. When the banks can no longer excite corporations or individuals to borrow, they begin lowering their interest rates until loan applications start to increase. With this new surge in borrowing, interest rates will eventually bottom out and start to rise again. The cycle continually repeats itself.

Preferred stocks are usually directly and quickly affected by changing interest rates. This is because preferred stock is purchased mainly for the fixed dividend rate. Rising interest rates, therefore, decrease the value of the preferreds, and falling rates increase the value, for the price of the preferred stocks must rise and fall so the dividend represents a competitive rate of return.

The effect of changing interest rates on common stock is less predictable as there are many variables which influence common stock movement. Nevertheless, rising interest rates create a bearish environment and falling rates a bullish one. For this reason bulls and bears pay close attention to the prime rate charged by banks to customers with excellent ratings. Upward movements in the prime rate scare the bulls and excite the bears; downward movements in the prime scare the bears and excite the bulls.

(The prime rate is generally affected by the discount rate charged depository institutions by the Federal Reserve. But this is not always the case. The discount rate sometimes changes more as a reaction to higher rates than as a signal of higher rates. The prime rate, in turn, affects the call money rate—the rate that banks charge brokers on stock exchange collateral. The call money rate is usually less than the prime rate.)

If you take pains to do some research, you will find that, generally, P/E ratios will fall as interest rates rise. (Table 5-13 reviews how to figure P/E ratios.) This is because investors are not willing to pay too high a price to get in on corporate earnings when rising interest rates are signalling that there may be better places for their money. And, as interest rates have pulled back, P/E ratios have increased. This is because the falling interest rates have encouraged investors to pay a little more for those corporate earnings.

In the past, the investment community has reacted pell mell to even just the news of changing interest rates, and we may expect this to continue today and tomorrow. Listen carefully to the financial news when changes in the prime rate are announced. When the change is down, the stock market will be up. When the change is up, the stock market will be down. A move of even a percent of a percent on treasury yields can drive the market hard one way or another. (See Table 5-14.)

The general rule: News of increasing interest rates is good news for short sellers.

Table 5-13
Figuring P/E Ratios

Stock	Stock Price Per Share	Earnings Per Share	P/E Ratio
A	$10.00	$1.00	10:1
B	$15.00	$1.50	10:1
C	$12.00	$1.50	8:1
D	$ 8.00	deficit	—
E	$21.00	$2.00	10½:1

In stock listings, the P/E ratio is expressed with only one numbe. Thus if the ratio is 8:1, under the P/E ratio column you would find the numeral 8.

Table 5-14
Sample Stock Listings

52 Weeks Hi	Lo	Stock	Sym	Div	Yld %	PE	Vol 100s	Hi	Lo	Close	Net Chg
		-B-B-B-									
43¼	35½	BCE Inc g	BCE	2.56	6.8	...	263	37⅞	37⅝	37¾	+ ⅛
16¼	7¾	BET	BEP	.43e	5.1	7	137	8½	8⅜	8½	...
20½	10	BJ Svc	BJS		...	41	426	17¼	16⅞	16⅞	− ⅛
12⅛	**6½**	**BMC**	**BMC**		**...**	**7**	**377**	**8¼**	**7⅞**	**8¼**	**+ ½**
32⅝	27¼	BP Prudhoe	BPT	3.15e	10.0	...	290	31⅜	31⅛	31⅜	+ ⅛
32¼	26⅝	BRE Prop	BRE	2.40	7.5	12	20	31⅞	31⅝	31⅞	+ ¼
8¼	**4⅞**	**Bairnco**	**BZ**	**.20**	**2.8**	**15**	**417**	**7¼**	**7**	**7¼**	**+ ⅜**
19⅛	15⅞	BakrFentrs	BKF	1.64e	8.9		142	18¾	18⅜	18½	...
26	15⅞	BakrHughs	BHI	.46	1.9	107	3646	24¾	24¼	24½	− ⅛
28½	19⅞	BaldorElec	BEZ	.52	1.8	22	12	28⅜	28⅛	28⅛	− ⅛
39½	31¼	Ball Cp	BLL	1.24	3.8	14	644	32⅜	31⅝	32¼	+ ⅜
8¼	3¼	BallyMfg	BLY		...	...	861	4⅞	4¾	4¾	...
9⅜	4⅛	BaltimrBcp	BBB		...	...	290	6¾	6¼	6⅝	+ ¼
24⅜	19¾	BaltimrGE	BGE	1.44	6.4	15	553	22⅝	22¼	22⅜	+ ¼
9⅝	2⅜	BancFla	BFL		...	...	45	8¾	8⅝	8⅝	+ ⅛
50	37¾	BancOne	ONE	1.28	2.9	13	3966	44	43⅝	44	+ ⅝
3¾	**5/16**	**BancTexas**	**BTX**		**...**	**...**	**380**	**1¾**	**1⅝**	**1¾**	**+ ⅛**
28½	24⅜	BancoBilV pf			...	...	55	27⅞	27¾	27⅞	...
30⅞	23⅛	BancoBilV	BBV	1.59e	6.2	6	79	25⅝	25½	25⅝	...
20¼	15⅛	BancoCentrl	BCM	1.02e	6.0	9	8	16⅞	16⅞	16⅞	− ⅛
17⅛	15⅛	BanComercial	BPC		...	...	30	16	15¾	15¾	− ½
49½	35	BancoSantdr	STD	2.26e	5.3	8	317	42½	41¾	42½	+1½
52	39⅜	BcpHawii	BOH	1.29	2.9	10	1065	44¼	42⅝	43¾	+1¼
73¼	51¾	Bandag	BDG	.60	.9	22	263	68¾	67½	68¼	+1
71	62⅜	Bandag A		.60	.9	22	195	65¼	64¾	65	...
19⅞	15¾	BangorHyd	BGR	1.32	6.7	14	39	19¾	19⅝	19¾	+ ⅛
25½	9⅛	BankBost	BKB		...	8	5582	19⅞	19¾	19⅞	+ ½
47¼	27½	BankBost pfA		3.20e	7.7	...	8	41¾	41½	41½	− ¼
43½	27	BankBost pfB		3.08e	7.5	...	11	41½	41	41	...
76¼	47½	BankBost pfC		5.62e	7.8	...	z720	72½	71	71¾	− ¾
25¼	24⅞	BankBost pfE			...	...	1160	25⅛	24⅞	25⅛	
43⅞	25¾	BankNY	BK	1.52	3.5	12	2798	43	42⅛	43	+1¼
49¾	30⅝	BankAmer	BAC	1.30	2.9	11	12587	44⅞	44¼	44¾	+1½

Which should be sold short? Stock listings give you little information to make a decision.

Endnotes

1. Some authors like to distinguish indexes from averages, but this distinction is being lost with time. Many refer to the DJ and other averages as indexes.

2. Numbers are rounded for simplification. Additionally, the conversation which follows is not verbatim, but is as can best be remembered by the investor. The stock at the time was on a steep decline. Harcourt, pressed for cash, had sold some theme parks for a lot less than the investment community expected.

3 What is an acceptable current ratio depends on the type of industry in which a company is entrenched. For example, real estate developers and hotel operators can get away with a lower ratio than most other companies because they have many loans secured by buildings and land.

6

Playing the Game

Procedures for selling short are relatively simple, and they were introduced in Chapter 1. Here in Chapter 6, a series of sample transactions will be described in order to give you some exercises that will answer most of your remaining questions.

Table 6-1 is a copy of federal income tax form Schedule D, on which stock investors must record their capital gains and losses every year. Notice that Part 1 is for short term trading and Part 2 for long term capital gains and losses. Currently, "short term" means one year or less and "long term" means more than one year. These definitions change as tax laws are revised.

For convenience, the transactions described in this chapter will follow the same format as that required by Schedule D. In fact, it is probably a good idea to keep a record of your transactions in this very same way. Then, at the end of the year when you fill out Schedule D, you can simply attach a record of your transactions and not have to fill in parts 1a and 8a. You need only scribble in a "see attached" note and staple to the schedule your list of transactions. On the other hand, if you have made only a few short or long term transactions and there is enough room on the schedule to record them, use sections 1a and 8a.

Table 6-1
Copy of Federal Income Tax Form Schedule D, Page 1

SCHEDULE D	**Capital Gains and Losses**	OMB No. 1545-0074
(Form 1040)	**(And Reconciliation of Forms 1099-B for Bartering Transactions)**	**19 91**
Department of the Treasury	▶ **Attach to Form 1040.** ▶ **See Instructions for Schedule D (Form 1040).**	Attachment
Internal Revenue Service (o)	▶ **For more space to list transactions for lines 1a and 8a, get Schedule D-1 (Form 1040).**	Sequence No. **12A**
Name(s) shown on Form 1040		Your social security number

Caution: *Add the following amounts reported to you for 1991 on Forms 1099-B and 1099-S (or on substitute statements): (a) proceeds from transactions involving stocks, bonds, and other securities, and (b) gross proceeds from real estate transactions not reported on another form or schedule. If this total does not equal the total of lines 1c and 8c, column (d), attach a statement explaining the difference.*

Part I Short-Term Capital Gains and Losses—Assets Held One Year or Less

(a) Description of property (Example, 100 shares 7% preferred of "Z" Co.)	(b) Date acquired (Mo., day, yr.)	(c) Date sold (Mo., day, yr.)	(d) Sales price (see instructions)	(e) Cost or other basis (see instructions)	(f) LOSS If (e) is more than (d), subtract (d) from (e)	(g) GAIN If (d) is more than (e), subtract (e) from (d)
1a Stocks, Bonds, Other Securities, and Real Estate. Include Form 1099-B and 1099-S Transactions. See instructions.						

1b Amounts from Schedule D-1, line 1b (attach Schedule D-1)						
1c Total of All Sales Price Amounts. Add column (d) of lines 1a and 1b ▶ **1c**						

1d Other Transactions (Do NOT include real estate transactions from Forms 1099-S on this line. Report them on line 1a.)

2	Short-term gain from sale or exchange of your home from Form 2119, line 10 or 14c	**2**			
3	Short-term gain from installment sales from Form 6252, line 22 or 30	**3**			
4	Net short-term gain or (loss) from partnerships, S corporations, and fiduciaries	**4**			
5	Short-term capital loss carryover from 1990 Schedule D, line 29	**5**			
6	Add lines 1a, 1b, 1d, and 2 through 5, in columns (f) and (g)	**6**	(	)	
7	Net short-term capital gain or (loss). Combine columns (f) and (g) of line 6		**7**		

Part II Long-Term Capital Gains and Losses—Assets Held More Than One Year

8a Stocks, Bonds, Other Securities, and Real Estate. Include Form 1099-B and 1099-S Transactions. See instructions.

8b Amounts from Schedule D-1, line 8b (attach Schedule D-1)						
8c Total of All Sales Price Amounts. Add column (d) of lines 8a and 8b ▶ **8c**						

8d Other Transactions (Do NOT include real estate transactions from Forms 1099-S on this line. Report them on line 8a.)

9	Long-term gain from sale or exchange of your home from Form 2119, line 10 or 14c	**9**			
10	Long-term gain from installment sales from Form 6252, line 22 or 30	**10**			
11	Net long-term gain or (loss) from partnerships, S corporations, and fiduciaries	**11**			
12	Capital gain distributions	**12**			
13	Gain from Form 4797, line 7 or 9	**13**			
14	Long-term capital loss carryover from 1990 Schedule D, line 36	**14**			
15	Add lines 8a, 8b, 8d, and 9 through 14, in columns (f) and (g)	**15**	(	)	
16	**Net long-term capital gain or (loss).** Combine columns (f) and (g) of line 15		**16**		

For Paperwork Reduction Act Notice, see Form 1040 instructions.   Cat. No. 11338H   **Schedule D (Form 1040) 1991**

Note that in the following examples, it is assumed that all capital gains and losses are short term.

Sample Transactions

You decide that despite the relative strength of the various stock indexes, banking stocks are going to be hit hard. It is 1988 and you have your eye on one stock that has had a remarkable climb. It is Citicorp, currently selling at $30 per share. It had been higher and you feel the current fall in prices will continue. Thus, you decide to play the stock short. You bid 300 shares at $30, and your broker is able to execute the trade at that price.

The broker's commission on the trade is $90. Because you are selling short instead of buying long, subtract this $90 from the proceeds to determine the true dollar value of the sale.

$$\begin{array}{lr} \text{Sold 300 sh., Citicorp at \$30} & = \$9,000 \\ \text{less Commission} & \underline{90} \\ \text{Sales Price} & \$8,910 \end{array}$$

In reality, you will not have to figure the sales price. When you receive your broker's statement , the above calculations will be done for you.

At a price of $8,910 for the 300 shares, the price per share is roughly $29.65. But do not assume that this is your break-even point, for there will be brokerage commissions again when you cover your position. You cannot be sure what that commission will be; it will depend on the value of the shares at buyback time. But as a rule of thumb, assume the closing trade commission will be the same as the opening trade. Thus, to figure your break-even point, subtract another $90 and divide the result again by 300 shares.

$$\$8,910 - \$90.00 \div 300 \text{ sh.} = \$29.40$$

As most stocks sell at one-eighth of a point increments, and one-eighth of a point is the equivalent of 12½ cents, your breakeven point on the Citicorp short sale will be $29⅜. This means the stock must be purchased at $29¼ per share or better, or you will lose money.

Aware now of your break-even point, you check the stock listings five days a week to keep an eye on Citicorp. The stock fluctuates a bit, then after some months falls to $23 per share, at which price you decide to sell all 300 shares. Because of the drop in price, commissions are less than expected ($75).

Congratulations! You have profited from your first short sale.

Description	Date Acq.	Date Sold	Sales Price	Cost or Other Basis	Loss	Profit
300 sh. Citi	5/25/90	10/17/89	$6,975	$8,910	—	$1,935

Note that in the above schedule the date acquired is later than the date sold. This is because the stock was sold first, then purchased later.

Equity Determination

When you sold short the 300 shares of Citicorp for $9,000, you were required to put up enough money to cover the brokerage commission and an additional $4,500 in order to justify the initial margin requirement set by the Federal Reserve Board. You may at anytime choose to deposit into your account more than the initial margin requirement, but never less.

Assume you deposited in your account the minimum amount required by the Federal Reserve. (Brokerage commissions will not be calculated as part of the following math because credit balances and margin requirements relate to the percent of the short market value of the stock sans commissions.) This amount is $4,500, and represents your starting equity. As the price of your stock moves up and down, so will the amount of equity you have in your account. Knowing how to calculate this equity is important so you will know when you must put up additional money or securities to cover your short position, and when you can borrow money from your account.

To determine your equity, simply subtract the short market value from the credit balance. The credit balance is the total of the short sale ($9,000) plus the amount deposited ($4,500).

Credit Balance	–	Short Market Value	=	Equity
($13,500)	–	($9,000)	=	($4,500)

Suppose Citicorp decreases $5 per share to $25 per share. This means you have a profit of $5 per share and your equity should increase.

Credit Balance	–	Short Market Value	=	Equity
($13,500)	–	($7,500)	=	($6,000)

On the other hand, suppose that the stock went up $5 per share; your equity would decrease.

Credit Balance	–	Short Market Value	=	Equity
($13,500)	–	($10,500)	=	($3,000)

Borrowing Power

When you have excess equity in your account, you may borrow it back from your broker. Your borrowing power at anytime, then, is the difference between the amount of deposit required by the Federal Reserve Board and the *increased* equity.

Simply put, if your equity has increased $1 over the initial margin requirement, you can borrow $1 from your account. If it has increased $10,000 over the initial margin requirement, you can borrow $10,000.

If your equity increases by $10,000, but this increase does not bring it above the original margin requirement, then you *cannot* borrow any money.

Table 6-2 gives some arithmetical examples for review.

Selling Power

Excess equity in your account can also be used to sell short additional stock. There is a different formula, however, for determining selling power. It is a bit difficult to grasp the formula at first. The trick is to remember that here we use the percent representing the original margin requirement.

Selling power is derived by dividing the initial margin requirement into the excess equity.

$$\text{Excess Equity} \div \text{Initial Margin} = \text{Selling Power}$$

Remember that the formula asks for "excess equity" and not simply "equity."

Given that the short market value of your position in Citicorp has increased by $1,500 (the stock has decreased $5 per share) and the initial margin requirement is 50%, you may sell short additional stock in Citicorp or sell short another stock up to an amount of $3,000.

Excess Equity	+	Initial Margin	=	Selling Power
($1,500)	+	(50%)	=	($3,000)

Table 6-3 gives additional examples for review.

Maintenance Margin Requirements

Most stock exchanges as well as the National Association of Securities Dealers (which runs the over-the-counter market) set the minimum maintenance margin for short accounts at 30 percent of the short market value. But often brokers will set these maintenance requirements somewhat higher to protect themselves in case the underlying securities move the wrong way too fast and the account cannot come up with the additional money to pay off sums borrowed from the

Table 6-2
Figuring Borrowing Power in Short Accounts

Current Market Price	Initial Margin Requirement	Initial Deposit	Increased Equity	Borrowing Power
$10,000	50%	$5,000	0	0
$10,000	50%	$6,000	$1,000	$1,000
$10,000	60%	$5,000	0	0
$10,000	60%	$6,000	0	0
$10,000	60%	$9,000	$3,000	$3,000

Borrowing power at any time is the difference between the deposit required to satisfy initial margin requirements of the Federal Reserve Board and the increased equity. Initial margin requirements may change from time to time. At this writing they are 50 percent for both short and long trades.

Table 6-3
Figuring Selling Power in Short Accounts

Excess Equity	Initial Margin Req.	Selling Power
$1,500	50%	$3,000
$2,000	50%	$4,000
$2,500	50%	$5,000
$3,000	60%	$5,000
$4,000	60%	$6,667

$$Formula: Selling\ Power\ = \frac{Excess\ Equity}{Initial\ Margin}$$

broker. Many brokers set the minimum maintenance requirement at 35 percent for two position accounts and higher for one position accounts. Additionally, stocks sold short at less that $5 per share have special maintenance requirements set by the exchanges, and brokers' requirements, again, may be even stricter. On stocks under $5, the maintenance requirement is usually 100 percent of the market value.

Given the absolute minimum maintenance requirement set by the exchanges and over-the-counter market of 30 percent, to determine the price at which additional money or securities must be deposited into a short account, multiply the credit balance in the account by the fraction $10/13$. *The credit balance is the total of the short sale plus the amount deposited.*

When you sold short the 300 shares in Citicorp for $30, the sale came to $9,000 and you deposited $4,500 to cover the initial margin requirement.

Short Sale	+	Amount Deposited	=	Credit Balance
($9,000)	+	($4,500)	=	($13,500)

Now, to determine how high the stock can appreciate before your broker will send a maintenance call, multiply $13,500 by $10/13$.

$$\$13,500 \times \frac{10}{13} = \frac{\$135,000}{13} = \$10,385$$

If the short market value increases to $10,385, then your equity will depreciate from the original $4,500 in the following way:

Credit Balance	–	Short Market Value	=	Equity
($13,500)	–	($10,385)	=	($3,115)

The amount of equity represented in the above equation is 30 percent of the short market value. Thus, as soon as the short market value goes above $10,385 (or your equity decreases below $3,115), you will receive a notice from your broker asking you to deposit additional money or equivalent securities in your account.

Table 6-4 gives additional examples for review.

Review of Formulas

A number of formulas have been thrown at you in rather quick succession. These were to help you determine in your short account: credit balances, equity, selling power, borrowing power, and maintenance margin requirements. Let's review them quickly.

Table 6-4
Figuring Minimum Maintenance Requirements
for Short Accounts

Short Sale	Amount Deposited	=	Credit Balance	x	Multiplier	=	Minimum Maintenance
$10,000	$5,000		$15,000		10/13		$11,538
$12,000	$6,000		$18,000		10/13		$13,846
$18,000	$9,000		$27,000		10/13		$20,769

A. Determine the credit balance so you can calculate equity and maintenance minimums:

Credit balance = Short sale + Amount deposited

B. Determine the equity in your account so you know how much money you will get if you sell your holdings:

Equity = Credit balance − Short market value

C. Determine your borrowing power so that you can withdraw money from your account when necessary:

Borrowing power = Equity − Initial margin

D. Determine selling power to see how much more stock you can buy without putting up additional money:

Selling power = Excess equity + Initial margin

E. Determine the minimum balance required before a maintenance call will be issued:

Minimum balance = Credit balance x 10/13

Stop Loss

In the transaction described at the beginning of this chapter, you managed a $1,935 profit in about seven months from roughly a $4,600 investment (remember commissions). This is because you sold short on margin and in effect had the advantage of having $4,500 do the work of $9,000. Short sales are not always profitable as this example may have implied. Short sales can go awry just as easily as regular way trades.

Generally, the dangers of extreme losses from short sales are prevented because of maintenance margin requirements. If the stock or stocks you own take a climb, your broker is on standby to notify you of due amounts as soon as your equity depreciates to a certain level. At this time, you can notify your broker to buy back as necessary to cover your positions at the same time that you send additional cash to cover balances due; or, of course, you can just send the required cash or securities to cover your debt. But sometimes you may be away when your broker tries to call you or reach you by mail and you are not able to take the appropriate action to cut your losses. And sometimes the stock you have shorted becomes a takeover candidate and explodes in price—in which case you are going to be out a lot of money.

Suppose, for example, that the 300 shares in Citicorp increased markedly in value in short time and you were unavailable to answer margin calls. The broker would ordinarily buy back the stock in your account to help cover amounts due—but the stock can climb even further before he realizes you cannot answer the margin calls and he must cover your position by depleting all your equity.

By the time the short position can be covered, the stock may double in price, in which case the stock would result in more than a complete wipe out for you.

Let's look at a step-by-step example.

1. You have $4,500 with which to sell short Citicorp common.

2. You decide to use margin to sell short $9,000 worth of stock. This means you owe your broker $4,500.

3. Citicorp's price doubles while your broker is trying to get to you with maintenance margin calls. Finally, he stops your continued losses by buying the stock. The cost is $18,000 because the stock has doubled in this very short time.

4. The stock was sold for $9,000 and bought back for $18,000. That is a $9,000 loss.

5. This $9,000 loss represents the amount lost on the trade. Remember, you sold short on 50 percent margin. Only $4,500 was your money. You not only owe the broker $4,500 for the initial amount he lent you, but you must also cover the loss on the trade: $9,000.
    $9,000 + $4,500 = $13,500 loss

6. In summary, because the stock doubled before it could be bought back and you had sold short on 50 percent margin, you lost three times your initial investment.

The extreme losses possible for short sellers using maximum margin makes it wise to "insure" your positions to some extent with stop loss orders. The stop loss order is simply an order to your broker to cover your short position when your stock reaches a certain price. (In regular way trading it is an order to your broker to sell the stock when it falls to a certain price.) It is not always possible for your broker to sell at the stop loss price you designate, but most of the time a broker can meet your order or come close to it.

In the previous example of a stock doubling in price and your losses tripling as a result, it is easy to see why a stop loss order (which is good until cancelled) can be a money saver. The broker would have closed out your position long before you lost all your money.

What guidelines should you use to determine where to put the stop? There is no set answer. A lot depends upon the trading range of the stock and the amount of margin being employed. Remembering that when you put up only 50 percent of the short sale you lose two dollars for every one dollar rise in share price, you will want your stop loss price ten to fifteen percent from the purchase price. If the stock does go up fifteen percent, this means a thirty percent loss for you.

Some investors will put in a stop loss order as soon as they short. Then they revise the order as necessary, sometimes on a daily basis. It is smart to continually revise the stop loss, but generally it is a good idea to wait and see how the stock moves after being shorted before the first stop loss order is placed.

Safety Play

The safest way for a short seller to play her game is to hedge by purchasing a number of calls equal to the number of shares she has shorted. That is, she sells short "x" number of shares and buys long at least 1/100th as many calls as she has stock. (100 shares of stock, 1 call. 900 shares of stock, 9 calls.) The call limits the risk and in some cases can even assure profit if the stock goes the wrong way.

Suppose that at the same time you purchased 300 shares of Citicorp at $30, you also purchased three January 30 calls for $100 each.

What does this mean? First of all, it means your break-even point on the short sale must take into account the $300 paid for the calls. So right away you know that hedging with calls is an expensive game—but often worth the extra money. Secondly, it means that should the stock go up instead of down, the money you would lose on each share of stock is just about earned by the calls, which will increase in price as the stock goes up. The term "just about" is used here because the movement of the call premium (price) may or may not be coincident with the movement of the underlying stock. Its movement depends on a number of factors described in the chapters on Puts and Calls.

As the call approaches the January expiration date it will decay slightly. To complicate matters even more, demand for the call as the stock rises and approaches the expiration date may offset or enhance the time decay. Time decay and call price movement will be explained in further detail in Part 4 of this book. For now, it is only important to realize that it makes sense to buy calls on the same stock in which you are selling short.

Sometimes short sellers will buy twice as many, or even more, calls as they have sold short shares. In this case, the calls are out of the money and selling sometimes for pennies. If the stock increases very strongly and rapidly in price, the calls can skyrocket as the rising stock price brings the calls in-the-money. The gain on the calls may more than offset the loss on the stock.

Another advantage of being long on calls while you are shorting the underlying stock is that if the stock climbs instead of going down, the rise in the value of the calls will be offsetting your losses and delaying any maintenance calls from your broker.

Dual Position Accounts and Margin Requirements

Generally, no one takes only short positions. Someone may be predominately a short seller but he or she will occasionally be long on some stocks. What about the minimum maintenance requirements for such an account? How are they figured?

For dual position, or what are referred to as mixed margin accounts, separate calculations are necessary for the long and short positions. This is because the maintenance margin requirements for long positions are figured slightly differently than they are for short positions. Thus, maintenance calls are initiated much more quickly for short accounts.

To begin with, note that the arithmetic for determining short equity is different than it is for long equity.

A. Determining long equity:
Long Market Value (current price of the stock)
− Debt Balance (money owed the broker)
= Long Equity   (your ownership)

B. Determining short equity:
Credit Balance (Short sale + Amount deposited)
− Short Market Value (current price of the stock)
− Short Equity (your ownership)

For those of you who have wondered exactly why those maintenance calls come so much more quickly on short sales, you now have your answer in the above formulas.

Now, what about the minimum maintenance requirement on a mixed margin account? Using the percents required by the exchanges and OTC and not those varying percents used by brokers, determining the requirement is simply a matter of multiplying market values by the required percents, 25 percent on the long side, and 30 percent on the short side; then adding the results.

Minimum maintenance requirements:

  A. Long accounts:
        25 percent of long market value

  B. Short accounts:
        30 percent of short market value

  C. Mixed margin accounts:
        A + B

Given the above formulas, if you are long $20,000 on stock and short $20,000, your minimum maintenance requirement would be calculated as follows:

$$(25\% \times \$20{,}000) + (30\% \times \$20{,}000) = \$5{,}000 + \$6{,}000 =$$
$$\$11{,}000 \text{ (minimum maintenance requirement)}$$

If you are long $20,000 and short $50,000, your minimum maintenance requirement would be calculated as follows:

$$(25\% \times \$20{,}000) + (30\% \times \$50{,}000) = \$5{,}000 + \$15{,}000 =$$
$$\$20{,}000 \text{ (minimum maintenance requirement)}$$

7

Common Misconceptions

There are a number of misconceptions that seem to stall investors selling short for the first time, or set these investors up for a great awakening.

A first misconception is that the stock market is the best place for one's money, whether he or she is a long or short player. This idea is usually the result of reading those many statistics that show how much better off one would be if he or she were in stocks over a given period instead of in other securities.

These types of statistics can be greatly misleading, because not every stock will have increased in those same time frames. Take for example the Dow Jones averages over the years. While it's true that the majority of those stocks have performed well over selected periods of time, some of those stocks have not, and an investor may very well have been invested in stocks that could not keep pace. Additionally, most independent investors cannot actually leave their money in the marketplace for many years. They need to cash in their stocks periodically to buy automobiles, homes, or vacations; or to pay outrageous tuition or taxes.

Actually, the types of securities that carry the lowest risk, and those which are the most popular with investors, are government securities and money market instruments. The government securities are bills, notes, and bonds which the U.S. Government issues in order to finance the U.S. Treasury. The money markets are made up of short term government and other debt instruments which mature in periods of less than one year. (See Tables 7-1 and 7-2 for money market instruments and their comparative rates.)

Table 7-1: Safety Plays

Name	Description	Trading Procedures/ Tax Data
T-bills (treasury bills)	Shortest term government security with 91 day, 182 day, nine month and one year maturities.	$10,000 denominations sold at a discount. Interest earned is taxed at maturity—earlier if the T-bills are sold. No state or local taxes apply.
TABs (Tax Anticipation Bills)	T-bills that mature one week after corporate quarterly taxes are due	Same as above.
Treasury Bonds	More than 10 years maturity; sometimes callable, long term debt obligations	Traded in round lots ($5,000) and on a percentage of par ($1,000). Annual interest is taxed but no state or local taxes apply.
Treasury Notes	Interest paying two to 10 year debt instruments.	Traded on a percentage of par value ($1,000). Annual interest taxed but no state or local taxes.
GNMAs (Ginnie Maes)	Securities offered by the Government National Mortgage Association to finance residential housing, and which have 25 to 30 year maturities.	$25,000, then $5,000 increments. Annual interest is subject to federal, state and local taxes.
FNMAs (Fannie Mae's)	Securities offered by the Federal National Mortgage Association and backed by the authority to borrow from the U.S. Treasury; money raised is used to purchase insured FHA and VA homes.	Traded like any common stock

Some of the safer plays in the securities markets. These securities offer competitive interest rates. Before plunging into the stock market it is always wise to measure other opportunities for your money. If you you can get 9 percent on your money with little or no risk, why chance gambling on the same return through speculation on stocks? In other words, before you speculate or invest in the stock market, consider the opportunity cost.

Table 7-2
Comparative Money Rates for Money Market Instruments

Discount Rate (that charged depository institutions by the Federal Reserve)	3.0%
Prime Rate (that charged by banks to customers with excellent credit ratings)	6.0%
Federal Fund Rate (that charged on overnight interbank loans, and basis for money market rates)	3.125%
Call Money Rate (that available to brokers)	5.0%
Treasury Bill Rate (that available on discounted short-term government securities)	2.90%
Certificates of Deposit (CDs of $100,000 or more that are issued by money center banks for six month periods)	3.05%
Commercial Paper Rates (that available on high-grade corporate promissary discount notes and dealer placed)	3.14%
Bankers Acceptance Rates (that available on short term negotiable discount time drafts)	2.97%

Additionally, there are other safe investments which, while they do not offer the extreme gains possible from stock and options investments, do offer substantial returns over the long term with much less risk. These are high-interest savings programs that take advantage of compounding. And in those cases where compounding can take place under a tax shelter—as in an IRA (Individual Retirement Account)—money can accumulate much quicker than would be expected. (See Table 7-3).

The point is that before you invest in the market, take a good hard look at what your money can do elsewhere. This is called looking at *opportunity cost*. Opportunity cost represents the dollar value of resources that are ignored because you have decided to sell short or buy long in the market. In other words, that $10,000 you decide to put in the market could also be put in CDs paying five percent per year. If your investment in stock loses only $100 over the course of a year, you have actually lost $400, because that money could have earned you $500 from the certificates of deposit. And if you do make 6 percent on that stock, think of the

Table 7-3
Results of Annual Compounding of Interest

Rate of Interest	Years to Double Money
6%	12.0
7%	10.3
8%	9.0
9%	8.0
10%	7.2

If you have $10,000 to invest, should you take a chance on the stock market or some savings instrument? Simple annual compounding at six percent would allow you to double your money in twelve years. Semiannual and quarterly compounding would allow you to double it in even less time. Can you do better as a short seller in the market?

To determine how your money can grow at various interest rates and compounding schedules, use this formula:

$$S = P(1 + i)^n$$

where   P = Original principal
           i   = Interest
          n = Number of interest (or conversion) periods
         S = Compound amount

risk you took to take profits only one percent more than you could have gotten with a little or no risk investment paying five percent.

The stock market is basically for gamblers—very educated and calculating gamblers, but gamblers none the less. If you can lose, you are gambling. But then, no great risk, no great gain. Thus, bear in mind that the methods of turning a profit discussed in this book are by no means a sales pitch to get you to invest in the market. Rather, this book is saying that if you are going to play the stock market, here are three additional ways in which you may be able to turn a profit.

A second misconception is that selling short is safer than buying long. What really counts in any investment game is knowing what stock to pick and when to pick it. An investor has no guarantees from the stock market other than, perhaps, the fact that when he writes options he will receive premium income. But, of course, if he is a naked writer (he does not own the underlying stock), and the option goes the wrong way, he can wind up losing much more than he ever earned fror writing.

Stocks can always go the wrong way after you buy them or short-sell them. What is particularly nice about the stock market is that you can always test your ideas on paper before putting them into practice. You can play a paper game. Pick a couple of stocks to sell short and then watch the newspaper every day to see how they move over a period of a couple of months; at the same time pick a couple of stocks to buy long and watch these for the same period. You might think that just by glancing at the 52-week high and low price in the listings for each stock is a quicker way to do your practice, but this listing does not show direction. Consider a stock that has a 52-week high and low of $30 and $10 and is currently selling for $20. Did the stock go from $30 to $10 and now to $20, or did it go from $10 to $30 and now drop back to $20? These questions can only be answered by going to your library and doing some research, not by merely glancing at the daily stock listings.

A third misconception is that only stocks on the major U.S. exchanges can be sold short. There are more than 100 stock exchanges in the world and a number of them in the United States. The financial papers and financial sections of large city daily newspapers list some of these.

Stocks on any U.S. exchange and some of the foreign exchanges may be sold short. But in the case of the foreign exchanges, each has its own rules and restrictions, and not all allow short selling. In addition to these exchanges there is also the OTC market, perhaps the largest market for stocks at this writing. Bear in mind, however, that the OTC market operates very differently from the stock exchanges, which are auction markets. This means you must be extra careful about your interpretation of stock quotes listed for the OTC stocks. The reason follows.

In the OTC market, stock prices are determined by negotiations which take place between remote market makers who are trading stocks for their own accounts. These market makers are entrusted with basically the same responsibility as the specialists on major or primary markets like the New York Stock Exchange or the American Stock Exchange. They must maintain an orderly market at all times. But there are some differences in their methods. A specialist on the primary exchanges matches one buy or sell order against another sell or buy order, but the OTC market maker is buying or selling from his firm's holdings.

NASDAQ bid and asked quotations represent the price at which someone is offering to buy and the price at which someone is offering to sell. But these bid and ask prices only represent the *highest* bid and *lowest* ask prices for the related issue. If you see a quotation of 5 – 5½, this means you can buy the stock at 5½. This might not be the only asking price for a round (100 shares) lot of stock, but the other asking prices would be higher. This type of quote is generally referred to as a "firm quote." There are other types of quotes such as the "workout order" which means the trader must work out his order before any order can be executed. There is the "subject quote," which is subject to confirmation.

A fourth misconception is that low trading volume in a stock is an indication that the price of the stock will fall. The price of any stock can go up or down on relatively high or relatively low volume. The number of shares traded for any issue is hardly the same from day to day. Volume can often fluctuate by hundreds of thousands of shares. However, if over a period of weeks, volume in a particular issue shows steady decline, then the stock *may* be in for a tumble. Low volume should only be considered a "flag" and not a certainty. *Remember that there is no single indicator which can be relied upon for price direction.*

A fifth misconception is that stocks reaching new highs are destined to decline in price. It is true in stock investing as well as in science that "what goes up must come down," but in stock investing "when" and "how far" are the determining factors in whether or not you will realize a profit. A stock may rise to new highs six or seven days after you sell it short, and though it will fall back when profit taking occurs, it may never fall back to your break-even price. A high closing price is no indication that tomorrow or the next day the stock is going to retreat. Daily closing prices are little more than the daily summary of trading activity in a stock, and are no direct measure of investor interest. If, however, the daily price fluctuations represent a significant spread, you might want to do some quick but relatively thorough research to determine whether or not to take a short position or, if already shorted, to buy back the stock.

A sixth misconception is that stocks reaching new lows are poor candidates for short selling. When a stock reaches a new low for the day, it should be a candidate for some research. Stocks hitting new lows are often in trouble and tend to fall even further. But do not base a short sale simply on the fact that the stock is on the "new low" list. Call your broker. Search the news to find out why it may be falling. A top executive may have passed away, a new accounting report may have come out, Moody's may have changed the company's debt rating. Many short sellers depend on the "new lows" list to find potential candidates.

A seventh misconception is that stocks which make the "most active" list are poor candidates for short sellers. Just checking the "most active" list for one week will indicate that not only do many stocks decline in price after making the list but they have also declined in price on the day that they were among the most active. The reply to this misconception is the same as that for the "fourth misconception" (trading volume): Stocks can go up or down on relatively high or relatively low trading volume.

Take for instance the case of Dow Jones (not the indicator but the common stock for Dow Jones, the publisher of *Barron's* and the *Wall Street Journal*). In January of 1990 it not only made the most active list but continued to soar in price, from about $33 per share to over $40 per share. Many uninformed investors, including some pros, rushed to get in on what they thought was the beginning of great things for Dow Jones common. There was exceptional volume as investors bought in at $38 per share, at $39, at $40, at $41 . . . But by May, just four months later, the stock was at a depressing $24 per share. The strong advance was simply the result of a major investment house taking heavy positions in order to meet money management objectives. A lot of the big money guys got hurt. Now, Dow Jones common fluctuates quite a bit and those that went in at $40 or more might still make a profit—but just think how much more they might have made if they sold short at $40, then went long at $24. Or, just plain stayed away until the stock dropped to $24 per share.

An eighth misconception is that stocks with high P/E ratios are good candidates for short selling and those with low P/E ratios are not. The P/E ratio is one of the most misunderstood and incorrectly used ratios by new, independent investors. This price-to-earnings ratio has little significance by itself. It is basically an historical review of a stock's trading pattern, and future performance is hardly ever guaranteed by past performance. Additionally, all stocks do not trade at the same ratios. Utility stocks like the Bell companies or Public Service and Electric often trade at lower P/E ratios than media stocks such as A. H. Belo or the New York Times. A high P/E ratio for one stock can represent too high a P/E ratio for another.

P/Es can be so very misleading. Consider the case for the Stephen Caes Machine Co. (fictitious) which is selling at 10 times earnings. As the stock is listed for $20, this means the earnings per share are $2. The stock may generally sell at an average price of $30 per share and a P/E ratio of 15. The latest P/E, less than the past average, may indicate investor dissatisfaction, or it may indicate gaining strength. Here you have the possibility of a candidate for short selling or regular way trading—or just something to stay away from now. The P/E ratio alone tells you nothing, except that the stock might be worth looking into.

A ninth misconception is that a stock on which a two for one or other split has been declared is a poor candidate for shorting. Usually before a stock split is declared, a stock starts advancing in price. Somehow, word always gets out. And about the time of the declaration and for some period thereafter the stock generally increases, but there is also usually a pullback about the time of the actual split. As a rule of thumb, stay away from stocks that are splitting unless you determine the stock has been overbought. Then do some research into projected earnings and historical and projected P/E ratios. There is often the chance that the news of the split has created an overbought situation and the stock will eventually pull back.

Bear in mind that the split does not mean that you will double your losses (if it's a two-for-one split). If you have sold short 100 shares of a stock for $20 and there is a split, you are now short 200 shares at $10. In the first and second cases, the amount of money you have in the stock has not changed. What you have after a split is the *potential* for losing more or making more. Take again a two for one split. Now that you have twice as many shares short, each one dollar increase in price means a $2 loss; and each decrease in price means a $2 gain.

A tenth misconception is that when you buy on margin, your broker shares your losses. When your broker loans you money to buy stock, he wants to be paid back in full, plus interest. Some investors new to margin buying and shorting are under the impression that if they short $10,000 worth of stock on 50 percent margin, and the stock goes up 50 percent the broker shares half that loss. No, absolutely not. When the broker loans you money to purchase stocks, she is not going in on the stock with you; and when you sell short on margin, she is not your partner. You are responsible for all losses that may be incurred; your broker is just your banker.

An eleventh misconception is that the marketplace is so regulated and watched that improprieties cannot occur. Ingenious minds bent on profit can find ways to get around anything if they don't mind getting on the wrong side of the law and spending years in prison. Stocks are sometimes manipulated by the big money traders. This became clearly evident in recent times by conspiracy and fraud charges brought against Michael Milken, Ivan Boesky, David Solomon, and others.

In one case involving MCA Inc. and Golden Nugget, Boesky had purchased almost 900,000 shares of MCA from Milken with the sole purpose of helping Milken disguise the fact that Golden Nugget was doing an about-face on plans to take over MCA. The large trade to Boesky was to give the marketplace the idea that there was still a great deal of demand for MCA and that the takeover might still take place.

A twelfth misconception is that buying calls to hedge on short sales is too expensive and not worth the investment. It certainly can be very expensive to load up on calls for stock you have shorted. The additional cost for the calls will lower your break-even point. But you do not have to buy the more expensive calls with close striking prices. You can buy calls which are far out-of-the-money (a term to be explained in our discussion of puts and calls in following chapters). This way you have "insured" your position to some extent. If the stock you have shorted rises drastically for reasons of takeover or unexpected increases in earnings, the calls will offset some of your losses on the stock.

8

Guidelines

There are basic rules related to investing that every shortseller must follow. Adherence to these rules does not ensure success but it at least limits the chance for failure. Making money in the stock and options markets is no easy task. Even covered call writing, which guarantees income, does not guarantee profit from your investment scheme, for the income from the calls can be offset by losses from the underlying security. The shortseller has absolutely no guarantees. Being careful about what and when to buy is all important.

1. *Be sure you have a good understanding of stock market arithmetic: how capital gains are figured, how brokerage commissions affect your break-even point, what dividends and stock splits mean for the shortseller, and how to calculate opportunity cost.* Knowing the basic arithmetic not only lets you know how to keep score but also helps you channel your efforts and establish your goals.

2. *Develop an understanding of basic economics, particularly the effects of inflation and employment on the national economy and the effect of interest rates on common and preferred stock prices.* Additionally, you should understand business cycles (Table 8-1) and how the market reacts or anticipates these cycles.

Table 8-1
The Business Cycle

Period	Description
Expansion	Business is booming, interest rates are low, and money for expansion is easy to get. The smart money waits for signs that interest rates will rise and begin selling their stocks. They want to sell while things are still hot and there are plenty of buyers.
Settlement	Business is leveling off, interest rates are on the rise, and money is becoming harder to get. Can the government manage the economy and prevent severe recession or depression? The smart money is on the sidelines, the not-so-smart money is wondering what to do with all those securities.
Contraction	The economy is retreating, but hopefuly the government will put in the controls to keep it from falling too far back. Meanwhile, the smart money is taking positions in the market again, anticipating the next phase, and taking advantage of low prices.
Recovery	The economy has turned around. All those investors who sold out to the smart money want to get back in. The smart money, however, will ride the bull until they feel they are at least one quarter of the way into the next expansion period. Then, the cycle begins again.

Generally, there are four periods in every business cycle. These are periods of expansion, settlement, contraction, and recovery. These are measured by changes in the gross national product (GNP), which is the total of all goods and services produced by a country. Know how the stocks you are considering shorting generally perform in these various business periods. But most of all understand that stock prices usually move in advance of the economy. This is because the investment community trades securities for what they will be worth in the future.

If prices are expected to be lower because of a downturn in the economy, investors sell; if they expect prices to be higher because of an upturn in the economy, investors buy. GNP projections help investors look into the stock market's future. But while there is a correlation between economic upturns and downturns and stock price movement, this correlation is not time dependable. That is, sometimes the GNP can indicate strength for the economy, but stock prices will be low. Again, this is because the investment community trades in anticipation of future events, so you can sometimes expect that economic performance and stock performance will not be coincident.

3. *Have a working knowledge of business finance so that you can read corporate reports, particularly balance sheets and income statements.* You don't have to be an accountant or an MBA to understand these reports. They are fundamentally simple. The balance sheet represents a snapshot of a company's financial strength on a given day; it lets the stockholder know what it owns and what it owes. The income statement is a snapshot of the company's activities to a given date.

These reports can help you get a feel for what your target stock is all about and whether it shows the kind of weakness that *might* make it a candidate for short selling. But these reports in themselves cannot become the sole basis for any decision. You will want to contact your broker for a report on forecasts for the company. Tomorrow is important in selling short or buying long, for we all invest for what something will be worth tomorrow.

4. *Understand the difference between the stock exchanges and the OTC market.* Remember that the exchanges are auction markets while the OTC is not. This is important to you as an investor when it comes time to interpret bid and asked prices, and to understand at just what price you may wind up buying and selling a stock. But because the OTC is not an auction market for stocks does not mean that you should underrate this tremendous investment arena. The OTC was created for the trading of *all* securities, not only those stocks which may be unlisted, but also those which are listed on the major exchanges.

Opportunities abound on the OTC, although the quality of the stocks differs markedly. In the past, it was particularly difficult to trade over-the-counter for a number of reasons, including the fact that investors could expect no minimum standard for the issues being offered. Now, however, the OTC has become an extremely orderly market where stocks can be traded almost as easily as on major U.S. and overseas exchanges.

The reason for the OTC's efficiency is an automatic quotation system commonly referred to as NASDAQ (National Association of Securities Dealers Automatic Quotation System), which provides the investment community with three levels of service. Level I gives the current best bid and ask prices for a security. Level II gives the bid and ask prices from all market makers and prices represent definite buy and sell opportunities. Level III allows the updating of bid and ask prices by market makers.

What investors particlarly like about this system is that before a security may be listed, the issuer must publish its total assets and the minimum number of stockholders.

5. *Never select a stock without getting additional opinions.* Always subscribe to a couple of investment newsletters. If you have a full-service broker, they generally have a couple—one which is free and lists certain stocks and other securities that may be of interest, and one for which there is a subscription fee. This second one gives specific detail and recommendations about market activity. If you subscribe to a number of investment guides and newsletters, you will often become confused, finding that they often offer opposing views of a specific stock, or of near-term general market performance. Consider this an advantage, for these different opinions will often dampen your enthusiasm, and it is best to make your investment decisions when you are cool and calculating and not caught in the heat of great anticipation.

Besides these investment newsletters, you may also want to seek out opinions from knowledgeable friends, and especially from your account executive at the brokerage house. If you use a discount broker which does not offer opinions or publish lists of recommendations, pay attention to the financial news, and study forecasts or recommendations to be found in specialized columns in such newspapers as *Barron's*, the *Wall Street Journal* and *Investor's Daily*.

6. *Be willing to pay the extra money to hedge your positions when possible.* Not all stocks are optionable stocks so you cannot always buy calls on a stock you are selling short. But when it is possible to hedge your short positions with calls, do so, even though it means your break-even point will be further away. As a rule of thumb, avoid selling short those stocks on which calls are not available. This is by far the safer way to go. The losses that can be realized on short sales can be extreme. As I've mentioned earlier, $10 stock can rise to $50 or more but it can only fall to zero.

7. *Be sure the return on your investment is worth the risk.* Even if you are hedging your position by buying calls on the stock you are selling short, you must ascertain whether the potential profit you are seeking is worth tying your money up. Unless you are a hard and fast speculator who knows the game, if you cannot hope for at least a 30 percent return on your short sale in six months, keep your money in the bank.

8. *Do not put all your money in one play.* In other words, spread your risk. But do not spread the risk so much that you are only able to buy such a small amount of stock, or sell short such a small amount of stock that it is not worth being in the market in the first place. Diversification makes sense unless you have only a small amount to invest, in which case you might as well stay out of the stock market altogether.

9. *Do not believe that stock listings present all the data you need to know to make a trade.* Stock listings are no more than a scoreboard showing the previous day's trading, the annual trading range and dividend amounts and rates. In the financial dailies

and larger city newspapers you will also find additional information such as P/E ratios and a whole menu of footnoted data, but all these listings really are is history. Remember that deciding on a stock to sell short necessitates studying its fundamentals and looking at its technical performance, then getting a couple of professional opinions.

10. *Remember that panics do happen on occasion and it's nice to be in a position to take advantage of them.* Investors get greedy and drive stocks to new highs, then they get scared and start bailing out in a hurry, thereby driving prices down.

Some panics are merely technical and quickly corrected as new buyers see oversold conditions and rush back in to the market, now driving prices up. There are many mini-panics that occur in the market, prices tumbling when economic news is threatening. Usually, in these little panics, it is nice to be short on selected issues or long on puts in these same issues. When stocks tumble in these mini-panics they tend to do so with a vengeance.

There have also been some very major panics (Table 8-2) in the history of the United States resulting from widespread mismanagement by both the government and industry. Some led to years of depression.

Bear in mind, however, that as a short seller it is not always easy to profit from these sudden market crashes. In the first place, it is often impossible to get through to a broker during these times. The brief panic of 1987 clearly illustrated that. Phones at brokerage houses were so tied up with panicky investors that the majority of accounts could not be serviced. Additionally, there were the short sale price restrictions—that is, price restrictions in regard to up ticks, zero ticks, etc.— that frustrated many a short seller.

Table 8-2
Financial Panics

Year	Background
1819	America was booming in the wake of the War of 1812. But in the year that Spain ceded Florida to the U.S. and Alabama became a state, the Second Bank of the United States called in its major loans and sent the economy into a nose dive.
1857	Speculators in commodities, railroads and land saw the U.S. as the end of the rainbow, but the "end" they saw was their own. They helped drive the economy into the ground at the same time that wagon trains were uniting the nation by bringing families across the plains and to the Far West for the first time.
1873	In the year that Buda and Pest were united as the capital of Hungary, Spain was declared a republic, and Tchaikovsky produced his Symphony No. 2, financial panics hit Vienna and then the U. S. The railroads that helped join together the new world were failing and tearing its economic base.
1893	In the same year that Henry Ford constructed his first automobile, European money lost its enchantment with American industry and withdrew its extensive investments; a four year depression followed.
1907	A country that had the year before witnessed the great San Francisco quake was now witnessing a record run on its banks that was halted only by J.P. Morgan's importing of $100 million worth of gold from Europe.
1929	Still unable to respond to, or ride the business cycle, the country let speculators run the economy into the ground. The result was the second worst market crash in the country's history. Investors experiencing the crash would forever be superstitious about the month of October. Margin requirements were later rightened and short-selling curtailed when these were interpreted to be the underlying causes of the crash.
1987	A record bull market was suddenly sabatoged by portfolio insurance programs and index arbitrage, but at the heart of the market crisis was probably an over-leveraged investment community. As this was a purely mechanical crash, no depression followed.

Part
3

Put Buying

9

Understanding Put Options

In the previous chapters, you saw how the short seller makes his profit. He has his broker borrow stock from another account so he can sell it for your account, and then he later purchases it back on your instructions. The difference between the selling price and the buyback price represents his profit.

Of course, if the stock does not go down in price, the short seller loses money instead of profiting. And in the previous chapters, you also saw not only how this can happen but also just how extensive the losses can be.

Because the short seller must have in his account—or pay within five days—cash or stock equivalent to whatever the margin requirements specify, he ties up a lot of cash at the same time that he puts himself at exceptional risk. Consider a short sale of 200 shares of Pepsi stock at $80 per share. The short seller must tie up about $8,000 in cash to meet original margin requirements while he waits—and prays—for the stock to decline in price.

Most small investors do not like to tie up their cash, nor do they like to expose themselves to unlimited risk. So, they sometimes turn to the buying of puts instead of the selling short of stock. Puts, like most options, are very low priced; many puts can be purchased for less than $1. In addition to providing the small investor with a great deal of leverage, puts also limit risk substantially unless they are sold short.

Take the case of the 200 shares of Pepsi selling at $80 per share. The short seller putting up the margin stands the possibility of not only losing the entire $8,000 but many times that amount if the stock increases substantially. Not so the put buyer, who may have the option of playing those 200 shares to go down for a mere $200 while at the same time resting assured that she cannot lose more than $200 if the stock doubles or even triples. The put buyer can never lose more than the price she pays for the put plus the broker's commission.

Disadvantages of Put Buying

Why then would anyone want to sell short a stock instead of playing the puts on that stock? The main reason is that there are time limits on the put contracts. The short seller can, theoretically, wait forever for the stock to fall in price but the put buyer has to see the stock fall in price by the expiration date of the contract. On the date the contract expires, the put buyer has a worthless option.

The put buyer is saddled with two other considerations that the short seller need not worry about. The first of these is the fact that the value of a put decays as time passes and the contract expiration date approaches. Of course, if the stock goes up in price during this time the put will increase in value instead of decay but if the stock movement is nil or just slight, that put will probably decrease in value, particularly in the last month of the contract.

The second of these considerations is that in many cases, particularly those involving lower priced puts, the stock has to fall a few points or more before the put starts to become profitable. And, here again, the inherent time decay feature of puts may negate the put's value even as the stock increases. This is because the lower priced puts are usually out-of-the money, meaning the price at which they can become profitable is far below the current price of the underlying stock. More on this in the next chapter.

While there is less risk of extreme loss from buying puts, it is generally harder to make a profit with put buying than it is with selling short a stock. (Table 9-1 looks at the relationship between put premiums and the price of the underlying stocks.)

Additional Advantages of Put Buying

There are some other very special advantages for the put buyer. Remember that it was explained how minimal his risk is? He cannot lose more than what he paid for the put plus the broker's commission. Well, despite the fact that his risk is limited, his profit potential is not. If he has purchased $200 worth of puts on Pepsi, he can only lose $200—but he can make $2,000 and possibly much more. Whereas the short seller has unlimited risk and limited profit (the stock can only go down so far), the put buyer has limited risk and offers the possibility of

Table 9-1
Put Premiums and Stock Prices

Underlying Stock	Market Price	Strike Price	Time to Expiration	Put Premium
Boeing	$85	$85	7 days	1½
Coke	$45	$45	7 days	½
Humana	$45	$45	7 days	⅝
CIGNA	$55	$55	7 days	¾

All of the stocks above are at-the-money. That is, their market price is the same as their strike price. But notice how the respective puts are available at different premiums although all the options are the same length of time from the expiration date. Current stock price and demand influence option premiums and even stocks at the same price and having the same striking prices and expiration dates, such as Coke and Humana, may have their options at different premiums.

percentage gains in thousands of percent. (See Table 9-2 for the differences between short sales on stock and buying puts.)

Additionally, because of the low price of puts, the put contract holder is unlikely to panic when the market for the underlying stock goes the wrong way. If Pepsi were to climb five, six or 10 points, you can bet the short seller will be on the edge of his seat, or already taking his losses; but the put buyer is not going to lose any more if Pepsi goes up 20 points than if it goes up one point, and so he is more likely to be in a position to profit if the stock eventually retreats, because he still owns the put contract until the expiration date.

Thus, the advantage to buying puts lies in the great leverage they afford, the diversity they allow, the tremendous profit potential they offer, and the minimal and limited risk they promise. Let's review these.

The tremendous leverage is the result of the low price of the puts and the fact that they move in some relation to the price of the underlying stock. In some cases a one point move in the underlying stock can be a one point move in the price of the put. If the stock is selling for $10 and the put for $1, while that price movement represents only a 10 percent gain in the stock, it represents a 100 percent gain in the price of the put. The put presents an opportunity wherein a few dollars can do the work of many dollars.

The great diversity that puts allow also comes as a result of their low price. Instead of tying his money up in one short sale, the investor has the prerogative

Table 9-2
Basic Differences Between Selling Stock Short and Buying Puts Long

Selling Stock Short	Buying Puts Long
No time limit governing the value of the stock. Stock sold short can be purchased whenever the short seller deems it most advantageous.	Each contract has an expiration date, at which time the options become worthless.
There is no limit on the amount of losses that may be incurred for a stock can, theoretically, go up in price forever.	Losses are limited to the cost of the option plus whatever trading commissions are involved.
Profits are limited to what can be achieved by the stock declining 100 percent, as a stock cannot depreciate more than 100 percent. (How much margin is used will determine if profits will possibly exceed 100 percent.)	Profits can be extensive, for the put can easily increase in value three or four times. Some may increase nine or 100 times or more in value.
Stocks may be sold short in odd-lots (less than 100 shares).	Each put represents 100 shares.
Margin is available.	All transactions must be in cash or equivalents.
Amount of cash tied up in a short sale is extensive because of the high price of stocks.	Little cash is required for puts as the options may sometimes cost less than one percent of the stock.
Amount of cash tied up in a short sale is extensive because of the high price of stocks.	Little cash is required for puts as the options may sometimes cost less than one percent of the stock.

of spreading that same amount of money over many investments, including other options and low priced stocks or even other securities.

The tremendous profit and limited risk result from the fact that an investor's loss is limited to the price paid for the put but his gain increases as the price of the put increases.

Contract Terminology

There are some terms (Table 9-3) with which you must become familiar to understand the basics of put buying. These are:

- Exercise Price (Striking Price)
- Premium
- Expiration Date
- Underlying Stock
- Writer

More freguently referred to as the striking price these days, the *exercise price* is the price at which the stock can be sold by the owner of a put. The exercise price never changes during the length of the contract. Where the exercise price is in relation to the current price of the stock is one of the determining factors for the price of the put, as you will learn in the next chapter.

The *premium* is the price a put commands, and it is what drives the options markets. As a put buyer, you want to try to purchase a put at the lowest possible premium and to sell it at the highest possible premium before the contract expiration date. That's right—you will be both a buyer and a seller of a put. It's the only way you can possibly realize a profit. *Remember, you want the underlying stock to go down in price, but you want the put to go up in price.*

> *Example*: You purchase a put option on Pepsi stock. The stock is at $80 per share and the cost of the put is $200. The striking price is $75, which means you cannot exercise the put until the stock falls below $75. If the stock never falls to $75, the put will expire worthless and you will lose $200. But, suppose the stock falls to $70 per share. In this case the put will be worth roughly $5 (the premium). As each put represents 100 shares of stock, if you sell the put for $5, you will receive $500 in premiums and thereby realize a gain of $300.

The *expiration date* of an option contract is the date the option becomes worthless. The day before this expiration date, the option can be worth hundreds of dollars, but on the day of expiration it is worth zero.

Unless there are unusual circumstances, if the price of the *underlying stock*, which is the stock on which the put contract is written, remains at or near the same price it was at when the option was purchased, the value of the put will decrease as the expiration date approaches. This puts the *writer*, or short seller of the put, at an advantage because he can always buy it back at the lower price and realize a gain. But it places the owner of the put at a disadvantage because the contract he is holding is depreciating in value for him. This depreciation because of the approaching expiration date is called *time decay*.

Chapter 9

Table 9-3
Options Terminology

Term	Definition
Put	An option giving the buyer the right to sell the underlying interest at a certain price and for a specified length of time.
Buyer	The person buying the put in hopes that it will increase in value as the underlying interest decreases in value.
Writer	The person selling an option to the buyer for the premium involved. The writer (seller, short seller) is legally obligated to honor the terms of the contract.
Exercise Price (Strike Price)	The price at which the put buyer can exercise his rights.
Expiration Date	The date an option contract becomes worthless. For most options, the expiration time is always 11:59 a.m. on the Saturday after the third Friday of the month.
Premium	The cost of an option, quoted in points and fractions of a point. Because each option represents 100 shares of stock, the true price for an option is the premium quoted x 100. To purchase a $2 put, then, you would need $200 plus whatever is the broker's commission.

Options Listings

Table 9-4 is a typical options listing from the financial section of a large daily newspaper. All options listings do not take this same format but this is the easiest layout with which to work. These listings are published daily except, perhaps, when the markets have been closed on the previous day. Usually the listings follow the stock listings in daily newspapers and financial weeklies.

When you trade stock options, you trade them in a secondary market created by the Options Clearing Corporation (OCC). Like the stock exchanges, the OCC

Table 9-4
Typical Newspaper Options Listing

PHILADELPHIA

Option & NY Close	Strike Price	Calls-Last Oct	Calls-Last Nov	Calls-Last Feb	Puts-Last Oct	Puts-Last Nov	Puts-Last Feb
12	12½	r	r	7/8	r	r	r
SvcCp	17½	r	1/2	r	r	r	s
Sprint	22½	1 11/16	2 1/8	r	r	r	r
24½	25	r	7/16	1	r	r	1 11/16
StaStB	40	r	r	r	r	r	5 1/8
TelMex	40	r	r	r	r	3/8	1 7/16
47¼	45	7/16	r	r	r	r	r
47¼	50	r	1/2	r	r	r	r
TritEn	30	r	8	r	r	r	r
37⅝	35	2½	4	r	r	r	r
37⅝	40	r	1¾	r	r	r	r
Un Pac	50	r	3¼	r	r	r	r
53	55	r	r	2	2⅛	r	r
WMS Ind	17½	1/2	1¾	r	3/16	3/4	1⅝
18⅛	20	r	1/2	r	2	2⅝	3½
18⅛	22½	r	1/8	r	r	r	r
Waste	30	6¾	r	r	r	1/16	1/4
37¼	35	2¼	2⅝	3½	1/16	3/8	1¼
37¼	40	r	5/16	1 3/16	r	3⅛	4¼
37¼	45	s	1/16	s	s	r	s
WebbD	17½	r	r	3½	r	r	r
21⅜	20	5/8	1⅜	r	r	13/16	r
21⅜	22½	s	1/2	r	s	r	r
21⅜	25	s	1/8	s	s	r	s
Wlwrth	30	2½	2¾	r	r	5/16	r
32½	35	r	r	1⅛	r	3	r
XOMA	10	1/16	3/4	r	1/4	15/16	1⅝
9¾	12½	r	1/4	r	2¾	2 11/16	r
9¾	15	r	r	1/2	r	r	r
9¾	17½	s	r	r	s	7½	r

Call vol 94,461 **Open int** 1,541,349
Put vol 67,267 **Open int** 1,126,357

PACIFIC

Option & NY Close	Strike Price	Calls-Last Oct	Calls-Last Nov	Calls-Last Dec	Puts-Last Oct	Puts-Last Nov	Puts-Last Dec
AdvTis	7½	1 1/16	1 11/16	r	r	r	r
8¾	10	r	3/8	15/16	1 3/16	r	r
Altera	10	r	r	r	1	r	r
AmtcCp	15	1¼	r	3¼	r	3/8	r
17½	17½	1/8	r	1 11/16	1/16	2	r
17½	22½	r	r	1/2	r	r	r
AnnTay	20	r	5/8	r	r	r	r
Bevrly	7½	r	3	r	r	r	r
10⅝	10	5/8	15/16	1 1/16	r	r	r
Bowatr	17½	r	r	r	r	r	11/16
18⅝	20	r	r	r	1⅞	r	r
Cirrus	30	r	3⅜	r	r	r	r
31¾	35	r	1 7/16	r	r	r	r
CrkBrl	30	r	r	7⅛	r	r	r
36¾	35	2¼	2¾	r	r	3/4	1¾
36¾	40	r	r	1⅛	3⅝	r	r
CrayCm	5	s	s	7/16	s	s	1¾
Cray	20	r	1⅝	r	r	1⅛	r
20	22½	r	3/4	1¼	2¾	2⅞	3⅛
20	25	r	1/2	r	5⅛	4½	5⅜
20	30	r	r	r	r	10	r
20	35	s	s	1/16	s	s	r
DataGn	7½	4¼	r	r	r	r	r
12¼	10	2¼	2¼	2 5/16	r	r	3/8
12¼	12½	r	9/16	15/16	1/4	13/16	r
Datscp	20	5⅛	r	r	r	r	r
24⅞	22½	2¼	r	r	r	r	r
24⅞	25	3/16	1 7/16	r	r	r	r

is regulated by the Securities and Exchange Commission (SEC). The OCC is owned by the stock exchanges that create the markets for options. These exchanges are the American Stock Exchange, the Chicago Board Options Exchange, the New York Stock Exchange, the Philadelphia Stock Exchange, and the Pacific Stock Exchange. The sixth member-owner of the OCC is the National Association of Securities Dealers.

Options listings only represent a scoreboard of yesterday's activities and should never be used as the basis for selecting an option. You must learn as much as possible about the underlying stock and the technical factors that may affect its short-term movement.

Note that in Figure 9-1, the listings contain both call and put activity. For now, you need only be concerned with puts, though the option listing headings described below pertain to both calls and puts.

You will notice that for any of the underlying stocks listed in the far-left column, there may be available a number of different contracts selling at different prices and having different strike prices and expiration dates. This variety of contracts on any given security is what adds to the dynamic nature and fun of option trading, and also adds to the safety of dealing in puts and calls. You always have the option, so to speak, of switching from one contract to another until it finally pays off—or of playing a number of different contracts at the same time.

Month. The months listed represent the expiration month of the contracts being offered. The specific date is not given because you are expected to know what it is. Currently all options made avaiilble by the six member-owners of the OCC expire on the first Saturday after the third Friday of the month. Expiration cycles may be monthly, quarterly, or some combination of monthly and quarterly expirations. As the underlying stock changes in price, new options contracts will be introduced. Higher priced stocks usually must move 10 points one way or the other before a new option is made available. The lower priced stocks, however, need only move 2½ to 5 points. One drawback with these tables is that they do not always list all available options, so it is usually a good idea to check with your broker before deciding to work with any particular expiration date or striking price.

As one expiration date expires, another is listed. All options on each exchange do not expire in the same months. If you take time to study Figure 9-1, you will note that all stocks are not on the same monthly or quarterly cycles. As mentioned earlier, as those expiration dates approach, the options, whether puts or calls, will most likely decrease in value. But the rate of the decay in premiums is not consistent and depends upon a number of variables, not the least of which are the relationship between striking prices and stock prices, and the ratio of the premiums to the stock prices. Another factor to consider in option decay is the number of days to expiration. An option three months from expiration will decay at a slower rate than an option one month from expiration. If the option is just days from expiration, the rate of decay can be greatly accelerated. Of course, stock price movement may inhibit any price decay, reverse it, as well as accelerate it.

In Figure 9-1, the premiums listed (¼, ½, etc.) represent the last prices at which the options traded. Generally, option premiums are quoted in terms of bid and ask prices and there is usually a ¼ to ½ point spread beteeen these bid and ask prices. As one-eighth of a point represents a large percentage of the price of an option, this spread is a disadvantage to the trader. If he wants to buy quickly, of course, he simply goes in at the ask price. Generally it is possible to buy a put or call at a price just between the current bid and ask.

Option & Close. In this column, you will find listed the underlying stock on which the options contracts are written. Notice the premiums for the different classes of puts. (Option contracts covering the same underlying interest are referred to as a "class" of options.) When the striking price for a put is higher than the stock price, the put premiums are generally higher. When this relationship occurs, the put is said to be "in-the-money," meaning that the underlying interest is at a price favorable to the option holder. If he wants to exercise his rights, he is in a position to do so, though not necessarily at a profit. (In-the-money has a different meaning in the case of calls. A call is in-the-money when the market price of the stock is above the striking price. Money positions are further clarified in the next chapter.)

Information about the underlying stock is critical to your success in trading puts. Always try to squeeze as much information as you can from your broker and other sources before purchasing any puts. You never want to be in a position of buying any put on a stock that is going to skyrocket in price. Your put may be in-the-money when you buy it but far out of the money minutes later. Remember that if you are buying long a put, you want a stock that looks weak and will probably go down in market value. (This is sometimes confusing to the new put player because when you buy a stock long, you want the stock to go up.) Again, it's the put you want to go up in value and it only goes up in value if the stock goes down in price far enough and fast enough to counter the time decay characteristics of an option.

Opening and Closing Transactions

While owners of puts have the right to exercise their options to sell the underlying stock at the market price and buy it back at the striking price when possible and practical, most investors trade puts as they would trade stocks. They either buy the puts long or sell them short.

Someone selling the put short is expecting that the underlying stock's market price will not be below the striking price before the option contract expires. His main interest is in the premiums he receives on the puts he has written (shorted).

Someone buying puts long hopes to realize a profit by eventually selling the puts at a higher price than he paid for them.

There are two types of transactions in options trading—an opening transaction and a closing transaction. But often there is only an opening transaction. That is, sometimes investors buy long and never sell, or sell short and never buy back.

An opening transaction can be either a buy or sell transaction. The long buyer uses the opening transaction to create an "opening buy." The short seller uses the opening transaction to create an "opening sell." The closing transaction can also be either a buy or sell.

Why do many trades consist of only opening transactions? The reasons differ for shorts and longs.

The short seller always has the option of buying back the put he originally sold. But if the stock on which the contract was written remains far above the striking price as the expiration date nears, the short seller may find it to his advantage to just let the contract expire. After all, his primary interest was in the premium he received for writing the contract.

The long buyer also has the option of selling his put. But if the price of the underlying stock remains above the striking price as the expiration date approaches, he may find it more to his advantage to just let the put expire. When the cost of the sell commissions are subtracted from the value of the put, the owner might lose more money from a sale than from expiration.

Here are two examples, one in which expiration is the smarter choice, the other in which a closing transaction is preferable.

Example #1. *You buy five puts on Coca Cola at $1.25 each. That is a total cost of $125 for each put and a total investment of $625 before commissions. The stock is at $48 per share and the striking price is $45. The day before expiration, the stock remains above the striking price and so the put has depreciated to $1/16$ of a point, or $6\frac{1}{4}$ cents. This means if you sell the puts you own, you will receive $31.25. Tack on sales commission of $40 and you actually lose your entire investment plus another $8.75 ($31.25 - $40.00). You actually lose less if you let the option expire.*

Example #2. *You own five puts on Coca Cola for which you paid $625. The day before expiration the stock is in the money by 50 cents and the puts for which you originally paid $1.25 each ($125 total) are now selling for $1/4$ point or 25 cents each. If you sell the puts you still stand to lose money but will at least walk away with $125 less commissions ($40). If you let the options expire, you walk away with nothing. Selling the puts is the wiser move.*

10

Value and Money Positions

The worth of an option is determined by its intrinsic value positions and its time value.

The intrinsic value is the amount by which an option is in-the-money. In the case of puts, this means the amount by which the underlying stock is below the striking price.

Market Price	Striking Price	Intrinsic Value
$20½	$25	$4½
$20½	$22	$1½
$20½	$20½	0
$20½	$18	0

The time value is whatever additional value is added to, or subtracted from, intrinsic value—as the result of the length of time remaining until expiration of the contract. (Puts decay as expiration dates approach.) The following is a simple illustration of how time value can add to the price of an option.

Market Price	Striking Price	Instrinsic Value	Premium	Time Value
$20½	$25	$4½	$5	$ ½
$20½	$22	$1½	$3½	$2
$20½	$20½	0	$2	$2
$20½	$20½	0	$1	$1

Types of Puts

In previous chapters, you were very briefly introduced to the different types of puts. Puts may be in-the-money, at-the-money or out-of-the-money, each of these money positions being determined by the relationship between the striking price and the market price of the underlying security.

In-the-money puts had their exercise price above the current market price of the stock. If you owned these puts and wanted to exercise your option selling the underlying security at the higher striking price (and then immediately buying it back at the lower market price), you would be assured of a profit before commissions. Generally, you would want to purchase only in-the-money puts.

At-the-money puts are those which have an exercise price equal to the current market price of the stock. If you wanted to exercise your rights under these conditions, you could only break even.

Out-of-the-money puts have an exercise price above the current market price of the stock. If you own an out-of-the-money put, you basically have a put with no intrinsic value and one which may expire worthless. But this does not mean you cannot profit, for you may be able to trade the put before expiration. Out-of-the-money puts will establish a trading range during the term of the contract and the difference between the high and low prices may be an opportunity for profit. Additionally, out-of-the-money puts can be big winners. They are usually very low priced while out-of-the-money and, therefore, sometimes good buys if the underlying stock is showing short-term weakness. When an option far out-of-the-money winds up in-the-money, the percent of increase that can follow can be highly impressive. Think for a second of a situation where you might buy an out-of-the-money put for $1/8 and then have it move far into the money, realizing an intrinsic value of $4. If you had purchased 10 of the options at ⅛, for a total outlay of $125, before expiration date you would have puts worth $4,000. This is the kind of return that attracts investors to the options market. Table 10-1 gives examples of the types of puts.

In-the-Money Puts

From the buyer's, rather than the seller's, point of view, in-the-money puts are the safer invesment. But do not assume that just because the puts are in-the-

Table 10-1
Types of Puts

A. In-the-Money: A put having an exercise price above the current price of the underlying stock.

Stock	Current Quote	Exercise Price
Boeing	84 ⅞	90
Shell	46 ¾	50
UAL	148 ½	150
CIGNA	55 ⅛	60

B. Out-of-the-Money: A put having an exercise price below the current price of the underlying stock.

Stock	Current Quote	Exercise Price
AMR	68 ⅜	65
Hershey	35 ¾	35
Contel	30 ⅝	30
Disney	130 ⅞	130

C. At-the-Money: A put having an exercise price equal to the current price of the stock.

Stock	Current Quote	Exercise Price
Marriot	25	25
Hilton	55	55
Wrigley	60	60

money, you are sure to realize a profit. The options market is highly volatile and you can be far in-the-money one day and the next day far out-of-the-money.

Example #1. You purchase a July 20 put on Chrysler Corporation for $4¼ when the stock is at $16¼. The option is in the money because the strike price ($20) is higher than the stock price. With still two months to go until the expiration date, the stock climbs to $21 and the put decreases in value to $1½.

*But before the expiration date, the stock falls again, this time to $18 and the
July 20s climb to $2. You decide to sell, for you are afraid the stock will climb
back up.*

Cost of put:	$425
Selling price:	$200
Loss:	$225

As the above example illustrates, the fact that you had purchased an in-the-
money put with an intrinsic value of $3¾ ($20 strike price minus the $16¼ stock
price), did not guarantee you a profit.

However, if you were still holding the put the day before expiration, because
you would be in-the-money you would have the following choices. You could
sell the option as you did in the example, or you could exercise your option and
sell the stock for $20.

Now, you could wait as long as necessary to try to profit from market deterio-
ration in the underlying stock. Let's see how the arithmetic would look if you did
exercise your option and eventually covered your short position by purchasing
Chrysler at $15 some weeks later.

Short sale of stock:	$2,000
Purchase of stock:	$1,500
Profit on stock trade:	$ 500
Less cost of put:	$ 425
Gain:	$ 75

That certainly was a lot of trading to mere $75, but it was better than trading
less and losing $225. And the profit was only possible because you were holding
an in-the-money put with enough intrinsic value to make exercising it worthwhile.

But do not believe that, with in-the-monies, if you do not profit from the
option, you can eventually profit from exercising the option and later buying
back. Suppose that after exercising your option and shorting Chrysler, the stock
went up to $21, and you decided to cut your losses and buy the stock. (Or, cutting
losses had nothing to do with it—you just needed the money.) Now, the arithmetic would look like this:

Short sale of stock:	$2,000
Purchase of stock :	$2,100
Loss on stock trade:	$ 100
Less cost of put:	$ 425
Loss:	$ 525

The lessons to be learned?

1. In-the-money puts represent favorable positions for an option buyer but they certainly do not guarantee profit.

2. Even in-the-money puts can be highly volatile in price movement, particularly when they fall out-of-the-money.

3. Exercising rights is an expensive trading plan and still does not guarantee the trader will come out on top.

Most options players realize that trading options is really a long term play despite the fact that contract life is so relatively short. This may sound like a contradiction but remember that options contracts have many expiration dates. That is, there are definite cycles for contract expirations. Most options trade on a quarterly cycle with only the three closest months trading at one time. Thus, when you look at options listings you will see that, for example, some American Exchange expiration cycles are May, June and July, and when the May options expire, the next month listed is October. In some cases, the cycle includes four months over two quarterly cycles (i.e, January through March and also July). However, the daily options listing in your newspaper will still list only three expiration months. You will need to touch base with your broker for additional expirations on any option of interest.

It is this cycle of expiration dates that allows options players to turn what would ordinarily be a short term play into a long term quest for profit. They can sell one put as it approaches expiration and buy the one with the next expiration date. This allows them to avoid the costs associated with exercising options and having to maintain a short position in the stock. Such a strategy is illustrated in the following example.

Example #2. *You purchase a July 20 put on Chrysler Corporation for $4¼ when the stock is at $16½. The day before expiration the stock is at $21 per share and your put is at $½ You still feel the stock is going to plumet, so you sell the July 20 at $½ and now buy on October 20 for $1. The stock moves up and down in an extremely narrow range then drops to $15, at which time your put increases in value to $5. You decide to take your profits. You lost on the July 20 but gained on the October 20.*

Cost of 1st put:	$425
Selling price of 1st put:	$ 50
Loss:	$375
Cost of 2nd put:	$100
Selling price of 2nd put:	$500
Gain:	$400
Total Profit:	$ 25

See Tables 10-2 and 10-3 for additional clarification of in-the-money puts.

Out-of-the-Money Puts

Out-of-the-money puts have no intrinsic value. The striking price is lower than the market price so the option holder is in an unprofitable position. Thus, out-of-the-money puts are generally very low priced. This low price is what attracts buyers. The rate of return can be impressive if the put goes in the money.

Example #1. You purchase a July 20 put on Chrysler Corporation for $1¼ when the stock is at $22 and the expiration date is four months away. Within a few weeks of your purchase, Chrysler stock falls in price to $17 per share. Your put, now in the money, is worth $3½. You decide to take your profit.

Selling price:	$350
Cost of put:	$125
Gain:	$225

Example #2. You now purchase a July 15 put on Chrysler Corporation for $1¼ when the stock is at $17 and the expiration date is two weeks away. Chrysler stock runs into difficulty again, at the same time that the overall market is falling. In three days the stock plummets to $12 per share. Your put, meanwhile, increases in price to $3. You sell the put.

Selling price:	$300
Cost of put:	$125
Gain:	$175

Now, in each of the above examples only one put was purchased—a highly unlikely situation as low-priced puts are usually purchased in quantity. So, to get a better picture of what the profits could have been, multiply the profit realized in each example by 10, as well as the purchase price. In the first example, then, a $1,250 investment would have returned $2,250; and in the second example, a second $1,250 investment in another put on the same stock would have yielded another $1,750. All of which illustrates why many options players are very satisfied to be dealing with low-priced out-of-the-monies.

But out-of-the-monies do not have to go in the money to be profitable.

Example #3. This time you purchase the July 20 puts for $1 when the stock is at $25 and the expiration date is five months away. Within weeks after purchase the stock falls to $21 per share. Though the put it is still out-of-the-money, demand for the option in anticipation of further decline in the stock drives the price of the put to $2¼, at which price you decide to sell.

Table 10-2
In-the-Money Puts

Stock	Current Quote	Exercise Price	Proceeds after Exercise and Stock Transactions
Boeing	84 7/8	85	$125.00
Shell	46 3/4	50	$325.00
UAL	148 1/2	60	$487.50

If the buyer exercises his rights and sells the above stocks for the exercise prices, then immediately buys them, his proceeds from the transactions—*before commissions*—are indicated in the last column. Remember that there are commissions from having purchased the put, then commissions for selling the stock and more commissions for buying the stock. Each exercise is per 100 shares of stock.

Selling price:	$225
Cost of put:	$100
Gain:	$125

There usually has to be some substantial price movement before the out-of-the-monies can increase in value. In this example the price of the stock fell $4 per share but the put only increased $1¼. In-the-money puts would increase almost four times as much on the same price movement, though they would have been more expensive.

It generally takes a long-term strategy to profit from in- or out-of-the-monies. That is, you must keep buying the next option with the same striking price but new expiration date until your game plan turns a profit, or until it becomes clear losses are inevitable. Speculators, however, prefer out-of-the-monies because of their low price and the resulting leverage they afford. From their point of view, the lower priced options make sense because they are inexpensive and highly volatile, a tempting combination for any speculator.

The lessons to be learned:

1. Out-of-the-money puts are highly speculative, but their lower price keeps them attractive.

2. Out-of-the-money puts require a greater movement in stock price before they increase in value and expiration dates work rather drastically against them.

Chapter 10

Table 10-3
Advantages, Disadvantages of
Buying In-the-Money Puts

Advantages	Disadvantages
Buyer is immediately in-the-money; the put has intrinsic value. (But this does not mean the buyer immediately has a profit.)	The higher price of in-the-monies and the higher commission costs usually prohibit buying in great quantity.
If the option is far in the money, the put will always have some intrinsic value.	In-the-money puts will advance and decline fairly close to a point-for-point coincidence with the underlying stock except in the very early and later stages of a contract. Thus, the percent of loss can be staggering when the underlying stock only increases a few points.
	Usual risks of dealing in options explained in Chapter 14.

3. Out-of-the-money puts can offer tremendous rates of return while limiting losses to the low price paid for them.

See Tables 10-4 and 10-5 for further clarification of out-of-the-money puts.

At-the-Money Puts

At-the-money puts have a striking price equal to the current market price of the stock. For all practical purposes, they are actually out-of-the-money puts because once you take into account broker commissions, the owner is in the red.

As a buyer of an at-the-money, you are walking the fence between profit and loss. If the underlying stock is relatively volatile, you can quite quickly be either in-the-money or out-of-the-money. Depending how far it is to contract expiration time, these options may be fairly highly priced, or extremely cheap.

Table 10-4
Out-of-the-Money Puts

Stock	Current Quote	Exercise Price of Option	Intrinsic Value of Option	Exercise Rights
AMR	68⅜	65	0	None yet
Hershey	35¾	35	0	None yet
Contel	30⅝	30	0	None yet
Disney	130⅞	130	0	None yet

The put contracts on the above stocks allow exercise at the prices in column three. None of the above puts have intrinsic value and they are worthless to their holders.

Table 10-5
Advantages, Disadvantages of
Buying Out-of-the-Money Puts

Advantages	Disadvantages
Low cost allows purchase in great quantity and the chance for exceptional profit.	Stock may have to move a number of ticks in relatively short time for the puts to increase in value.
Amount of loss is relatively little compared to the possible profits. Often a mere one-quarter of a point move in the put can result in a 100 percent gain.	The change of the option expiring worthless is extremely high.
The underlying stock does not have to go into the money for the buyer to profit.	Usual risks of dealing in options explained in Chapter 14.

Higher priced at-the-monies will generally show small percentage increases unless there is a relatively strong decline in the underlying stock. The lower priced options, with built-in leverage because of their lower price, stand to offer a greater percent of return on investment. After all, an option purchased at one-eighth of a point that advances to three-eighths has tripled in value. Table 10-6 gives examples of at-the-money stocks and Table 10-7 compares some of their advantages and disadvantages.

Table 10-6
At-the-Money Puts

Stock	Current Quote	Exercise Price	Intrinsic Value	Exercise Rights
Marriott	25	25	0	No advantage
Hilton	55	55	0	No advantage
Wrigley	60	60	0	No advantage

Theoretically, the put owner has the right to sell the above stocks at their exercise prices. But where is the advantage? He cannot make any money as a result of the exercise, and commissions will assure he walks away a loser.

Table 10-7
Advantages, Disadvantages of
Buying At-the-Money Puts

Advantages	Disadvantages
Cost is less than in-the-monies with the same exercise price.	A relatively small movement upward in the price of the stock will put the option out-of-the-money and in danger of expiring worthless.
A relatively small movement downward in the price of the stock will put the option in-the money.	Time-decay accelerates considerably as the exercise date approaches.
	Usual risks of dealing in options explained in Chapter 14.

11

Basic Strategies

As a regular way buyer of puts, you are after the tremendous leverage provided by their low price, the portfolio diversification they allow just because of this low price, and the minimal risk they guarantee because you can lose no more than what it cost you to purchase the puts.

Your interest in any specific put has to do with your bearish observations about the underlying stock. If you are of the opinion that the stock will plummet, then the puts on that stock are of interest to you. You will always be seeking out the weaker members of any exchange or on the OTC.

As you get ready to place your buy order with your broker, you must make a mental note to be sure you give him all those special instructions necessary to assure your order is placed correctly and with economic efficiency.

Recalling the special instructions listed in Chapter 3, you need to specify to your broker not only the particular put you want, but also the number of puts you want to purchase. Additionally, you will want to define the striking price, underlying security, and expiration month. You will also want to specify the premium at which you want the trade to be executed, whether or not you require the entire order to be placed at the same time, and whether your order is an opening or closing one. Opening orders are those which represent the first position in an option. If you are buying long, then your opening order is a buy. When you sell an option with an equivalent striking price and expiration date to the option you purchased, then you are making a closing transaction. (For those selling short an option, the reverse is true. The opening transaction is the sell order and the closing transaction is the buy order.)

There are other special instructions which option traders may include with their orders. These are contingent, day, fill-or-kill, good-till-cancelled, immediate or cancel, limit and market.

The *contingent orders* not only specify the price at which the option may be purchased but may also specify the price of the underlying stock. "Mr. Broker, if Citicorp drops to $22, buy the July 25 puts."

Day orders are cancelled if they are not executed the same day they are placed. Usually a broker expects that, unless otherwise specified, an order is for the day only.

Good-till-cancelled orders remain in effect until executed or cancelled. Not every options exchange, however, allows good-till-cancelled orders. But some brokers will oblige you by placing your order every day until it is executed.

Fill-or-kill orders require that the complete order be executed immediately upon reaching the floor or else be cancelled.

Immediate-or-cancel orders also require immediate execution but here the entire order does not have to be executed.

Limit orders establish the price limit for the trade and *market orders* specify execution of the trade as soon as possible and under any conditions.

For example, now, let's look at the puts on a given day for IBM.

IBM Puts

Stock Price	Strike Price	June	July	Sept
120 7/8	95	1/8	1/8	3/16
120 7/8	100	1/8	1/8	3/8
120 7/8	105	3/16	3/8	3/4
120 7/8	110	3/16	1/2	13/16
120 7/8	115	1/4	7/8	2 1/8
120 7/8	120	1 1/16	2 3/16	3 3/4
120 7/8	125	3 7/8	5	6 1/8

In the case of IBM, you have quite a selection of puts to choose from, so your instructions to your broker must be very explicit to avoid any mistake. The striking prices range from $95 to $125 and the puts are available for as low as $.12½ to $6.12½.

Which put you select will depend upon how much money you have and how far down in price you guess IBM might go by a certain date. The expiration dates you have to choose from are the Saturdays after the third Fridays in June, July, and September. Notice how much higher the September puts are than those at the same striking price for June and July.

But before you place your order, you must decide on your basic strategy (Table 11-1). That is, will you just play naked puts, or hedge your positions by buying the stock or buying calls?

The Naked Buy

Just playing the option requires tying up the least amount of money, but it can leave you at greater risk. But as the whole point of playing the options market is to get leverage—that is, to get a few dollars to do the work of many—a lot of investors feel that naked buys are the better way to go.

Let's assume you agree and are now ready to place your order. After scanning the tables and doing a little more research, you feel that IBM, which has just had a bit of a run-up in price, is ready for a pull-back. You think the stock can pull back to about $110 by July. That means the July 115s will move into the money and bring you profit.

You give the broker your order.

Table 11-1
The Basic Strategies

Type	Description
Long Put	Purchase of a put on the underlying stock. If the stock declines in value, the put will probably increase in value, depending on strike price and expiration date.
Long Straddle	Purchase of a put and a call having the same strike price and expiration date. Stock must usually move substantially before a profit is realized.
Long Put, Long Stock	Purchase of a put and the purchase of 100 shares of stock. If the stock goes up in price to more than cover the premium for the put, profit can be realized. If the put goes up enough to more than cover the loss on the stock, profit can be realized.

"Mr. Broker, I'd like to open a position in the IBM July 115 puts. I'd like to buy 10, all or none, at 7⁄8, good-till-cancelled."

The broker is able to execute your order. For $875 plus commissions, you have purchased 10 IBM puts.

Over the next 10 trading days, the stock fluctuates and your puts move up and down as the stock approaches and retreats from the strike price; the expiration date gets closer; and the marketplace finds or loses interest in the option.

Stock Price	July 115 Put Price
120⅞	⅞
121	⅞
121¼	¾
120⅞	¾
120¾	¾
120½	¾
120	⅞
118½	1
118⅛	1
117½	1⅛
116	1½

(Note that these prices represent the last sale. Actually, the premiums for the put will be expressed in terms of bid and ask prices, and the spread can easily be ½ point for more)

Figuring a bird in the hand is worth two in the bush, you decide to sell your options when the July 115s are at 1½.

Proceeds from sale:	$1,150
Cost:	875
Profit:	$ 275

A profit of $275 is not a great gain, and generally an options player is in the market for a much larger return. Still, when the expiration date is drawing closer, it is often wise to take your profits when you can.

A $275 profit on an $875 investment, however, is nothing to take lightly. It represents a little better than a 35 percent profit in ten days.

Even though the put remained out of the money, it still managed to gain strength and allow you to realize a profit. Of course, you may argue that if instead of buying the puts you sold short the stock at $120⅞ and bought it at

$116, you would have realized a profit of $487.50 instead of $275. When dealing in out-of-the-money puts that remain out-of-the-money, this is often the case. But consider the following before you pass final judgment. Selling short the stock would have required (given 50 percent margin) over a $6,000 investment. Not only would you have had to tie up a great deal of money, but your rate of return would actually have only been about 8 percent.

Now, so that you can fully understand the messages in the next two subsections, let's look at a naked put purchase that does not pay off.

Consider the same IBM puts but now assume that you hold them another 10 days before closing out your position.

Stock Price	July 115 Put Price
116	1½
116 ½	1⅜
116 ¾	1⅜
117 ⅛	1⅛
118	⅞
118 ¾	¾
119 ⅛	⅝
120	⅝
120 ¼	½
120 ½	½

Deciding it is best to unload the puts, you sell the ten that you own at $½. Proceeds are $500. As the cost to buy the puts was $875, you have a loss of $375. In this case, if you had sold short the stock at $120⅞ and bought it at $120½, you would have had a gain of $⅜ per share. Clearly in this case, you would have been better off to sell short the stock.

In these two examples, the investment was in out-of-the-money puts, which have a rather unpredictable and somewhat slow movement while they remain out of the money. In-the-money puts are a bit more predictable and consistent, particularly to the nearest expiration date, and particularly when they are far in the money.

Long Stock and Long Put Hedge

Investors will sometimes buy puts mainly as a hedge for their long positions in stock. In this case, the puts are used to insure the investment rather than as a means of obtaining profit from a decline in the price of the underlying stock.

Consider again the IBM options:

IBM Puts

Stock Price	Strike Price	June	July	Sep
120⅞	115	¼	⅞	2⅛
120⅞	120	1⅛	2³⁄₁₆	3¾
120⅞	125	3⅞	5	6⅛

The investor might purchase 200 shares of IBM at 120⅞ and purchase two puts with the nearest strike price, in this case the June 120s. The idea is that if the stock rises in price, the most the investor will lose is the $225 he paid for the puts. And if the stock should decline, the profit from the puts will offset losses from the stock.

There is a substantial investment to make here. There is not only the $24,175 in stock plus commissions but also the cost of the options plus commissions. However, for a sizeable stock investment such as this, the cost of the puts is relatively low and serves as nothing more than cheap insurance.

If IBM increases to $127⅞ per share, the investor gains $1,400 on the stock but can lose no more than the $225 he paid for the put. Subtracting the loss on the put from the gain on the stock ($1,400 - $225), we find the true profit before commissions: $1,175.

If the price of the stock retreats $5 per share, the put could increase to about $6. In this case, the investor loses $1,000 on the stock but gains $1,200 on the put. Here the stock has plummeted 5 points, but the investor, having hedged with long puts, still comes out ahead.

Investors extremely bullish on a stock but reluctant to run naked with their investment might hedge with lower priced puts—and in such quantities that if the stock should fall drastically, the puts will more than ensure minimal profit.

Consider again those same IBM puts. But this time the investor buys 20 June 115s at ¼ when he buys 200 shares of the IBM stock. The puts will cost $500 but the investor feels that for a high-priced stock like IBM, which can sometimes fluctuate widely in price over a period of a couple of months, the puts do not present a costly hedge.

The stock must move at least 2½ points north to meet the investor's break-even point, for the puts cost $500. IBM often swings a couple of points in one direction or another in very short time, so gambling on a 2½ point move to break even on this hedge is not at all unrealistic. If IBM jumps five points, then the investor realizes a $1,000 profit on the stock but a maximum loss of $500 on the puts. There is a gain of $500.

If IBM drops two points, the puts will probably increase to at least $1.50, depending on the time until expiration. If this does happen, the investor loses $400 on the stock but gains $3,000 on the puts. He's $2,600 ahead.

Should the stock drop 10 points, the puts will probably increase to at least $5 or $6, for now they will be in-the-money, and once in-the-money their value will increase at about one point for each point the stock drops in price. A 10-point drop in the stock adds up to a $2,000 loss ($10 x 200 shares) on the stock, but the corresponding gain on the puts can add up to $9,500 to $11,500. That not only makes up for the loss on the stock, but assures a hefty profit besides.

It is possible that the stock will show little movement through an expiration date and the options might expire worthless or wind up being sold for 10 percent of their original worth just prior to expiration. But the investor can now purchase the puts having the next expiration date so that he continues to hedge his position. He can continually sell puts and buy new ones as long as he feels it is to his advantage and as long as puts with new expiration dates are available.

A strategy such as this is particularly advantageous with higher priced stocks that often fluctuate by five or more points during the life of an option.

Hedging in this fashion, as you have noticed, requires tying up a great deal of money for sometimes extended periods. This is true even when maximum margin is used. For the small investor with only a couple of thousand to invest at any time, being able to hedge with long stock and long puts is rarely possible and is another example of how much harder it is for Little Money to be successful in the market. Big Money can insure its positions, play combinations, take its time. But Little Money has to be on target with the right picks and little diversification.

Long Put and Long Call Hedge

This is also called a straddle, and it is designed for an option holder who anticipates a major move one way or another in the underlying interest. He is playing bear and bull at the same time. Because the strategy entails *buying* the put and the call, it is referred to as a long straddle.

In the case of IBM, a straddle would be a very expensive proposition. In the long straddle, the strike price and expiration date must be the same and the entire straddle must be purchased or sold, not just parts of it. Given the premiums below, consider the investment required for a straddle on IBM:

IBM
120 7/8

	Calls				Puts	
June	July	Oct	Strike Price	June	July	Oct
11 3/4	12 3/8	14 5/8	110	1/16	3/8	1 3/16
6 3/8	7 3/4	10 1/4	115	1/4	7/8	2 1/8
2 3/16	4 1/4	7 1/8	120	1 1/16	2 3/16	3 3/4

As the safer play entails designing a straddle that is close to being in-the-money, the minimum investment on the June 120s would be $350 ($237.50 for the June call and $112.50 for the June put). To design the straddle around the July 120s would require a minimum investment of $662.50.

To cover the eost of the June 120 puts and calls, the stock would have to move about 3½ points before the break-even point would be reached; in the second ($662.50 for the July 120s), the stock would have to move about 6⅝ points.

The Long Put

Option combinations and stock and option combinations are expensive for the independent investor with minimal money to invest. Thus, he usually just buys naked puts. But if he makes his put option buying a long term program, he will generally do well. But even a long-term approach requires exceptional luck in selecting right combinations of strike prices and expiration dates, as well as selecting the right option.

12

Common Misconceptions

Investors with little experience with options trading often misinterpret some facts about options and their applications. It is only when they have been involved in the buying of puts and calls for some time that everything begins to fall in place for them.

Here are some of the usual misconceptions that handicap new and infrequent traders.

A first misconception is that buying puts is always preferable to shorting the underlying stock. This idea is born of the option's low price, leverage, and the fact that the investor can lose no more than the cost of the put. The truth, however, is that puts have a short life; these contracts expire after a period of months at most, and if the buyer has not been able to unload these puts by that expiration date, he is left with a worthless contract.

Besides expiration dates, there are some other major reasons why shorting the stock may be preferable. For one, a put buyer needs a stomach of iron, as the value of a put can drop suddenly. Put buyers often see their contracts drop 100 percent in market value—and in very short time. One thing about a put or call, however, is that zero market value does not mean they may remain worthless; they can still regain value, but only as long as that contract expiration date has not arrived.

A second major reason shorting a stock may be preferable is because put action in that stock is relatively weak and there are few contracts available. This means the economies of scale and additional profits that can be achieved by buying in quantity are not there; neither will there be the chance to buy subsequent contracts as the current ones approach expiration.

A second misconception is that puts always move up in price as the underlying stock moves down in price. This is not always, but usually, true of in-the-money options but is a chancy thing with out-of-the-monies. In fact, far out-of-the-money options may require a substantial move in the value of the stock before the option premiums start to increase. In the case of at-the-monies, the change in the price of the option may also trail the change in the price of the stock; it depends upon the market's expectations for the underlying stock as well as the put. This last is also a consideration in all cases regarding option price movement, regardless of money positions.

A third misconception is that as long as a put is in-the-money, the owner of the put stands to profit. Being in the money means that the option has intrinsic value; it does not guarantee profit for the owner. For example, the put may have been purchased at three dollars and, despite the fact that it is still in the money, it is currently at a premium of two dollars.

A fourth misconception is that if an option is purchased out-of-the-money, the buyer is assured a profit if it goes in-the-money. An option can very possibly have been commanding a higher premium when it was out-of-the-money than when it later came in-the-money. A lot depends on what time during the contract period the put came in-the-money. Consider the following wherein an option was purchased out-of-the-money on June 18, and is in-the-money on August 15 with only three days until expiration.

Striking Price: $20   Expiration Date: Aug 22

Date	Stock Price	Option Price
June 18	$18.00	$2.25
June 20	$18.25	$2.25
June 25	$18.12½	$2.25
July 2	$17.50	$1.87½
July 9	$18.50	$2.00
July 16	$19.25	$2.12½
July 23	$19.00	$2.12½
Aug 6	$20.25	$2.00
Aug 13	$21.00	$1.87½
Aug 15	$21.25	$1.67½

As you may have noticed by studying the above table, despite the fact that the increasing stock price was exerting upward pressure on the option premium at various times, the approaching expiration date was steadily decaying the option so that, by the time it was in-the-money on August 6 for the first time, it was already worth less than it was on June 18 when it was out-of-the-money.

A fifth misconception is that an investor must be either a buyer or a seller of a put. Actually, he may be both. Options may be bought long or sold short just as the underlying stock may be bought long or sold short. With a put, however, it gets a bit tricky because you do just the opposite of what you might do with the underlying stock. This is, with a put you buy long if you expect the stock to decrease markedly in value, and you sell short a put if you expect the stock to remain at about its current price *or* go up in price. On the other hand, you would short the stock when you expect it to decline, and you would buy long the stock when you expect it to decrease in value.

Stock going up?   Buy stock long or sell short put.

Stock going down?   Buy put long or sell short the stock.

Stock going no place?   Sell short the put (as time decay of the option
                             will work to your benefit).

A sixth misconception is that in the case of stock splits, the exercise value is affected. Actually, what changes is the strike price and the number of options you have. For instance, if you own two Citicorp January 30 puts and there is a two for one split, then afterward you will own four January 30 puts. The value at exercise will not be affected.

In the case of a *stock split involving an odd number of shares*, it gets a bit tricky. Just remember that the number of shares covered by each option, as well as the strike price, is adjusted, but *the exercise value remains the same.*

For example, assume you own one Citicorp July 30 put. Because each put is for 100 shares and the strike price is $30, the exercise value is $3,000. Now, suppose that a three for two split is declared. As that means a distribution of an additional ½ share for each one that you own, the contract now represents 150 shares at a strike price of $20. This keeps the exercise value the same, as 150 x $20 = $3,000.

A seventh misconception is that stocks making the "new highs" list are good candidates for put options as they are bound to come down in price. The stocks can very easily establish a new trading range somewhere above the last price at which they were available. Remember, there are no "sure things" about stock or options price movements, and a number of factors must be heavily weighed before deciding which options have the chance of becoming winners. (Review Chapter 5 for approaches to selecting stocks for short selling or options trading.)

An eighth misconception is that if you own puts and calls with the same striking price and exercise date, you are bound to profit because the calls will make money when the stock goes up and the puts will make money when the stock goes down. The first question to challenge this concept is: "What happens if the stock does not move at all or moves in a very narrow trading range?" What happens is that both the calls and the puts depreciate in value, for remember these are wasting assets and they will continually disintegrate as that expiration date nears. A second question is: "Suppose the stock does not move one way or the other far enough to cover all premiums paid for this straddle (owning a put and call with the same strike price and expiration date)?" The answer, of course, is a loss on the investment.

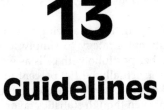

13

Guidelines

Many of the recommendations given in Chapter 8 for short sellers of stock are just as applicable for put buyers. The put buyer needs to understand basic stock market arithmetic and especially how to calculate breakeven points. He needs to know basic economics and be able to grasp the way interest rates, inflation and unemployment interact; tied in with this is an understanding of the business cycle and how the stock market prepares for each successive stage in the cycle. He has to be sure he knows what he is getting himself into, whether the potential gain is worth the risk and whether or not his money can be making just as much or more elsewhere.

Additionally, there are these guidelines for the buyer of long puts:

1. *Understand the goals of put writers as well as put buyers.* Knowing how the game is played by opposing teams helps develop additional instinct for the game and full measurement of the odds you are up against.

Now, as an investor who wants to benefit from market declines in stock prices, you will primarily be a long buyer of puts. Your goal is exceptional gain on your investment wherever and whenever possible. You would like to see the put that you have purchased for a mere one-eighth of a point skyrocket to $9 or $10 by the time the contract runs out. Such a gain is not unlikely in the options markets, but only those with an exceptional understanding of the underlying stock, good timing, and some luck will realize it. Most investors long on options do not fare very well, and most brokers like to tell stories about how many losers they have seen in their careers.

Put writers, on the other hand, are not looking for exceptional capital gains, but rather for additional and frequent income from the puts that they write. They know the odds favor the writer more than the buyer. They know they will be able to pick a lot of little winners, but they also know they can quite easily pick one loser that will make up for dozens of premiums earned by more careful writing strategies.

It would be no easy task trying to earn a living as a put buyer, but then nobody actually limits their investment strategy to simply long positions in puts. The average investor sprinkles her portfolio with calls as well as long and short positions in stock; never will she actually be 100 percent in puts. But as she instinctively knows that the market retreats with force every so often, she must include puts as part of her strategy even though statistics favor writers.

2. *Understand the basic terminology used in option trading.* But most of all, understand the way these terms relate to puts. For example, *in-the-money* has a different meaning in the case of puts than in the case of calls. A put is in-the-money when the striking price is higher than the market price of the underlying stock. A call, on the other hand, is in-the-money when the striking price is below the market price of the underlying stock.

3. *Understand that it is the premium that drives the market for a particular option.* When the premium is too high, long buyers are not willing to take a chance, and so the market becomes stagnant. When the premiums are low enough to excite buyer interest yet not so low as to scare away writers, then the market begins to take off.

4. *Understand how different the quote for an option is from the quote for a stock.* If a stock is quoted at 2½, this means the stock can be purchased for $2.50 per share. If an option is quoted at 2½, this means the option can be purchased for $250. This is because, unless otherwise noted, each option represents 100 shares of stock.

5. *Do not buy puts simply because they have been listed in the "Most Active Options"* tables. The majority can be wrong and often is when it comes to buying options. Additionally, sometimes an option makes the most active list because the big money is simply hedging its bets.

6. *Be sure of your goals and their practicality.* An option player always has lots of choices to make. There are usually a number of puts and calls available on some underlying stock, each of these options having different striking prices and expiration dates. What do you think the underlying stock will do from one option cycle to another? Do the potential movements in the stock price make the far

out-of-the-monies worth the gamble, or should you stay with at- or in-the-monies which, though more expensive, are less of a gamble? Do not buy an option just because it is cheap, and don't buy it just because it happens to be in-the-money. Weigh what the underlying stock can do and take your positions accordingly. You can select many different options at one time on any underlying stock.

7. *Keep abreast of options recommendations.* Many of the financial papers have columns dedicated to option writing and buying and there are newsletters for investors that specialize in options trading. Read everything you can.

14

Special Risks

There are special risks associated with playing the options markets. These have to do with market disruptions, exercise restrictions, secondary market cancellation, and broker insolvency.

Market Disruptions

Equity options are dependent upon active trading in underlying securities. Their premiums are in one way or another related to the price of some stock or other security. Now, if for some reason, trading should be halted in an underlying stock, trading in all options based on that stock must also come to a close.

Why would trading in a stock suddenly be halted? The reasons can be many, including unusually heavy demand causing tremendous backlog, bankruptcy filings, or major retreats or crashes, such as those that occurred in October 1987. When trading in any stock is suddenly halted, not only is the marketplace unsure of when trading will begin, but it is also unsure what the reopening price will be. This is particularly true during tender offers and bankruptcies when reopening prices can be double or half what they had been previously. Imagine the havoc among options holders and writers when this happens. Someone holding ten puts worth $2,000 on a company entering Chapter 11 can find her options off the board when the stock reopens. Worse yet, consider someone who has shorted 10 puts in expectation of a stagnant or rising market, sees her underlying stock stop trading, and then learns at reopening that fraudulent reporting has been discovered and the stock has dropped 15 points; if she shorted 10 puts, she could lose $10,000 or more from trading halt to reopening. This is because the puts would go up in price as the stock went down and she would have to put up additional margin or cover her position. Consider also the call writer whose stock is being taken over; as she tries to cover her position, she finds she is too late and trading has been halted. As she waits in panic for the stock to reopen so she can immediately cover her position, she fully realizes that her losses can be thousands of percent, even tens of thousands of percent!

Secondary Market Cancellation

The options markets are managed in such a way that everything possible is done to secure investor confidence. Though many of the rules and regulations governing the options markets are unknown to the average investor, they are clearly there on her behalf. For example, so that no one can monopolize the marketplace, the Securities and Exchange Commission limits the number of options contracts that can be owned by any single investor or any investment group. The limit is based on the trading volume for the underlying stock over a six-month period, and applies to contracts on the same side of the market. Thus, a very heavily traded stock such as CPC International would have a position limit of 8,000 but a less heavily traded stock such as Zenith Labs would have a position limit of 5,500. Others may have a position limit as low as 3,000 contracts.

Market control by any single investor or group is not the only major concern of the options markets; liquidity is another. When an investor takes a position, long or short, in any put or call, she wants to know she can enter a closing order whenever she needs or wants. If she does not have this privilege, she is not going to be interested in gambling her money on any options. Thus, without some insurance that the marketplace is liquid, the options markets would collapse in little time.

Nevertheless, as important as liquidity is to the investor and as important as it is to the stability of the markets, it cannot be absolutely guaranteed. Certain options from time to time must necessarily be cancelled. Sometimes markets become so volatile and active that they cannot be managed efficiently and cancellation is necessary. Sometimes there is just no market for a particular series of options and there is no justifiable reason to keep the series active. However, cancellation is not usually immediate. What the markets usually do is refrain from cancelling until the series expires. This presents some difficulty for the long term player currently in the red, because she cannot trade out of one expiration date into another *ad infinitum* until she finally realizes a profit; but if there is no continued interest in the option series she would very unlikely ever be in a position to profit.

Exercise Restrictions

Occasionally, the OCC or one of the options markets intervenes in normal clearing operations to prohibit the exercising of certain options or series of options. When this happens, put and call traders cannot close out their positions and will not be able to do so until the options, having been cancelled, are trading again or the exercise restrictions are lifted.

Exercise works differently for puts and calls. When a put is exercised, the owner of the put *sells* the stock at the strike price with the intention of buying it immediately or at any time that he feels it will be advantageous. When a call is exercised, the owner of the call *buys* the stock at the strike price with the intention of selling it immediately, or at some time in the future.

Broker Insolvency

Bankruptcies are rare in the brokerage industry but they can, and have, happened—and will happen. The early 1970s was a particularly difficult time for small brokerages, as was the period following the October '87 "crash." Few stock investors really suffer when a broker goes under, for their accounts are protected by the SIPC and usually by additional insurance taken out by the broker. Still, the delays and complications that result are serious enough to have every financial counselor recommend that the investor always be aware of the financial condition of his broker.

For options traders, brokerage financial trouble is a lot more serious. They can find that each and every one of their positions have been closed out without their knowledge. The Options Clearing Corporation has initiated safeguards to prevent this from happening, but the threat is always there. The OCC's safeguards have to do with the financial requirements it imposes on its member firms. Members must have minimum net capital, special margin deposits with the clearing corporation, certain assets pledged as collateral, and must maintain periodic and sufficient contributions to the clearing fund. (Payments to the clearing fund must be in cash or in U.S.-backed securities that meet maturity requirements.)

The broker's balance sheet and income statement should not be the only considerations in selecting that broker. There are two other very important factors:

- Mandatory arbitration
- Selection of account representatives

Mandatory arbitration refers to a clause in many brokerage contracts that states the investor *may not* sue the broker for any reason. What would prompt an investor to take a broker to court? Among other things: incorrect placement of orders, deliberately making unapproved executions, supplying false or misleading information, or incorrectly accounting for transactions. The recommendation is, if at all possible, to avoid using brokers that require mandatory arbitration.

The second, which refers to the investor's right to select account representatives, is important because when an investor first signs up with a broker, the account representative assigned to her is usually whichever one is available. Yet the trader may have little experience and need a much more knowledgeable representative, or she may find, for any number of reasons, that she would prefer to work with someone else. There are always those account executives that go beyond the limits set for them by the house in which they work; others treat customers carelessly, except for their larger accounts; they are constantly trying to sell the investor on certain stocks or other securities, or they are relentless in their churning of discretionary accounts.

The rule is to be as selective of an account representative as you are of the brokerage.

PART
4

Call Writing

15

The Writer's Perspective

The call writer is a short seller of calls. A call gives legal right to its owner to purchase the underlying security at a specified price for a specified period. Anyone can either be a writer or a seller of calls.

What is the advantage of being a call writer rather than a short seller of stock, or a put buyer?

As the short seller of stock, you must generally invest a great amount of money and the stock must go down in price before you can realize a profit. The put buyer, also, must want the stock to drop in price, for this is the only way his put will appreciate in value.

The call writer, however, benefits if the stock stays near its current trading range, even if it moves slightly up or down in price. The call writer is immediately in the black when his order is executed. His account is immediately credited for the price of the call less the broker's commission. For the put buyer or short seller of stock, however, that first transaction is a debit. Call writing is quick income, but may or may not be a safe strategy depending upon how far out-of-the money the call is, and what may happen to the underlying stock.

Intrinsic Value

Let's look at some of the same terms discussed in previous chapters about puts, but now we must apply those terms in a very different way, for puts and calls are opposite sides of the investment coin.

The value of a call, like the value of a put, depends mainly on its intrinsic value, but intrinsic value is interpreted differently for calls. The call has intrinsic value when its striking price is lower than the market price of the underlying stock.

Stock Price	Strike Price	Intrinsic Value
$30.00	$35.00	No
$33.50	$35.00	No
$35.00	$35.00	No
$35.12½	$35.00	Yes

When a call has intrinsic value, it is in-the-money. Its striking price is lower than the market price of the stock. This means that if you owned the calls and wanted to sell the stock immediately after exercising your option to do so, you would be assured a profit. Why? Because you would be in the enviable position of buying the stock at a much lower price than that for which it is currently selling.

But you are going to be a short-seller of calls. You are going to write them first—then *maybe* buy them back later. And what is good for the option buyer is not good for the option writer. Under most circumstances, then, you would not want to write in-the-money calls.

Besides intrinsic value, calls, like puts, also have a time value which is derived mainly from the life remaining on the contract, but which is also greatly influenced by a number of other factors, including investor interest and interest rates.

Consider the case for calls on Citicorp stock given below.

Stock: Citicorp

Stock Price	Strike Price	Difference	Option Price
$30.00	$25.00	$5.00	$5.75
$36.00	$35.00	$1.00	$2.00
$40.00	$45.00	($5.00)	$ .75

You will notice that if only the intrinsic value of an option were the determining factor for its market price, the option prices would be significantly less in the first two examples and actually zero dollars in the third. The additional value is considered the *time value*.

An Example of Call Writing

Call writers generally operate under the philosophy that the future value of a stock will probably be its current price, give or take 15 percent. So, they look for underlying stocks that may recently have had a fairly sizeable run-up in price and may now be settling in a narrow price range, or falling back in price 10 or 15 percent.

They certainly do not want a stock that is going to move steadily or suddenly upward in price, because if this happens the call they have sold short will also increase in value. If it does increase in value, they may be forced to buy it back at a higher price, or else deliver the underlying stock if the owner exercises her rights.

Consider the following calls on Disney.

Stock: Disney   Price: $130

Strike Price	June	July	October
$115	16	16¾	20⅞
$120	10¼	12⅜	16
$125	5⅝	8⅝	13⅜
$130	2¼	5¼	10
$135	¾	3	7¾
$140	⅛	1⅞	5¼

Suppose you are looking for income and have zeroed in on Disney. The stock has marched to $130 in short time from about $105. Because of the price of the stock and the demand for the calls, premiums are fairly high. You go down the list.

1. You can sell 10 June 115s and receive $16,000 credited to your account. If the stock drops a few points and the June 115s fall accordingly, you can then turn around and buy back the option at a lower price. The result will be a capital gain of a few hundred dollars. You can do this also with the July and October 115s, in which case you will receive even more money when you write. But the calls are in the money and, theoretically, the owner of the calls can exercise his option at anytime. If the calls have increased in price when the owner exercises his rights, you will lose money. You decide to stay away from writing any of the 115s.

2. You look at the other in-the-money calls and nix them for the same reason. The 120s and 125s can be called at anytime. Besides, if the stock

increases in price even one-eighth of a point, like the 115s, these options will be a minus for any writer (and a plus for any seller).

3. You look at the at-the-money June, July and October 130s. Again, you have no advantage. A minor upward movement in price will threaten your short position.

4. Now, you look at the 135s and the 140s. The 140s seem relatively safe because the chances of Disney reaching $140 per share by June or July seems pretty slim. But reaching $140 by October? Well, that's a possibility. However, these calls do not command very high premiums and you are uninterested.

5. For you, the July 135s seem to offer the best trade-off between safety and income. The Junes are too low priced and the Octobers too far off; Disney might be able to make it to $135 by October.

You phone your broker and tell him you want to short (write) two (to play it safe) July 135s on Disney. The broker executes the order and $600 is credited to your account.

Bear in mind that you have chosen the July 135s because you feel comfortable that the premiums are worth the risk. Another investor might only feel comfortable with the 140s; and yet another investor might prefer the October 115s because he is very sure the stock will decline and prefers the lower leverage afforded by the higher priced options, meaning the percent of loss is less with each point the option may go up. This is what makes the options markets so attractive—there is usually something available for every level of risk an options player is willing to take.

Having taken your opening position, you now watch the stock and the call premium.

Trading Day	Stock Price	July 135 Premium
1	$130	3
2	$130¼	3
3	$131	3¼
4	$131⅛	3¼
5	$131	3¼
6	$131¼	3¼
7	$132	3½
23	$133⅛	1¼
24	$133⅞	1⅜
25	$134½	1½

Trading Day	Stock Price	July 135 Premium
26	$135	1⅝
27	$136	1¾
28	$136½	1⅞
29	$137	2⅛
30*	$137½	2⅜

*Day before expiration

Notice the relationship between the premium for the July 135 and the stock price, and notice when you were showing profits and losses. On the first seven days of trading after you wrote the July 135 calls, the premiums climbed a bit. If you decided to buy the options back, you would lose ¼ of a point on each option. But why buy them back? There is no need. Your position is unthreatened—after all, the options are still out of the money. The stock had to move above $135 per share before you were in danger of being called. But by the time the option did move into the money, the time value pretty much wasted away the value of the option and the call was selling at only a little more than its intrinsic value. If you kept the calls until the 30th day, the worst that could happen would be that you had to buy them back for $475 (2 calls x $237½). Because you wrote the contracts for $600, you would still have a gain of $125 before commissions.

Disadvantages of Shorting Calls

Why then would anyone want to short stock or buy puts when selling out-of-the-money calls provides such quick income and such safety?

The main reasons are that buying puts is safer because you cannot lose more than your investment in the put, buying puts offers greater potential for exceptional gains, and selling short stock is not complicated by contract expiration dates that can leave the original investment worthless.

Remember that when you short a call (or a put), you can never make more than the premium you receive. But losses can be staggering if the put or call takes off.

Consider the following wherein a stock is selling for $30 per share, at which point someone shorts the stock, someone buys an out-of-the-money put, and you sell an out-of-the-money call.

Trading Day	Stock Price	Call Strike Price	Call Premium	Put Strike Price	Put Premium
1	$30.00	32½	¾	25	¾
4	$31.50	32½	⅞	25	⅝
7	$33.50	32½	1½	25	¼
11	$35.00	32½	2¾	25	—
13	$36.00	32½	3¼	25	—

Each of you was expecting the stock to decline, but, as it turned out, the stock went up instead. The put buyer lost $75 ($¾ x 100) by the 13th day of trading, which we will assume is the last trading day for the option. The short seller lost a hefty six points; this means a loss of $600 if she had shorted 100 shares. But she is still in the ball game. The options expired but certainly not her stock. She can continue to hold on until the stock drops in price and she can cut her losses.

But you? What happened to you? You sold short the call for $75, then had to buy it back on the 13th day or go through the additional expense of delivering the stock. Suppose you bought the call back at $3.25; your loss is $250 ($325 – $75).

At first glance, it appears that selling the call was much smarter than shorting the stock in terms of cash loss, and that is true because options are so very inexpensive. But here we are not comparing the same amounts. The initial investment to short the stock was $1,500 because we are assuming 100 shares were shorted on margin. If you had sold short 20 of the calls ($1,500) instead of just one, you would have realized a loss of $5,000.

Now, let's assume the stock goes the other way. Instead of increasing in price, it goes down in price as anticipated.

Trading Day	Stock Price	Call Strike Price	Call Premium	Put Strike Price	Put Premium
1	$30.00	32½	¾	27½	¾
4	$29.50	32½	¾	27½	¾
7	$28.00	32½	⅝	27½	1⅛
11	$25.00	32½	—	27½	2¾
13	$23.50	32½	—	27½	4⅛

On the 13th day of trading, the put buyer realizes a gain of $337.50 ($412.50 – $75.00). The short seller of the stock realizes a gain of $650, determined by subtracting $2,350 from $3,000. But you could only realize a gain of $75, the result of the premium income you received when you wrote the call.

The writer of a call, then, limits his gain to the premium received, but cannot limit his losses.

16

Income and Capital Gains

Income is realized from the premium received when the call is written. Before looking at some necessary considerations for profiting from writing calls, let's review the basic terminology for those who have skipped the chapters on puts to learn about shorting calls.

Basic Terminology

The options markets have a language very different from what the stock investor may be used to. Getting these terms down pat will aid in understanding options trading.

It is not unusual to find the neophyte losing money because she misinterpreted terms like striking price or exercise date, or did not understand how the different money positions relate to puts and calls.

For those of you who have read the chapters on put options in which the following terms were introduced, pay special attention to them now in regard to how they pertain to calls and call writing.

In-the-money

For a call, this refers to the situation when the striking price is lower than the market price of the stock. In-the-money calls are usually risky for the call writer. However, this does not mean that the writer cannot profit eventually by writing an in-the-money call, for the price of the call can retreat after it was sold short (written), and the trader can buy it back at the lower price. (See Table 16-1)

Out-of-the-money

For a call, this refers to the situation when the striking price is higher than the market price of the stock. Out-of-the-money calls are generally less risky for the call writer, not only because they are lower priced but because while they are out-of-the-money there is no chance of exercise. If the holder exercises his option, the writer would have to make good on his contract and deliver the underlying stock. But do not assume an out-of-the-money call means certain profit for the call writer, for they can increase in price and move in-the-money. (See Tables 16-1 and 16-2 for further clarification.)

At-the-money

For either a call or a put, this refers to the situation when the striking price is the same as the market price of the stock. At-the-money options are relatively risky for call writers (or put writers) because they can move in the money on the slightest change in the price of the underlying stock. (See also Table 16-1.)

Opening transaction

For the *call writer*, this represents the short sale of the option. For the *call buyer*, this represents the purchase of the call. For writers of out-of-the-money calls, as long as the option does not increase in value, there is no need to ever enter a closing (buy) transaction—unless the trader is afraid the option will eventually go in-the-money, and therefore wants to take his profits while he can.

Closing transaction

For the call writer, this represents closing out his contract by purchasing an option similar to the one he wrote. For the call buyer, the closing transaction is the selling of the option to close out his current position.

Class of options

All the call options, or all the put options on the same underlying stock, are said to be of the same class of options.

Table 16-1
Types of Calls

A. Out-of-the-Money: A call having a strike price above the current market price of the underlying stock.

Stock	Market Price	Strike Price
Seagate	$12½	$15
Valero	$14	$15
Wendy	$ 6½	$10
Wrigley	$57	$60
Xerox	$58¼	$60

B. In-the-Money: A call having a strike price below the current market price of the underlying stock.

Stock	Market Price	Strike Price
Seagate	$12½	$12
Valero	$14	$10
Wendy	$ 6½	$ 5
Wrigley	$57	$55
Xerox	$58¼	$55

C. At-the-Money: A call having a strike price equal to the current market price of the underlying stock.

Stock	Market Price	Strike Price
Seagate	$10	$10
Valero	$15	$15
Wendy	$5	$5
Wrigley	$55	$55
Xerox	$60	$60

Series of options

All options on the same underlying stock that have the same striking price and the same expiration date are said to be of the same series.

Table 16-2
Basic Differences Between Selling Stock Short
and Selling Calls Short

Selling Stock Short	Selling Calls Short
No time limit governing the value of the stock. Stock sold short can be purchased whenever the short seller deems it most advantageous.	Each contract has an expiration date, at which time the call becomes worthless. This works to the advantage of the call writer unless his option has moved in-the-money and it is called just before expiration.
There is no limit on the amount of losses that may be incurred, for a stock can, theoretically, go up in price to the nth degree.	True also of shorted calls.
Profits are limited to what can be achieved by the stock declining 100 percent, as that is the maximum a stock can depreciate.	Profits are limited to the premium received for writing the call.
Margin is available.	Margin has a different meaning for shorting calls. (See last subsection of Chapter 16.)

Expiration date

The date the option contract expires. The holder of an option must exercise his rights by the expiration date, or his contract is worthless. Options generally expire on the Saturday following the third Friday of the month at 11:59 am. However, the actual trading of the options is halted on that preceding Friday at 4 p.m.

Expiration cycle

This is the cycle of issuance and expiration for options contracts. Options are usually for three months in every other calendar quarter. Usually only the three closest trading months are listed.

Premium

The cost of the option, or its market value, is the premium. Though premiums are quoted in points like stock, the quoted premium multiplied by 100 is the true cost of the option before commissions. The 100 multiplier is required because each option normally represents 100 shares of stock.

Transaction statement

This is the written verification of the options trade to the writer and/or seller; it specifies the premium paid or received, the name of the underlying stock, the expiration date, and the striking price. The transaction statement is the only proof of sale or purchase. Options traders never actually see a contract. This is because so many opening and closing transactions take place every day that it would be cumbrous and uneconomical for both brokers and traders to get involved with formal legal contracts. As options contracts are generally all the same in terms of legal obligations of the parties, and only the specifics change, using a standard-ized transaction statement speeds the handling and verification of trades.

Secondary market

This is the market for puts and calls created by the options exchanges. This term "secondary market" is often misinterpreted to mean a less than viable market. Remember that when you buy and sell stocks and bonds, you are almost always dealing in the secondary markets created by the exchanges. (See the last chapter in this book for descriptions of how the exchanges work.) The very stock exchanges themselves, as well as the over-the-counter market, are, plain and simple, secondary markets.

For instance, when corporations issue stock for the first time in order to raise money, they sell it to investment bankers who then make it available to the financial community. Unless you are on a dividend reinvestment plan or an employee stock purchase plan, you are not actually making a stock purchase that will result in money being put in some corporation's treasury. The company sold the stock you just purchased a long time ago, and you are buying it now from your broker's or some other broker's account through that secondary market created by the exchanges.

Order information

To buy or sell an option, your broker generally requires the following informa-tion:

1. Number of options and kind (put or call)

2. The specific option

    a.   underlying security
    b.   striking price
    c.   expiration month

3. The premium

4. The type of order
    a.   all or none, partial, contingent, day, immediate or cancel, limit, market
    b.   opening or closing

Closing Transactions

When to close out a position is a decision the naked call writer must always be weighing. Should she wait out the contract, cut her losses, or take her gains now?

The answers to these questions depend upon the money position of the call, new expectations for the underlying stock, and the trader's game plan.

In the introductory example of naked call writing in the previous chapter, you chose to write an out-of-the-money call offering a relatively high premium for the safety offered by the striking price and expiration date. But, while your original plan was to hold your short position until the contract expired, when the stock increased in price and the option went in-the-money, you found it wise to enter a closing transaction. And so it is with all option writing: The trader must be ready to change her strategy when necessary.

Generally, naked call writers are interested in the premiums they receive from their writing strategies and are expecting their contracts to remain out-of-the-money until expiration. But this is not always the case. Some writers may short calls in lieu of shorting the stock, and because they are expecting short-term depreciation in an underlying stock that may rebound they are expecting to cover their positions long before contract expiration.

Strategies can differ markedly among traders. Those who may be interested in shorting calls for capital gains might *gamble* on calls close to the money or in-the-money; those who are mainly interested in the income the premiums represent will most likely write far out-of-the-money calls.

But every writer of options has her own game plan.

Out-of-the-Money Calls

For the covered call writer, out-of-the-money calls are usually the safest bet, for the writer not only earns the premium but can also profit on the stock. For the naked writer, out-of-the-monies represent a dilemma; they offer extra safety because of the high striking prices but offer extensive risk because of their low price and explosive potential. (See Table 16-3 for advantages and disadvantages of writing naked out-of-the-money calls.)

Following are two examples. Each represents a situation in which a call moves into the money. In the first example, the writer owns the underlying stock; in the second, the writer is uncovered.

(Bear in mind that when an option is in-the-money and close to expiration, it usually has only intrinsic value and is priced by about the amount it is above the striking price. The closer it gets to the expiration date, the more the value of the option will decay.)

Example #1. Karen Rigg owns 200 shares of Disney stock currently selling at $120 per share—the same price she paid for the stock. Wishing to earn some additional money from her portfolio, she sells two July 125 calls at 7½.

Table 16-3
Advantages, Disadvantages of Writing
Naked Out-of-the-Money Calls

Advantages	Disadvantages
The chance of the underlying stock being called, or of the writer having to close out her position, is less than that for other money positions.	The relatively low price for these calls means there is potential for losses in the thousands of percent. The tendency for investors to buy these calls in great quantity because of their low price increases the chances of exaggerated losses.
Time decay of the call is relatively rapid in the last weeks of the contract.	The writer does not own the underlying stock, so if the stock should suddenly surge beyond the strike price, it will be costly for the writer to cover himself if the option is exercised.
If the stock does not advance beyond the strike price, you stand to profit regardless of how much the option may have increased in value.	Usual risks of writing detailed in Chapter 14.

She receives $1,500. The stock climbs to $145 per share and the calls to $20
by expiration. Thus, her stock is called, which means she must sell it at the
striking price of $125.

How did Karen make out? Not badly at all. Selling the stock for $125 per share
meant a $5 per share gain, or $1,000 for her. On top of this, she had already
earned $1,500 from writing the call. Her total profit: $2,500. Hers was a relatively
safe strategy. Even if the stock went down, she would still have had the income
she received from writing the two calls.

Example #2. Dan Gaber writes two July 125 calls on Disney for 7½ He does
not own the underlying stock. His account is credited for $1,500. The stock
climbs to $145 per share and the calls to $20 by expiration. It is the day before
expiration.

What are Dan's options? (1) He can buy back the calls at $20 for a total cost of
$4,000 and a trade loss of $2,500 ($4,000 - $1,500). (2) He can deliver the stock by
purchasing it at the market price of $145 and selling it at the striking price of $125,
for a loss of $20 per share, or $4,000 on the stock trade. (But as he earned $1,500
from writing the calls, this amount must be subtracted from the stock trade loss
for the true result, which is a loss of $2,500.)
As you can see, having shorted out-of-the-money calls that make it well into
the money can mean heavy losses. But this is not the only danger for the naked
writer of calls. Far out-of-the-monies, which are extremely low priced and usually
purchased in large quantities, can bring financial havoc to even the wary naked
writer.

Example #3. Citicorp July 30 calls are selling for ¼ when the stock is at
$24½. As the expiratoin date is about 60 days away, you feel the calls are a
fairly safe bet. So, you sell 20 for a total of $500. But, as bad luck would have
it, the stock advances with strength and reaches $35 the day before expiration.
The calls, meanwhile, have advanced to 4¾. You have little choice but to
enter a closing transaction and buy the July 30s back for a total of $9,500 (20
x $475). Your total loss: $9,000.

The lesson to be learned: Be careful about writing low priced naked calls and
do not buy them in great quantity. A mere one-quarter of a point move in the
wrong direction can put you in the red by 100 percent. Of course, as long as the
call remains out-of-out-of-the-money, it makes little difference how much the
price moves against you. But as soon as it slips into-the-money, watch out!
"But," you might argue, "the option can always be bought back before it goes
out-of-the-money or gets too high in price."
The answer is that it is very tough to take a loss and inexperienced writers of
naked calls will procrastinate. They hope that the underlying stock will fall back

in price. After all, the underlying stock was selected for call writing because of its expected weakness, and it is hard for anyone to admit she made a mistake.

If you do not believe this little fact of life, or feel you are above getting caught in the same trap, consider the following.

Example #4. Expecting Xerox stock, currently at $47, to plummet, you sell five October 55 calls at ½ each. Your proceeds: $250. The stock price and option premiums then take the following swings:

Trading Day	Stock Price	Call Premiums	Paper Gain or Loss
3	$49	5/8	($60)
6	$51	7/8	($187.50)
9	$54	1¼	($350)
12	$56	2¼	($875)

Would you have sold on the third day to cut your losses? Probably not, for the call was still way out-of-the-money and there was still a good chance it would expire worthless. How about on the sixth trading day? As the option was still out of the money, the chances of your entering a closing transaction would be somewhat slim. By the ninth trading day, however, you might be worried enough to close out your position. But faced with the prospect of a $350 loss while the option was still out of the money, you might hesitate. By Day 12 you are deeply in trouble but you still might decide to hold your position; after all, the stock has just had a run up in price and should fall back.

But think about it. What would you do? Would you have sold at anytime to cut your losses, or held on to the very last? Do you see the dilemma the option writer faces, and why he rarely knows when to cut his losses until it is too late?

The objective is to be as careful as possible about the underlying stock selected for call writing, and to choose a far enough out-of-the-money striking price to offer additional protection. Bearing this in mind, observe the following examples which show how writing out-of-the-money calls can be profitable. Example #5 allows expiration, and example #6 brings the option into-the-money, but in both cases profit results.

Example #5. You sell five July 25 calls for $1 each on a stock currently selling for $20 per share. Your account is credited for $500.

Trading Day	Stock Price	Call Premiums	Paper Gain or Loss
1	$20	1	—
4	$21	1⅛	($62.50)
7	$19	¾	$125

Trading Day	Stock Price	Call Premiums	Paper Gain or Loss
11	$22	1½	($250)
20	$25	1¾	($375)
30	$26	1¾	($375)
40	$24	⅛	$437.50
Exp. Date	$24	0	$500

On Day seven you were realizing a gain and could have profited by closing out your position. But you would certainly profit much more by waiting until the expiration date. On Day 11, you are having some regrets. You are saying to yourself that you should have taken your profits when you could. On Days 20 and 30, when the calls were in the money and you were down $375 (notice how the time value holds the option premium to what it was 10 days earlier despite the $1 increase in stock price), you might have been considering closing out your position and cutting your losses. But it is clear your hesitation paid off, for on the 40th day of trading, the option was out-of-the-money again and you were in the profit zone. As the table indicates, the option eventually expires worthless and your paper gain becomes a real one. But what would *you* really have done?

Example #6. You sell five July 50 calls for $1.50 each on a stock presently selling for $47 per share. Your account is credited for $750.

Trading Day	Stock Price	Call Premiums	Paper Gain or Loss
1	$47	1½	—
7	$50	2½	($500)
14	$52	3½	($1,000)
21	$53	4	($1,250)
28	$51	1½	—
35	$51	1¼	$125
36	$51	1	$250

Allowing that Day 36 is the day before expiration, we see the call premium settling at $1, which is ½ point less than the price at which you had sold them.

There was reason enough for you to panic anytime from Day 7 until Day 28. The stock was not only above the striking price, but your calls were also demanding greater premiums. More nervous investors might have bailed out as soon as the ink began turning red—but not you. You waited for prices to retreat. When time finally eroded the call premiums to a profitable level by the day before expiration, you successfully closed out your position for a gain of $250. Lucky!

In-the-Money Calls

The naked writer of in-the-money calls is immediately in harm's way, for the underlying stock can be called at any time. However, the writer assumes the stock will not be called until the expiration date, and this is true almost all of the time.

For the covered call writer, there is often some safety built into his in-the-money writing strategies. This occurs when the premium exceeds the intrinsic value of the option by enough points to assure a gain if the stock is called. But as the naked writer does not own the underlying stock, he is at risk immediately and continues to be at risk until the premiums have fallen enough for him to realize a profit.

The naked writer, then, may be looked upon as a short seller who must decide between shorting the underlying stock or shorting the calls. If he has a limited amount of money to invest and anticipates a near-term drop in the price of the underlying stock, or a very minimal advance at best, then he will short the call. If he is unsure of the length of time he will have to maintain his position and he can tie up a lot of money for an extended period, he will want to short the stock.

Example #1. You feel that Syntex common is overbought and is about to fall back in price by 20 or 30 percent. You would like to short the stock but it is a relatively expensive one, currently selling for $59 per share. Margin considered, the minimum you would have to deposit in your account is $2,950. However, there are July 55 calls selling at 4½. As the expiration date is about one month away, you expect that the calls will begin decaying rapidly unless the stock makes its way further north. You write two calls for $900 in premiums. The action is as follows:

Trading Day	Stock Price	Call Premium	Paper Gain or Loss
1	$59	4½	—
3	$60	5½	($200)
5	$61	6½	($400)
7	$59	4¼	$50
9	$58	3¼	$250
11	$58	3⅛	$275
13	$57	2¼	$475

(This would be a good time to close out your position, but let's assume you decide to stay in the game.)

Trading Day	Stock Price	Call Premium	Paper Gain or Loss
14	$57	2¼	$450
16	$58	3⅛	$275
18	$58	3⅛	$275
20	$59	4¼	$50

(What would you do now? The stock is climbing again and so is the price of the July 55s.)

Let's assume that you decide to play it safe and enter a closing transaction to buy two July 55s at 4¼. Before commissions, you have a profit of $50.

Notice the lessons here. (1) You would have made more money if you weren't so greedy; after all, on the 13th day of trading you were $450 in the black. (2) You *did* profit although you had written an in-the-money call. (3) You *did* profit although the stock was at the same price when you closed out your position. *Time,* slowly decaying the options as the expiration date approached, worked to your advantage.

Now, let's assume that the stock's price action takes a different swing. What decisions would you make as you move into the red or black, given that there are 25 trading days until the calls expire?

Trading Day	Stock Price	Call Premium	Paper Gain or Loss
1	$59	4½	—
5	$57	2¼	$450

(Would you get out now? Twenty days remain until expiration.)

9	$55	¾	$750

(How about now? Why get greedy?)

13	$55	¾	$750
17	$54	½	$800

(The option has now fallen out of the money. Will you take the $800 profit? How much more can you make? If the option expires, your profit is $900.)

Trading Day	Stock Price	Call Premium	Paper Gain or Loss
21	$54	½	$800
22	$55	¾	$750
23	$55	⅝	$725
24	$56	⅞	$775
25	$57	1¾	$650

If you at least took your profits on Trading Day 25, you would be a winner again. However, if for some reason you failed to enter a closing transaction and the contract expired, you would have lost $900.

The lessons here are that once you write a call, you cannot forget it. Pay attention to its daily price movements. Realize that not only must you make many decisions on whether to stay in or close out during the life of the contract, but you must be careful not to let the option run to 4 p.m. on the third Friday of the expiration month, at which time the option becomes worthless.

Example #2. You decide to write two in-the-money calls on Storage Technology, which is currently selling at $32. You favor the July 30s, currently at 3 ½, because you feel a small drop in the price of the stock will pull the calls out-of-the-money, thereby reducing their value substantially. Twenty-five days of trading remain until expiration. You purchase only two calls to reduce risk.

Trading Day	Stock Price	Call Premium	Paper Gain or Loss
1	$32	3½	—
5	$33	4½	($200)
9	$34	5½	($400)

(Would you close out now and cut your losses or wait in expectation that the stock will still lose some ground?)

13	$36	7¼	($750)

(The stock is showing unexpected strength. Can there be a takeover in the making? If so, uh-oh! What will you do? Hang on?)

17	$35	6	($500)

(The stock is backing off in price, and the option is losing time value. Should you wait longer or close out?)

Trading Day	Stock Price	Call Premium	Paper Gain or Loss
21	$34	4½	($200)
22	$35	5½	($400)

(Things were beginning to look up, but now you are falling deeper into the red. What will you do?)

23	$34	4¼	($150)
24	$35	5	($300)
25	$36	5¾	($450)

Here the stock increased a mere four dollars per share, so the amount of the loss was not unmanageable. However, it is important to note that if you had sold short the stock instead of the calls, you would still have only a paper loss. There would be no need to purchase back the stock because your trading would in no way be affected by any expiration date.

What would have happened if the stock climbed higher in price? Well, the option premium would also have climbed in price and your losses would have been much more exaggerated. Consider the following case:

Original Premium	Total Income from Writing	Current Premium	Current Value	Gain or Loss
4½	$900	7½	$1,500	($600)
4½	$900	10	$2,000	($1,100)
4½	$900	15	$3,000	($2,100)

Losses can mount quickly. When to close out? The big question!

It takes nerves of steel to be a writer of naked calls. (See Table 16-4 for a summary of the advantages and disadvantages of writing in-the-money calls.)

At-the-Money Calls

Calls are at the money when the striking price and the market price of the underlying stock are equal. At-the-money is an extremely temporary state of affairs, for, usually, the slightest movement in price of the underlying stock will bring the option either out-of or into-the-money.

Table 16-4
Advantages, Disadvantages of
Writing Naked In-the-Money Calls

Advantages	Disadvantages
Premiums tend to move in a fairly determinable relationship to the underlying stock.	The stock can be called at any time. Thus, the writer is immediately at risk when his order is executed.
If the stock is highly volatile, it is possible to realize impressive capital gains by writing, closing out and later rewriting—provided the price swings are impressive and predictable. Few investors, however, have the experience and timing to play this game.	The risks of writing detailed in Chapter 14.

The short-term prospects for the related options can be highly volatile, for once the option moves into the money, its value may increase markedly, and when it moves out of the money its value can *decrease* markedly. How much the options may actually swing in price will depend a great deal on the life left in the contract period. Once again, covered call writers are in a much more advantageous position with at-the-monies than are naked writers. This is not only because the covered call writer already has his margin requirements filled through ownership of the underlying stock, but because this ownership allows safer approaches to the writing strategy. For one, the covered call writer may ride the underlying stock for a paper profit of $5, $10 or more before she decides to write an at-the money call on the stock. And she may choose to write at a premium high enough to assure a profit when the stock is called. For example, consider the following:

Stock	Market Pr.	Call Prem	Strike Pr.	Advantage
GM	$50	1⅞	50	$187.50

Suppose the writer had originally purchased GM at $40 per share. After realizing a $10 per share paper profit on the stock, she decides to write an at-the-money call. If the stock should happen to be called, the premium of $187.50 will cover the sell commissions and she will still earn $10 per share on the rate of the stock.

The naked writer is more limited in his program. His first trade is in the option; he trades the stock only if he has to meet his contract obligations.

Let's play with some more trading activity.

Example #1. *You are expecting Pepsi common stock to decrease in price. A number of analysts have judged the stock to be overpriced based on expected earnings. You sell two calls on the stock with an expiration date 60 trading days away. These are October 75s and they are at-the-money. The calls traded for 5½.*

Trading Day	Stock Price	Call Premiums	Paper Gain or Loss
1	$75	5½	—
6	$72	4	$300
11	$70	2½	$600

(If you close out your position now, you will realize a $600 profit. However, if the option, already out of the money, expires worthless, you will make $1,100. What would you do?)

16	$72	4	$300
21	$76	6½	($200)

(Now, you are in the red. Will the stock continue to go north, or will it drop again? The expiration date is getting closer and you know if the option goes out-of-the-money, it will decay quickly.)

26	$78	8½	($600)
31	$80	10½	($1000)
41	$75	3½	$400

(You have returned to profitability. The stock has returned to the price it was at when you wrote the calls, and time decay of the options has brought the premiums down two points. It is an ideal time to take your profits. But you won't. You'll go for broke!)

51	$80	5¼	$50
56	$83	8	$500
57	$83½	8	$500
58	$84	9	($700)
60	$84	8½	($600)

Table 16-5
Advantages, Disadvantages of
Writing Naked At-the-Money Calls

Advantages	Disadvantages
The chances of the underlying stock being called is less than that for in-the-monies, though more than that for out-of-the-monies.	Only a small upward movement of the underlying stock's price will put the call in the money.
The value of the call will depreciate rather quickly as the expiration date nears, as long as the underlying stock has not advanced much beyond the strike price.	Usual risks of writing detailed in Chapter 14.
If the stock is highly volatile, it is possible to realize impressive capital gains by writing, closing out and later rewriting—provided the price swings are impressive and predictable, and in the right direction. Few investors, however, have the experience and timing to play this game.	

As it turns out, *you lose*, although there were a number of points during the contract time that you could have realized a profit. How do you know when to hold a position and when to close out? The answer is "from experience." In the early stages of your naked call writing career, however, the best answer is to take your profits as quickly as you can and to cut your losses just as quickly. (See Table 16-5 for the advantages and disadvantages of writing naked out-the-money calls.)

Margin Math for Naked Writers

Writers of naked equity options traded on the major exchanges must meet strict margin requirements. For each trade, the writer must put up the total value of the premium plus 20 percent of the stock price less any amount the option is out of the money. But the margin can never be less than the premium plus 10 percent of the stock price.

Premium	Stock Price	Strike Price	Amount Out-of-the-Money	Margin Requirement
$2	$30	$35	$500	$300
$3	$40	$42.50	$2½	$950

Note: As each call represents 100 shares of stock, the premium is multiplied by 100 and the stock price is multiplied by 100. Thus, the margin requirement in the first example is calculated in either of the following ways: $200 + (.20 x $3000) - $500, OR $200 + $600 - $500.

For OTC naked options, the formula is the full amount of the premium plus 45 percent of the underlying stock price less the out-of-the-money amount. The minimum margin requirement is the same as it is on the major exchanges.

Hedging

The safest hedge for the short seller is to own the underlying stock, in which case he becomes a covered call writer. He is long on the stock and short on the call.

Covered call writing on out-of-the-monies is an extremely safe way to begin an options trading career because if the stock is ever called, the options trader already owns it and can deliver it without additional expense. If the stock *never* goes beyond the striking price, then the covered call writer is in the enviable position of having earned the premiums from writing the calls and yet being able to keep his stock.

However, the covered call writer is playing two games at the same time. He is playing the underlying stock as well as the calls. This means the stock can depreciate more points than the call, in which case the trader has taxable income from the premium, and a paper loss on the stock.

> *Example #1.* You sell two July 30 calls on Golden Nugget for $200. The calls expire worthless (meaning you are $200 ahead) but the stock falls to $25 per share (meaning you have lost $1,000 on paper). Unless you sell the stock for tax purposes, you have $200 in premium income which may be taxed. If you do sell the stock, then your covered call writing effort actually turns out to be a losing proposition: $1,000 in losses on the stock and only a $200 gain on the expired call.

> *Example #2.* You buy 200 shares of Grumman at $27 per share and at the same time you sell two July 30 calls on the stock. The short sale on the options

brings you $200 in premiums. The options expire worthless and the stock is at $29 per share on the expiration date. You have earned $200 on your covered calls and if you decide to sell the stock will earn another $400.

Example #3. You write two calls on Grumman; the stock, which you own, is currently selling at $27 and the calls are at $1 each ($100, actually, for remember each call represents 100 shares of stock). The striking price is $30. An assignment is received when the stock is at $35 per share. You must deliver the stock at $30, thereby forfeiting an extra $5 per share gain. Nonetheless, you have gained $3 per share on the stock; that brings your total gain to $800 ($600 from the sale of the stock, $200 from writing the calls).

As the above examples indicate, there are a number of ways to profit from covered call writing, but as covered call writing entails also playing the market for the underlying stock, any gain achieved from writing the call can be reduced by the paper or cash losses on the underlying stock.

Order Strategies

The different types of orders discussed in the beginning of Chapter 11 are also used in call trading. For call writers, however, market orders (which specify execution of the trade as soon as possible and under any conditions), and good-till-cancelled orders (which leave the order in effect until cancelled) should be avoided.

Generally, it is recommended that call writers place limit orders; these orders establish a price limit for the trade. Additionally, and if possible, writers should also make use of contingent orders; these not only specify the price at which a call should be shorted, but also specify at what price the underlying stock price must be at before the option order can be executed.

Spreads

Spreads are complex strategies using puts and calls, different puts, or different calls. You were introduced to those of special interest to put buyers in Chapter 11. With spreads, the trader is gambling on the future relationship between the different options bought or sold at the same time.

Spreads are not recommended for the neophyte or for the occasional trader, and are mentioned here only for educational purposes. Those that entail writing calls follow:

There is the *time spread* (also referred to as the horizontal or calendar spread). It entails buying calls with the same strike price but different expiration dates.

Buy five XYZ June 30 Calls
Short five XYZ July 30 Calls

The income from the July 30s should be enough to cover the cost of taking the long position, and leave the trader in the black should the underlying stock retreat in price. If the underlying stock price jumps, the long position should allow large percentage gains to reduce or cover losses from the short side of the transaction. Time spreads are by no means a sure thing for the investor. Break-even points are high because of the multiple transactions, and call values on either side of the transaction are usually moving in an unpredictable relationship.

The *price spread* is used in the same way as the time spread, except the calls have the same expiration date, but different strike prices. If the trader is long the lower strike price, then he is expecting the underlying stock to gain in price. If he is short the lower strike price, then he is bearish on the underlying stock.

Diagonal spreads contain options with different strike prices and different expiration dates, but, of course, the underlying stock is the same.

Here again it is the relationship between the different options that will determine profit or loss for the trader, and if the spread will be profitable in a rising market, it may be considered a bull spread; in a declining market, a bear spread.

17

Common Misconceptions

A first misconception is that shorting calls is always preferable to buying puts because your account is immediately credited. If the underlying stock falls substantially in price, you would make much more money as a result of owning the put. If the underlying stock moves up enough in price, bringing the call in the money or keeping it in the money, you would lose far more from shorting the call than you would if you owned a put. Remember that you cannot lose any more than the cost of a put you buy long. The call shorted, on the other hand, can go up hundreds of percent by the expiration date, thereby compounding your losses.

A second misconception is that shorting calls is always preferable to shorting the underlying stock. Shorting the stock does require a greater cash outlay because generally you have to put up at least 50 percent of the value of the stock in cash or securities. However, there are no time restrictions when dealing in the stock. Calls have expiration dates. There is a limited amount of time for the trader to make a profit. Additionally, margin *is* required for shorting calls. For each trade on one of the major exchanges, the writer (short seller) of a call must put up cash or securities equal to the total value of the premium plus 20 percent of the stock price less any amount the option is out-of-the-money. On the OTC market, the margin requirement is the full amount of the premium plus 45 percent of the underlying stock's price. This still amounts to much less than the trader would have to deposit for shorting stock but it is, nonetheless, an expense often overlooked when a writer is considering a naked option.

A third misconception is that the further the underlying stock falls in price, the greater the profit for the naked writer. The maximum profit the call writer can ever expect to make is represented by the premium she receives when she writes the call.

A fourth misconception is that an out-of-the-money call sold short always means a loss for the writer if that call goes into the money. Untrue—the writer may still possibly realize a profit. Remember that any option is a wasting asset. As the expiration date approaches, the call may retreat in price even if the underlying stock increases slightly in price. But don't count on this!

For instance, you might sell short out-of-the-money calls having only a time value (no intrinsic value) of $1½. By the expiration date when they are in the money, they may now have an intrinsic value of $¾ but their time value will have been completely wasted. In this case, you stand to profit $50 on each call you sold short.

A fifth misconception is that a trader can only be a buyer or a seller of a call. The trader may be *both* a buyer and a seller. Calls may be bought long or sold short just as puts or stock may be bought long or sold short.

Stock going up?	Buy a call.
Stock going no place?	Write a call.
Stock going down?	Buy a put or short the stock.

A sixth misconception is that in the case of stock splits, the exercise value is affected. No, it is the strike price and the number of calls that you have that changes.

A seventh misconception is that stocks making the "new highs" list are good candidates for call writing as they usually retreat in price. What holds true for buying puts in this regard also holds true for selling calls. Stocks can very easily establish new trading ranges above the last "new high." That is, they may continually set new highs over a period of weeks.

An eighth misconception is that writing a call is the same as buying a put. This very common misconception is born from the realization that both put buyers and call writers profit when a stock goes down. *But* call writers also profit if a stock does not move at all, and sometimes even when it goes up in price. Put buyers generally only profit if there is a substantial downslide in the stock price.

A ninth misconception is that the underlying stock is always called as soon as it moves far enough beyond the striking price to make exercise profitable. Actually, it is very rare for a stock to be called before expiration.

A tenth misconception is that options listings provide enough data on which to make a trade. Option listings, just like stock listings, simply represent a daily score sheet. What went up? What went down? What are current puts and calls selling for? A great deal of research is required before any opening transaction can be made. The naked call writer wants to write on stocks that will decline in price, or remain at about their current price throughout the contract period. Knowing that underlying stock is important. What is its potential? More specifically, what is its potential during any one of the contracts available?

18

Guidelines

Following are some guidelines for writing naked calls. Bear in mind that some brokers or financial advisors might expand the list.

1. Be sure you understand how the stock options game is played. This means knowing contract terminology, types of orders, and how to determine break-even points. Remember that the objective of the naked writer is to get income from premiums. This is the writer's sole motivation because whatever that premium is, it represents the very most she can hope to make on her trade. Call buyers have unlimited profit potential. Writers do not. They have, instead, unlimited risk. Only the value of the premiums makes them willing to take that risk.

Premiums are the primary force behind the options markets. Nothing much happens until the premiums are high enough to attract writers yet low enough to excite buyers. If premiums are too high or too low in relationship to strike prices, exercise dates or the possible performance of the underlying stock, then options are not going to trade.

If the options are too highly priced, potential buyers, who want to maximize their capital gains by buying very low and selling very high, are going to be disenchanted. If options can only command very low premiums, what writer is going to want to gamble on them? In some cases, of course, buyers of options are not quite as interested in trading the options as in eventually acquiring the unlying security. For instance, an investor may be very interested in owning a couple of thousand shares of McDonalds because she expects a special dividend to be declared or because she is expecting a takeover at any time. But she does not have the money to buy on cash or margin, so she takes out call options with the intention of exercising her rights just before the dividend declaration or at any time during the contract period. In a case such as this the buyer may be less interested in the cost of the calls, but pricing will still play a major factor in the amount of calls she finally purchases. And she would, of course, want these calls to be far in-the-money.

2. Avoid writing in-the-money calls unless you have an exceptional track record for picking stocks that head south in short time. Writers of in-the-monies are always immediately at risk; the stock can be called at anytime.

3. Spread your risk. Do not write calls in any great quantity no matter how sure you seem to be about the underlying stock. Sometimes a trader may let greed or past success go to his head, and he will write 20 or 30 calls because they are out of the money and low priced. He stands to gain handsomely if the calls remain out of the money, but should they move into the money, his losses can be devastating.

   Consider a situation in which *you* write 20 July 30 calls at ½ when the underlying stock is at $25. Your income is $1,000 (20 calls at $50 each). But now assume the stock advances to $35 per share and the calls now have an intrinsic value of $5 and a time value of $1. You are now in the red to the tune of $11,000. (The 20 calls are now worth $600 each, or a total of $12,000. Subtract from this value the $1,000 you received from writing and you are $11,000 in the red.)

4. Understand the importance of good timing. Options have time limits. You have to make your money in months, weeks or days. You need to develop the kind of instinct and skill that lets you sense what stocks may decline and during what period. It is not enough to select an underlying stock that will *eventually* halve in price; you want to select it for your writing strategy when it will fall in price *while your option is still alive.*

5. For your first dozen or so trades, do not select the underlying stock on which you wish to trade options by yourself. Take advice from at least one or two investment newsletters and solicit advice from your broker. Your opinion also counts. Sometimes you will find that the opinions you receive from different sources will be highly contradictory. One brokerage house may highly recommend a stock, another may be telling its customers to sell it; one newsletter may see a possible takeover occurring, another may see imminent danger. If all the contradictory information takes away your motivation to trade, consider this as healthy a sign as being inspired to buy or sell. Not doing anything at all is often the safest approach to investing or speculating in the stock and options markets.

6. Stick to your game plan. Carefully weigh your strategies for different stocks and options, then play your game. But at the same time keep on top of the news, continue to do your research, have contingent plans. In this way, if the variables which prompted you to develop a specific game plan change noticeably, you can close out your positions or re-evaluate your goals.

7. Immerse yourself in the financial world. Read the financial papers, listen to the financial news. Anyone with money in the stock and options markets has to stay tuned to the world. Search the dailies and weeklies for news of that stock you shorted, or chose for buying puts or selling calls.

PART
5
The Markets

19

Stock Markets

There are more than one hundred stock markets throughout the world. They all do not have the same rules and regulations and on some of these markets you are not allowed to sell short. On others, you are not allowed to trade at all if you are a foreigner.

For the most part, your short selling efforts will be done on one of the exchanges in the United States. These exchanges are listed in Table 19-1, though you will rarely find the smaller U.S. exchanges listed in the *Wall Street Journal* or other financial dailies. Not all of the foreign exchanges are listed in the financial papers, either. Generally, the only foreign exchanges listed are the Tokyo, London, Sydney, Hong Kong, Johannesburg, Frankfurt, Brussels, Milan, Amsterdam, and Stockholm. And only a few of the stocks on these exchanges are actually listed. The London Stock Exchange, for instance, is far larger than the New York Stock Exchange, but generally only about 150 stocks of international interest are listed in the *Wall Street Journal* every day. Exchanges in countries like Greece, Denmark, India, Indonesia, Norway and others are generally of little interest to U.S. investors.

Table 19-1
Location of U.S. Stock Markets

Boston:	Boston Stock Exchange, 53 State Street, Boston, Massachusetts 02109
Chicago:	Midwest Stock Exchange, 440 South LaSalle Street, Chicago, Illinois 60605
Cincinnati:	Cincinnati Stock Exchange, 205 Dixie Terminal Building, Cincinnati, Ohio 45202
New York:	American Stock Exchange, 86 Trinity Place, New York, New York 10005
Philadelphia:	Philadelphia Stock Exchange, 1900 Market Street, Philadelphia, Pennsylvania 19103
Salt Lake City:	Intermountain Stock Exchange, 39 Exchange Place, Salt Lake City, Utah 84111
San Francisco:	Pacific Stock Exchange, 301 Pine Street, San Francisco, California 94104
Spokane:	Spokane Stock Exchange, 225 Peyton Building, Spokane, Washington 99201
Washington, D.C.:	National Association of Securities Dealers, 1735 K Street, N.W., Washington, D.C. 20006

Corporate New Issues

There are three types of chartered stock that a corporation issues (Table 19-2) but when you trade stocks, you usually trade them in the secondary market created by investment bankers and underwriters. Investment bankers may be individuals, but are usually securities firms that specialize in raising money for corporations or local governments. When the investment banker is satisfied that a corporation is sound and its securities are marketable, it purchases the securities at what it hopes is a discount from what the general public is willing to pay for it. The investment banker then tries to sell those newly issued securities for the best possible price.

Table 19-2
Chartered Stock

Authorized Stock:	Amount of stock that a corporation may issue without revising its charter.
Issued Stock:	The percent of authorized stock actually sold to the public, or which has been repurchased by the corporation.
Outstanding Stock:	Stock actually in the hands of the public.

Underwriting Procedures

There is a middle step to bringing new securities to the public. This is the formation of an underwriting syndicate by the investment banker. The syndicate is designed to spread the risk, for in underwriting any corporate issue extremely large amounts of money are involved and to take a loss on any public offering can put an investment banking firm in harm's way.

Other investment banking firms or individuals may make up the underwriting syndicate. In most of these syndicates, each member is legally bound to share the responsibility for outstanding balances. This is usually referred to as an Eastern syndicate.

This means that if you and I participate, as investment bankers, in an underwriting effort to sell $50 million in securities issued by Giallella Corporation, and each of us has a 10 percent obligation, we must sell $5 million each. Now if you fall short of your commitment by $2 million, even though I and everyone else met his quota, we are responsible for your shortfall as well.

In another type of syndicate, known as a Western syndicate, each banker is only responsible for his share of the distribution. In this case, if you were responsible for 10 percent of a $50 million offering, the extent of your obligation is $5 million in sales.

Members of the underwriting syndicate do not get directly involved in selling to the public. They invite brokers and dealers to be the middlemen. Dealers differ from brokers in that the broker works for his customer's account and the dealer works for his own account. Neither dealers nor brokers have any obligation to buy securities from the syndicate. They are simply salesmen who work on a commission.

The brokers will immediately begin contacting customers they feel may be interested in the new issue. You may have received some of these phone calls yourself. The objective is to create a sea of interest so that by the time the sale of the securities is initiated, the brokers can begin earning their commissions.

If your broker has contacted you about a new issue and you express interest, you may not always actually get the opportunity to buy in. This is because the selling group is usually instructed to solicit interest for more shares than will actually be made available. This little trick helps keep the price of the issue as stable as possible. If you do get a chance to buy in, you generally do not have to pay a buy commission although you will be required to buy in lots of 100 shares.

No matter how far back you and your broker go, do not jump on a new issue until you have seen a preliminary prospectus. It always sounds like a hot tip when the broker calls about a new oportunity, but while every effort is usually made to keep the price at or above the offering, these issues can tumble in price once the offering is completed. You might wonder if any effort at price stabilization isn't illegal—well, new issues are an exception, and the Securities and Exchange Commission allows underwriters to take the necessary steps to support new issue prices. In the case of demand outweighing supply, the result is usually upward pressure on the price of the issue. But if supply outweighs demand, then the underwriters must interfere by purchasing the shares at the issuing price.

Should you take a position in a new issue without having the chance to review the preliminary prospectus, you have a legal "out" should you change your mind. According to the law, unavailability of a preliminary prospectus necessitates that your broker deliver a final prospectus within 90 days. Otherwise you can back out of the deal. Additionally, if you had not seen the preliminary prospectus and the final prospectus contains information which would have steered you away from the stock, you again have the legal right to cancel your order.

The preliminary prospectus is not usually as detailed as the final and does not contain such information as the size of the offering or the discounts offered to dealers. But it will contain:

- Financial information regarding corporate activity in the last two years

- Descriptions of the securities being offered

- Pertinent data about the company

- Names, ownership, and compensation for directors, upper management and others

Public Trading

Now that the offering is in public hands, buyers and sellers will continually negotiate its value. They will do this in those highly active and hectic auction markets known as the stock exchanges. The trading that now takes place in that new offering has nothing to do with those investment bankers and underwriting syndicate. The game now continues with brokers, dealers, and little guys such as you and I. We will also trade in the OTC (over-the-counter market), the market for stocks managed by the National Association of Securities Dealers.

When you call your broker to short stock, he borrows it from his own account, some dealer's, or maybe some other broker's. The corporation that issued the stock has no interest at all in your specific trades, though it is always interested in what is happening to the price of the stock.

Why should the corporation have any interest in the price of the stock after the original public offering? Because the company may want to issue additional shares at some future date, and the current market value of its stock will be a direct influence on the price of the new issue.

Now, you may think that this is just a superfluous numbers game because no matter how much the stock is currently valued for, the company can reach its goal by simply issuing additional shares. This is very true, but the more shares a company has to issue to raise money, the more the earnings per share are diluted. Dilute earnings per share and traders will pay less for the stock. Stockholders are thereby cheated.

Let's look at an example. Suppose that the current price for Exxon is $55 per share. Because Exxon will deal with underwriters rather than the general public, it entices interest by discounting the shares to, perhaps, $50.

If the goal of the corporation is to raise $50 million, then it must issue one million new shares.

$$\$50 \text{ million} : \$50 = \text{one million shares}$$

There are now one million additional common shares of Exxon available, one million additional shares over which earnings must be distributed. If Exxon could have sold those shares for $100 instead of $50, it would have had to issue only a half million shares. *There would be a half million fewer shares over which to distribute earnings. Each shareholder would be richer.*

Exchange Requirements

The exchanges listed in Table 19-1 require that certain conditions be met before a company may have its stock listed. These conditions specify:

- the minimum number of shares that must be held publicly
- a minimum number of round-lot shareholders
- minimum pretax earnings
- minimum trading volume
- minimum common stock value
- wide geographic holdings

The OTC market generally only has listing requirements for those securities that will be included in its automatic quotation system: NASDAQ (National Association of Securities Dealers Automatic Quotations). These listing requirements are not as rigid as those of the exchanges but require:

- a certain amount of assets

- a minimum number of shareholders

- a minimum number of market makers dealing in the stock or other security

The OTC, although not considered an exchange because it is a negotiated rather than auction market, may for all practical purposes be considered one (and is listed along with other exchanges in most reference books). Despite its separate status, the OTC represents the largest trading market for stocks in the U. S.

Very often you will hear a broker say a stock is traded in the "second market." The second market is the OTC market, the first being that created by the exchanges. A third market also exists—the market for stocks on the OTC that are also available on one or more of the major exchanges.

20

Put and Call Markets

Options are nothing new either to business or to the securities markets, but it was not until 1973 that the first major effort was made to allow investors to trade puts and calls as easily as they trade common and preferred stocks. Prior to this, attempting an opening or closing transaction in an option was sometimes similar to trying to buy or sell a rare book.

The Chicago Board Options Exchange

The Chicago Board Options Exchange pioneered the development of an efficient and orderly market for stock options trading. Far-sighted members of the CBOE realized that options had great appeal to stock traders, but were generally being ignored because finding buyers and sellers was such a cumbrous business.

Today, when we think of stock options, we think of a marketplace for increasing our wealth. Depending on our history of experience and level of sophistication, we immediately think of puts, calls, warrants, and stock rights. But two decades ago, only a relatively few traders knew or understood the option markets and relatively few played at the game. Actually, until the mid-1970s, the term stock option was mainly used to describe an additional type of incentive that corporations gave to its higher ranking employees.

Instead of giving many key employees additional increases in salary which would only be eaten away by the higher taxes associated with their new income bracket, the corporation gave these employees the right to buy corporate stock at a certain market value anytime within a specified time frame. If the stock went up, the employees would benefit accordingly by taking advantage of their "option" to buy the stock at the lower price.

In a time when capital gains are treated very differently from salaried income, these stock option programs are particularly attractive. Corporations see the options as a work incentive; the executives and employees will work that much harder to make the corporation thrive so that the stock increases in value—and their options are that much more valuable.

With the founding of the Options Clearing Corporation (OCC) in 1973, the Chicago Board began to change the way the general public thought of stock options. Suddenly there was a whole new marketplace for investing, and one which functioned somewhat like the stock markets about which they knew.

Many independent and small traders were enthused about the CBOE's plans. The easy availability of options trading would help them "insure" their positions by covered writing, and increase their chances for extraordinary profits when they bought puts or calls.

Extraordinary profits were what attracted investors to the stock market in the first place. Few investors, however, were able to realize their goals. One of the major obstacles standing in their way of large capital gains was the fact that it takes money to make money. If IBM or Litton was so high-priced that they could only buy a few shares, they were more likely to turn to lower priced and probably more speculative stocks. However, the easily available options promised by the CBOE would give traders the low-priced action that would allow them to trade in quantity. Okay, so they could not afford the big guys like IBM or Litton, but they could afford the calls and puts on their stocks. The chance for big percentage gains was again being made available to them.

The Chicago Board was right about investor interest. The little guy, often strapped by his limited finances and borrowing power, was indeed looking for a way to spread his risk, gain additional income, or realize greater capital gains. Additionally, he wanted to know that whatever market offered him these opportunities also offered him guarantees that the market in general—and particularly the market in specific options—would be secure. The CBOE promised the investor all of these things when it established the OCC as the guarantor of any listed option in U.S. markets and, through associate memberships, the same for many options traded on foreign exchanges. (Table 20-1 lists many of the options currently available from U.S. markets.)

Along with this new and efficient system for trading options came a need for educating the general trading public about the availability of options on certain stocks, how these options could not be traded, and the level of integrity now afforded options traders. Most of the education came through the account representative at the local brokerage office. Particularly since 1975, every new account was told about options and their potential. Additionally, other frequent traders on the broker's customer list were told about the new opportunities afforded by the new options market. Especially stressed was the fact that there was an organization formed specifically to back every option trade. There were four parties involved in every option trade: the buyer, the seller, the broker, and a guarantor. As part of its major responsibilities, the OCC assures that there are matching positions for all puts and calls, and that there are both sellers and buyers for all options being traded.

OCC Membership

Membership in the OCC now includes some major exchanges, but until 1975 the Chicago Board Options Exchange was going it all alone. That year, the American Stock Exchange became a member-owner, thereby giving additional strength and credibility to the marketplace. (See Table 20-1 for current Exchange listings.)

Now OCC membership includes also the National Association of Securities Dealers and the New York, Pacific, and Philadelphia Stock exchanges. With the addition of the New York and Philadelphia exchanges as owner-members, the OCC gained a lot of history as well as the additional respect that goes along with being supported by institutions that go back to the beginnings of the country.

Few people realize it, but the Philadelphia Stock Exchange was actually the first formal exchange in this country. For many years before its formation, the Philadelphia Exchange hosted a loose community of traders very similar to that growing in the still-spacious, barely inhabited (less than 40,000 citizens) city of New York. But by 1790 they saw the need for a formal organization and the Philadelphia Exchange was born.

Years later that hungry group of securities traders in New York would finally establish their own official exchange, but it would not be until the early part of the 19th century. They originally called themselves the New York Stock Exchange Board and put stringent requirements on membership. As the country grew and the securities industry with it, brokers were anxious to become members of the exchange; but as most professional organizations do to eliminate competition and keep the money for themselves, the New York Stock Exchange Board severely curtailed the number of new applicants accepted. Another exchange was formed by those who could not get membership and this was named the Open Board of Brokers, eventually to merge with the original New York exchange, resulting in the New York Stock Exchange.

The American and Pacific exchanges also go back into the last century, though not by the names they are known by today. Officially, the Pacific Stock Exchange was born of the merger in 1957 of the Los Angeles and San Francisco Stock Exchanges. But the Los Angeles Exchange, then the Los Angeles Oil Exchange, was formed in 1899 and the San Francisco exchange in 1882. The American Stock Exchange, founded in 1849, was originally known as the New York Curb Exchange, and actually conducted business outside until their first indoor quarters were established in 1921.

OCC Operation

The OCC is a very complex corporate system. If your take a moment to think about how many options are traded every day, you can understand why the OCC needs to have complex banking and other financial support systems in place. Imagine if writers of options were unable to get the money for their opening transactions, or buyers for their closing transactions. The marketplace would be in havoc, lawsuits would abound, and traders would avoid the options markets! What if the marketplace could not get the latest prices, cancellations, new offers, or general trading information? The marketplace would become a maze of confusion and no one would trust it! The OCC is chartered to prevent these problems and reactions through the efficient management of not only money, but also information.

The financial safeguards start with the extensive network of over 200 clearing banks located in the U.S. and foreign countries. These banks provide the OCC with the monetary muscle for not only backing up the marketplace but also assuring that foreign funds can be transferred and delivered with speed and efficient handling. Remember that the options markets are cash markets and settlements must be made quickly. Thus the need for a banking network and management system that allows all payments of U.S. and foreign funds to be completed on the same day delivery is made by an agent bank. This brings such liquidity to the market place that even the short-term cash flow problems that OCC clearing members may experience will not prevent settlement payments from being capably handled during the normal banking day.

OCC clearing members are the brokerage firms that you and I use to do our trading. These clearing members are especially important to the OCC system because the OCC has no direct contact with the trading public, and without them the OCC could not assure that the contractual obligations of options traders will be met. It is up to each clearing member to back up writers' obligations with the necessary collateral. To protect the public from those instances when a clearing member is caught in a cash bind and cannot provide the necessary collateral, the OCC charges each clearing member a fee on each contract, with the proceeds then deposited into a fund. When OCC revenues exceed those actually needed to cover operational costs and reserve requirements, the clearing member may expect a percent of this contract fee to be refunded. Besides the contract fee, each member firm is required to have a certain amount of net capital, must be a registered broker-dealer under the Securities and Exchange Act of 1934, and be staffed and managed in such a manner that options trades can be executed quickly and in an orderly fashion. Through a system called C/MACS (Clearing Management and Control System), the OCC is able to provide a check on clearing members' back office operations. C/MACS allows the OCC to audit members' account and trading data; send and receive information almost immediately; and change, correct, or update records if and when required.

Other Services

Equity options are only one of the products offered and backed by the OCC. Other products are index, debt, and foreign currency options.

In equity options, each put and call is for a specific number of shares of an underlying stock. In index options (Table 20-2 gives a typical listing), each put and call relates to the value of the underlying index and whatever multiplier is used for that index.

"Index" refers to the value of a select group of securities. For instance, the value of all the stocks in Standard & Poor's 100 make up one currently popular index, the value of which was originally determined by placing some arbitrary starting value on the stocks as a group. The starting value represents the index's base value, but it must necessarily be adjusted every so often to reflect such changes as the deletion or addition of stocks, and any recapitalization that may take place. All stock indexes are not valued in the same way. In some cases, this value is determined by calculating the average price of each stock, by totalling the price of the stocks in the group, or by any other way the sponsors of the index may find suitable and acceptable.

A "multiplier" is the number used to determine what each point movement in the index means in terms of real money. An index using a multiplier of 10 would change in value by $10 with each increase or decrease of one point. If the multiplier were 100, each point would represent $100.

Exercise and settlement procedures for Index options are very much the same as those for stock options; but in the case of index options, settlement is only in cash and takes place the day following exercise. Index options have special risks associated with them over and above those discussed in Chapter 14 for equity options.

Debt options, too, have their own special risks. Price information is not always readily available and individual dealers will set their own prices. Also, equity options represent 100 shares of the underlying stock, but debt options can represent millions of dollars.

Foreign currency options also require a different scope of knowledge and range of skills than do equity options. In the trading of foreign currency options, the trader must be familiar with the relative value of foreign money, especially in relation to the U.S. dollar. She must also be versed in the political and economic background of the issuing country as well as understanding that the huge amounts of money involved in round-lot currency transactions can force her to deal with the more expensive and cumbrous odd-lot market. (See Table 20-3 for a typical listing of foreign currency options.)

For all these additional options products designed by the OCC or backed by it, lots of research and advice are required before that first informed trade can be made. Even being "expert" in the equity options market does not make one potentially successful in these other options markets.

Table 20-1
Sampling of U.S. Listed Options

STOCKS	CHICAGO	AMERICAN	PHILADELPHIA	PACIFIC	NEW YORK
A G EDWARDS INC	•				
A H AHMANSON & CO		•			
AAR CP			•		
ABBOTT LABS			•		
ACUSON CP				•	
ADAPTEC INC		•			
ADC TELECOMMUN				•	
ADOBE SYSTEMS INC				•	
ADOLPH COORS				•	
ADT LTD	•				
ADVANCED MICRO				•	
ADVANCED TISSUE				•	
ADVANTA CORP		•			
ADVANTA CORP	•				
AETNA LIFE & CAS		•			
AGENCY RENT A CAR		•			
AIR PRODUCTS & CHEM			•		
AIRBORNE FREIGHT		•			
AIRBORNE FREIGHT	•				
ALASKA AIR GROUP		•			
ALBERTSONS INC			•		
ALCAN ALUMINUM		•			
ALCO STANDARD					•
ALDUS CP				•	
ALEX & ALEX SERV	•				
ALEX BROWN INC			•		
ALLERGAN INC			•		
ALLIANCE PHARMA	•				
ALLIANCE PHARMA		•			

STOCKS	CHICAGO	AMERICAN	PHILADELPHIA	PACIFIC	NEW YORK
ALLIANT TECHSYSTEMS	•				
ALLIANT TECHSYSTEMS					•
ALLIANT TECHSYSTEMS			•		
ALLIED SIGNAL CP			•		
ALLTEL CORP				•	
ALTERA CP				•	•
ALUMINUM CO AMER	•				
ALZA CP				•	
AMAX INC		•			
AMDAHL CP	•				
AMER BARRICK		•			
AMER BRANDS INC		•			
AMER CYANAMID		•			
AMER ELECTRIC PWR	•				
AMER EXPRESS CO	•	•			
AMER FAMILY CP		•			
AMER GEN CP	•				
AMER HOME PROD		•			
AMER INFOTECH	•				
AMER INTL GROUP	•				
AMER POWER CONV	•				
AMER PRESIDENT				•	
AMER SOFTWARE INC			•		
AMER STORES	•				
AMER TEL & TEL	•				
AMER TELEVISION COMM	•				
AMERADA HESS			•		

STOCKS	EXCHANGE				
	CHICAGO	AMERICAN	PHILADELPHIA	PACIFIC	NEW YORK
AMERITRUST CORP				•	
AMETEK INC			•		
AMGEN		•			
AMOCO CP	•				
AMP INC	•				
AMR CP			•	•	
ANADARKO PETRO	•				
ANALOG DEVICES			•		
ANHEUSER BUSCH			•		
ANN TAYLOR STORES				•	
ANTHEM ELECTRONICS		•		•	
AON CORP				•	
APACHE CP					•
APPLE COMPUTER		•			
APPLIED BIOSYSTEMS				•	
APPLIED MAGNETICS	•				
APPLIED MATERIALS				•	
ARCHER DANIELS			•		
ARCO CHEMICAL		•			
ARKLA INC		•			
ARMCO INC			•		
ARMSTRONG WORLD IND			•		
ARROW ELECTRONICS		•			
ASA LTD		•			
ASARCO INC		•			
ASHLAND OIL INC			•		
ASK COMPUTER SYS			•		
AST RESEARCH INC		•			
ATLANTIC RICHFIELD	•				
ATLANTIC SOUTHEAST	•				
AURA SYSTEMS	•				
AUTO DATA PROCESSING			•		

STOCKS	EXCHANGE				
	CHICAGO	AMERICAN	PHILADELPHIA	PACIFIC	NEW YORK
AUTODESK				•	
AUTOZONE INC	•				•
AVERY INTL CP			•		
AVNET LTD		•			
AVON PRODUCTS	•				
BAKER HUGHES INC.				•	
BANK ONE CP				•	
BANK OF BOSTON CP			•		
BANK OF NY	•				
BANKAMERICA	•				
BANKERS TRUST			•		
BARD C R INC			•		
BARNETT BANKS		•			
BATTLEMOUNTAIN GOLD	•				
BAUSCH & LOMB INC		•			
BAXTER LABS	•				
BAYBANKS INC	•				
BCE INC	•				
BEAR STEARNS	•				
BECKMAN IND INC	•				
BECTON DICKINSON			•		
BELL ATLANTIC	•				
BELLSOUTH CP		•			
BELMAC CORP		•			
BENEFICIAL CP				•	
BERGEN BRUNSWIG	•				
BEST BUY CO INC	•				
BETHLEHEM STEEL	•				
BETZ LABORATORIES				•	
BEVERLY ENTER				•	
BHC COMMUN INC	•				
BIO-TECHNOLOGY GEN	•				
BIOGEN INC	•	•		•	

STOCKS	EXCHANGE				
	CHICAGO	AMERICAN	PHILADELPHIA	PACIFIC	NEW YORK
BIOMET INC	•				
BIRMINGHAM STEEL					•
BLACK & DECKER MFG	•				
BLOCKBUSTER ENTER	•	•			
BMC SOFTWARE	•			•	
BOATMEN'S BANCSHARES	•				
BOEING CO	•				
BOISE CASCADE CP	•				
BOLAR PHARMA	•				
BORDEN CHEM & PLAS					•
BORDEN INC				•	
BORLAND INTL	•				
BOWATER INC				•	
BRIGGS & STRATTON			•		
BRINKER INTL			•		
BRISTOL MYERS	•				
BRITISH AIRWAYS			•		
BRITISH PET ORD ADR				•	
BRITISH STEEL PLC					•
BROAD INC			•		
BROWNING FERRIS		•			
BRUNO'S INC	•				
BRUNSWICK CP	•				
BUFFETS INC	•				
BURLINGTON NORTH	•				
BURLINGTON RESOURCES			•		
C & S SOVRAN				•	
CABLETRON SYSTEMS	•			•	
CABLETRON SYSTEMS			•		
CADENCE DESIGN SYS	•	•			
CAESARS WORLD			•		

STOCKS	EXCHANGE				
	CHICAGO	AMERICAN	PHILADELPHIA	PACIFIC	NEW YORK
CALFED INC				•	
CALGENE INC		•			
CALGON CARBON CP			•		
CAMBRIDGE BIOTECH	•				
CAMPBELL SOUP					•
CAPITAL CITIES COMM	•				
CAPITAL HLDG CP					•
CARNIVAL CRUISE	•				
CARTER-WALLACE	•				
CASTLE & COOKE				•	
CATELLUS DEVEL	•	•			
CATERPILLAR INC		•			
CBI INDUST			•		
CBS INC	•				
CDN PACIFIC		•			
CENTEL CP		•			
CENTERIOR ENERGY				•	
CENTEX CP					•
CENTEX TELEMNGT				•	
CENTOCOR INC	•				
CENTRAL & SOUTHWEST				•	
CERIDIAN CP	•				
CETUS CP		•			
CHAMBERS DEVEL CO	•				
CHAMPION INTL CP	•				
CHARLES SCHWAB	•				
CHASE MANHATTAN		•			
CHECKERS DRIVE-IN	•	•			
CHECKPOINT SYSTEMS				•	
CHEMICAL N Y		•			
CHEMICAL WASTE MNGT		•			
CHEVRON CP		•			

STOCKS	CHICAGO	AMERICAN	PHILADELPHIA	PACIFIC	NEW YORK
EXCHANGE					
CHIPS & TECHNOLOGIES		•			
CHIQUITA BRANDS INTL			•		
CHIRON CORP	•	•		•	•
CHRIS CRAFT IND	•				
CHRYSLER CP	•				
CHUBB CP					•
CIGNA CP	•				
CINCINNATI BELL	•				
CINCINNATI FINAN		•			
CINCINNATI MILACRON			•		
CINEPLEX ODEON CP			•		
CIRCUIT CITY STRS				•	
CIRCUS CIRCUS ENTER		•			
CIRRUS LOGIC	•			•	•
CISCO SYSTEMS	•			•	
CITICORP	•				
CLAIRES STORES					•
CLARK EQUIPMENT			•		
CLAYTON HOMES			•		•
CLEARLY CDN BEV		•			
CLOROX CO			•		
CML GROUP			•		
CMS ENERGY CP					•
CNA FINAN CP		•			
COASTAL CP	•	•			
COCA COLA CO	•				
COCA COLA ENTER	•				
COLGATE PALMOLIVE	•				
COLLAGEN CP		•			
COLUMBIA GAS SYS		•			
COMCAST CP CL A			•		
COMDISCO INC				•	

STOCKS	CHICAGO	AMERICAN	PHILADELPHIA	PACIFIC	NEW YORK
EXCHANGE					
COMERICA INC			•		
COMMODORE INTL LTD			•		
COMMONWEALTH ED	•				
COMMUNICATIONS SAT			•		
COMMUNITY PSYCH CNT			•		
COMPAQ COMPUTER				•	
COMPRESSION LABS	•				
COMPUTER ASSO INTL	•				
COMPUTER SCIENCES CP	•				
CONAGRA INC		•			
CONAGRA INC		•			
CONNER PERIPHERAL				•	
CONSECO INC		•			
CONSL ED		•			
CONSL FREIGHTWAYS					•
CONSL NAT GAS		•			
CONSL PAPERS				•	
CONSL RAIL CP			•		
CONTL BANK CP	•				
CONTL CP			•		
CONTL MEDICAL			•		
CONVEX COMPUTERS			•		
COOPER IND		•			
COOPER TIRE & RUB			•		
COPYTEL INC		•			
CORDIS CP			•		
CORESTATES FINAN		•			
CORNING GLASS	•				
COSTCO WHOLESALE		•			
COUNTRYWIDE CREDIT			•		

STOCKS	CHICAGO	AMERICAN	PHILADELPHIA	PACIFIC	NEW YORK
CPC INTL				•	
CRACKER BARREL				•	
CRANE CO		•			
CRAY COMPUTER					•
CRAY RESEARCH INC			•		
CRESTAR FINANCIAL			•		
CRITICAL CARE AMER			•		
CROWN CORK & SEAL			•		
CSX CP				•	
CTL CENTURY TEL				•	
CUC INTL INC			•		
CUMMINS ENGIN					•
CYPRESS MINERALS	•				
CYTEX CP		•			
CYTOGEN CP		•			
DANA CP					•
DANAHER CP			•		
DANEK GROUP	•				
DATA GENERAL				•	
DATASCOPE CP				•	
DATASCOPE CP			•		
DAYTON HUDSON CP				•	
DEAN FOODS CO				•	
DEERE CO		•			
DEL WEBB CP			•		
DELL COMPUTER CORP			•		
DELTA AIRLINES	•				
DELTA WOODSIDE	•				
DELUXE CHECK PRINTER			•		
DEPRENYL RES		•			
DETROIT EDISON CP			•		
DEXTER CP		•			

STOCKS	CHICAGO	AMERICAN	PHILADELPHIA	PACIFIC	NEW YORK
DIAGNOSTEK INC		•			
DIAL CP		•			
DIAMOND SHAMROCK	•				
DIASONICS INC	•				
DIEBOLD INC	•				
DIGITAL COMMUN					•
DIGITAL EQUIPMENT	•	•			
DIGITAL MICROWAVE				•	
DILLARD DEPT STRS				•	
DISNEY WALT	•				
DOLE FOODS				•	
DOLLAR GENERAL				•	
DOMINION RESOURCES			•		
DONNELLY RR & SONS			•		
DOVER CP			•		
DOW CHEMICAL	•				
DOW JONES			•		
DRESS BARN	•				
DRESSER IND			•		
DREYERS ICE CREAM				•	
DREYFUSS	•				
DSC COMMUN		•			
DU PONT CO		•			
DUKE POWER CO			•		
DUN & BRADSTREET		•			
DURACELL INTL	•	•	•		•
DURR-FILLAUER MED		•			
DUTY FREE INTL		•			
DWG CP			•		
E SYSTEMS INC				•	
EASTERN ENTERPRISES			•		
EASTMAN KODAK	•				

STOCKS	EXCHANGE				
	CHICAGO	AMERICAN	PHILADELPHIA	PACIFIC	NEW YORK
EATON CP	•				
ECHLIN INC				•	
ECHO BAY MINES				•	
ECI TELECOM LTD	•				
ECOGEN INC	•				
ECOLAB INC					•
EDISON BROTHERS					•
EG & G INC			•		
EGGHEAD SOFTWARE		•			
ELAN CP	•				
ELECTRONIC ARTS	•				
EMC CORP	•				
EMERSON ELEC		•			
ENGELHARD CP	•				
ENRON CP	•				
ENSEARCH CP				•	
ENTERGY CP	•				
ENTERRA CP			•		•
ENVIRONMENTAL SYS			•		
ENZON INC		•			
EPITOPE INC	•	•			
EQIUFAX INC				•	
ETHYL CP				•	
EXABYTE CORP	•	•		•	
EXXON CP	•				
FED HOME LOAN MTG		•			
FED MOGUL CP				•	
FED PAPERBOARD				•	
FEDDERS CP					•
FEDERAL EXPRESS CP	•				
FEDERAL NATL MTGE			•		
FEDERATED DEPT STORE	•				
FERRO CP				•	

STOCKS	EXCHANGE				
	CHICAGO	AMERICAN	PHILADELPHIA	PACIFIC	NEW YORK
FHP CORP	•	•			
50-OFF STORES					•
FILENE'S BASEMENT	•				
FIREMANS FUND	•				
FIRST BANK SYSTEM	•	•			
FIRST CHICAGO CP	•				
FIRST DOLLAR STRS			•		
FIRST FIDELITY BANCO	•				
FIRST FINAN MNGT					•
FIRST INTERSTATE	•				
FIRST MISS CP				•	
FIRST OF AMER BANK			•		
FIRST UNION CP				•	
FISHER PRICE		•		•	•
FISHER SCIENTIFIC	•				
FLEET FINAN GRP		•			
FLEETWOOD ENTER		•			
FLEMING COS				•	
FLIGHT SAFETY INTL			•		
FLOWERS INDUSTRIES			•		
FLUOR CP	•				
FMC CP					•
FOOD LION INC		•			
FORD MOTOR CO	•				
FOREST LABS	•				
FOSTER WHEELER CP				•	
FOUNDATION HEALTH		•	•		
FPL GROUP				•	
FRANKLIN RESOURCES				•	
FREEPORT MCMORAN CORP	•		•		
FREEPORT MCMORAN RES		•			

STOCKS	EXCHANGE				
	C H I C A G O	A M E R I C A N	P H I L A D E L P H I A	P A C I F I C	N E W Y O R K
FRUIT OF THE LOOM					•
FUQUA IND INC	•				
GANNETT CO				•	
GAP INC	•				
GAN INC 93	•				
GATX CORP			•		
GEN CINEMA CP	•				
GEN DYNAMICS CP	•				
GEN ELECTRIC CO	•				
GEN MILLS				•	
GEN MOTOR CP	•				
GEN MOTOR CP CL E			•		
GEN PUBLIC UTIL				•	
GEN RE CP		•			
GEN SIGNAL			•		
GENCORP INC	•				
GENELAB TECH INC	•				
GENENTECH INC				•	
GENETICS INSTITUTE					•
GENETICS INSTITUTE					•
GENETICS INSTITUTE				•	
GENRAD INC			•		
GENSIA PHARM	•				
GENUINE PARTS				•	
GENZYME CORP	•	•	•		•
GEORGIA GULF CP			•		
GEORGIA PACIFIC			•		
GERBER PROD		•			
GERBER SCIENTIFIC			•		
GIANT FOODS		•			
GIBSON GREETINGS			•		
GILLETTE CO		•			
GLAXO HOLDINGS		•			
GLENFED INC		•			

STOCKS	EXCHANGE				
	C H I C A G O	A M E R I C A N	P H I L A D E L P H I A	P A C I F I C	N E W Y O R K
GLOBAL NATURAL RES	•				
GOLDEN WEST FINAN			•		
GOODRICH BF	•				
GOODYEAR TIRE RUB		•			
GOULD PUMPS INC					•
GRACE W R & CO		•			
GRAINGER W W		•			
GRAND METROPOLITAN		•		•	
GREAT ATL & PAC		•			
GREAT LAKES CHEM	•				
GREAT WESTERN FINAN	•				
GREEN TREE ACCEPT	•		•		
GREENWICH PHARM	•				
GROUND WATER TECH					•
GROW GROUP INC				•	
GTE CP		•			
GTE P		•			
GULF STATES UTIL					•
H & R BLOCK		•			
HALLIBURTON CO	•				
HANDLEMAN CO	•				
HANSON TRUST	•				
HARLEY DAVIDSON			•		
HARNISCHFEGER IND			•		
HARRIS CP	•				
HARSCO CP	•				
HASBRO INC				•	
HBO & COMPANY				•	
HEALTH IMAGES INC				•	
HEALTHCARE COMPARE	•			•	
HEALTHDYNE INC				•	

STOCKS	CHICAGO	AMERICAN	PHILADELPHIA	PACIFIC	NEW YORK
HEALTHSOUTH REHAB					•
HEALTHTRUST INC	•	•			
HECHINGER CO CL A			•		
HECLA MINING CO		•			
HEINZ H J	•				
HELMERICK & PAYNE					•
HERCULES INC		•			
HERSEY FOODS		•			
HEWLETT PACKARD CO	•				
HILTON HOTELS				•	
HITACHI LTD	•				
HMO AMERICA	•				
HOME DEPOT			•		
HOME FED S & L	•				
HOME INTENSIVE CARE		•			
HOMESTAKE MINING CO	•				
HONDA MOTORS			•		
HONEYWELL INC	•				
HOSPITAL CO OF AMER				•	
HOUGHTON MIFFLIN			•		
HOUSEHOLD INTL INC		•			
HOUSTON IND					•
HUMANA INC	•				
IBP INC			•		
ICN PHARMACEUTICALS	•		•		
ICOS CORP	•				
ILL TOOL WORKS			•		
ILLINOIS CENTRAL			•		
IMC FERTILIZER				•	
IMMUNEX CP				•	
IMMUNOGEN INC		•			

STOCKS	CHICAGO	AMERICAN	PHILADELPHIA	PACIFIC	NEW YORK
IMMUNOMEDICS	•				
IMPERIAL CHEM IND					•
IMPERIAL OIL CL A	•				
INCO LTD		•			
INFO RESOURCES	•				
INFORMIX CP	•	•			
INGERSOLL RAND					•
INLAND STEEL				•	
INTEL CP		•			
INTELLIGENT ELECT				•	
INTERGRAPH CP		•			
INTERPUBLIC GROUP CO					•
INTL BUSINESS MAC	•				
INTL FLAVORS & FRAG	•				
INTL GAME TECH		•			
INTL MOBILE MACH				•	
INTL PAPER	•				
INTO RECTIFIER	•				
INTL SPEC PRODUCTS		•			
INVACARE CP		•			
ITEL CP	•				
ITT CP	•				
IVAX CORP	•				
JAMES RIVER					•
JAN BELL MARKETING	•				
JEFFERSON PILOT CP		•			
JOHN H HARLAND					•
JOHNSON & JOHNSON	•				
JOHNSON CONTROLS			•		
JOSTENS INC					•
JWP INC		•			
K MART CP	•				

STOCKS	CHICAGO	AMERICAN	PHILADELPHIA	PACIFIC	NEW YORK
KAUFMAN & BROAD HOME			•		
KAY JEWELERS			•		
KELLOGG CO		•			
KEMPER CP			•		
KERR MCGEE	•				
KEYCORP			•		
KEYSTONE INTL INC				•	
KIMBERLY CLARK		•			
KING WORLD PROD				•	
KLM ROYAL DUTCH AIR	•				
KNIGHT RIDDER INC			•		
KNOWLEDGEWARE INC			•		
KNOWLEDGEWARE INC					•
KOMAG INC				•	
KROGER CP		•			
L. A. GEAR INC	•				
LAC MINERALS	•				
LAIDLAW TRANS LTD		•			
LAM RESEARCH CP				•	
LAND'S END INC	•				
LANDMARK GRAPHICS		•			
LAWTER INTL INC			•		
LEGENT CP	•				
LENNAR CP		•			
LESLIE FAY			•		
LILLY ELI & CO		•			
LIMITED INC	•				
LIN BROADCASTING		•			
LINCOLN NATL CORP		•			
LINEAR TECH				•	
LIPOSOME CO	•				

STOCKS	CHICAGO	AMERICAN	PHILADELPHIA	PACIFIC	NEW YORK
LIPOSOME TECHNOLOGY		•			
LITTON IND INC	•				
LIZ CLAIBORNE	•				
LOCKHEED CP				•	
LOCTITE CP			•		
LOEWS CP	•				
LONG ISLAND LIGHTING					•
LONGVIEW FIBER CO	•				
LORAL CP	•				
LOTUS DEVELOPMENT		•			
LOUISIANA LAND EXP			•		
LOUISIANA PACIFIC		•			
LOWES COMPANIES			•		
LSI LOGIC CP	•				
LUBRIZOL			•		
LUBY'S CAFETERIAS	•				
LYONDELL PETROCHEM					•
MA HANNA					•
MAGNA INTL CL A	•				
MANOR CARE			•		
MANPOWER	•				
MAPCO INC				•	
MARGARETTEN FINAN	•				
MARION MERRELL DOW				•	
MARK IV INDUSTRIES					•
MARRIOTT CP			•		
MARSH & MCLENNON			•		
MARTIN MARIETTA			•		
MARVEL ENTERTAINMENT	•				
MASCO CP		•			

STOCKS	EXCHANGE					STOCKS	EXCHANGE				
	CHICAGO	AMERICAN	PHILADELPHIA	PACIFIC	NEW YORK		CHICAGO	AMERICAN	PHILADELPHIA	PACIFIC	NEW YORK
MATTEL INC		•				MESA LTD PART		•			
MATTEL INC		•				MGI PHARMA INC		•			
MAXTOR CORP				•		MGIC INVESTMENT		•			
MAXUS ENERGY				•		MICHIGAN NATL CORP		•			
MAY DEPT STRS	•					MICRON TECHNOLOGY	•			•	
MAYTAG CO					•	MICROPOLIS CP				•	
MBIA INC			•			MICROSOFT CP				•	
MBNA CORP		•				MID-AMER WASTE			•		
MCCAW CELLULAR		•				MIDWAY AIRLINES	•				
MCCORMICK & CO			•			MILLER HERMAN					•
MCDERMOTT INTL INC			•			MILLIPORE CP			•		
MCDONALDS CP	•					MIPS COMPUTER SYS	•				
MCDONNELL DOUGLAS			•			MIRAGE RESORTS			•		
MCGRAW HILL			•			MITCHEL ENERGY				•	
MCI COMMUNICATIONS	•					MNC FINAN INC		•			
MCKESSON CP				•		MOBIL CP	•				
MEAD CP	•					MOBILE TELECOMMUN	•				
MEDCO CONTAINMENT				•		MOLECULAR BIO SYS		•			
MEDCO RESEARCH		•				MOLEX INC	•				
MEDICAL CARE INTL	•					MONSANTO CO	•				
MEDTRONIC INC	•					MORGAN JP & CO				•	
MELLON BANK CP					•	MORGAN JP & CO 95				•	
MELVILLE CP				•		MORGAN STANLEY				•	
MENTOR CP		•		•		MORRISON INC					•
MENTOR GRAPHICS		•				MORRISON KNUDSEN				•	
MERCANTILE STORES			•			MORTON INTL INC				•	
MERCK & CO	•					MOTOROLA INC			•		
MEREDITH CORP			•			MULTIMEDIA INC				•	
MERIDIAN BANCORP		•				MURPHY OIL CP				•	
MERISEL INC	•					MYCOGEN CP		•			
MERRILL LYNCH		•				MYLAN LABS		•			
MERRY-GO-ROUND	•	•	•			NALCO CHEM CP				•	
						NASHUA CP		•			

STOCKS	EXCHANGE				
	CHICAGO	AMERICAN	PHILADELPHIA	PACIFIC	NEW YORK
NATIONSBANK			•		
NATL CITY CORP		•			
NATL DATA CP			•		
NATL HEALTH LABS			•		
NATL MEDICAL ENTER		•			
NATL SEMICONDUCTOR	•				
NATL SERVICE IND			•		
NBD BANCORP			•		
NCR CP	•				
NEIMAN MARCUS GROUP				•	
NELLCOR INC					•
NETWORK SYSTEMS		•			
NEUTROGENA CP			•		
NEWBRIDGE NETWORK				•	
NEWELL CO					•
NEWMONT GOLD CO			•		
NEWMONT MNG CP			•		
NIAGARA MOHAWK PWR		•			
NICOR INC				•	
NIKE INC				•	
NL IND INC				•	
NOBLE AFFILIATES		•			
NORD RESOURCES		•			
NORDSTROM INC		•			
NORFOLK SOUTHERN CP	•				
NORTH AMER VACCINE	•	•			
NORTHERN TELECOM	•				
NORTHERN TRUST CP	•				
NORTHROP CP	•				
NORWEST CP				•	

STOCKS	EXCHANGE				
	CHICAGO	AMERICAN	PHILADELPHIA	PACIFIC	NEW YORK
NOVA PHARMACEUTICAL				•	
NOVA PHARMACEUTICAL	•				
NOVACARE				•	
NOVELL INC		•			
NOVELLUS SYS				•	•
NOVELLUS SYS	•				
NUCOR CORP	•				
NWNL COMPANIES	•	•			
NY TIMES CL A				•	
NYNEX					•
OCCIDENTAL PET	•				
OCEAN DRILL & EXPLOR		•			
OCEANEERING INTL INC				•	
OCTEL COMMUN CP				•	
OEA INC		•			
OFFICE DEPOT INC		•			
OGDEN CP	•				
OHIO EDISON CO				•	
OLD REPUBLIC INTL			•		
OLIN CP		•			
OMNICOM GROUP INC				•	
ONEOK INC				•	
ORACLE SYSTEMS	•				
OREGON STEEL MILLS				•	
ORGANOGENESIS	•				
ORYX ENERGY	•			•	
QUAKER OATS 95				•	
OUTBOARD MARINE	•				
OWENS CORNING FIBER				•	
OWENS ILLINOIS	•				
PACCAR INC					•

STOCKS	CHICAGO	AMERICAN	PHILADELPHIA	PACIFIC	NEW YORK
PACIFIC ENTERPRISES		•			
PACIFIC GAS & EL		•			
PACIFIC TELESIS				•	
PACIFICORP				•	
PAINE WEBBER	•				
PALL CORP	•				
PALL CORP	•				
PANHANDLE EASTERN			•		
PARAMETRIC TECH			•		
PARAMOUNT COMMUN	•				
PARKER HANNIFIN			•		
PEGASUS GOLD	•				
PENN CENTRAL			•		
PENNEY J C CO		•			
PENNZOIL CO	•				
PEP BOYS					•
PEPSICO INC	•				
PERKIN ELMER				•	
PERRIGO CO	•				
PET INC	•				•
PETRIE STORES			•		
PFIZER INC		•			
PHELPS DODGE		•			
PHILA ELEC				•	
PHILIP MORRIS		•			
PHILLIPS N V					•
PHILLIPS PETROLEUM		•			
PHILLIPS VAN HEUSEN	•				
PHM CORP			•		
PIC N SAVE				•	
PICTURETEL CP			•		
PIER 1 IMPORTS					•
PINELANDS INC		•	•		

STOCKS	CHICAGO	AMERICAN	PHILADELPHIA	PACIFIC	NEW YORK
PINNACLE WEST CAP				•	
PIONEER HI BRED INTL		•			
PITNEY BOWES		•			
PITTSTON			•		
PLACER DOME			•		
PLAINS RESOURCES	•	•			
PNC FINAN CP			•		
POLAROID CP	•				
POTLATCH CP					•
PPG IND			•		
PRECISION CAST PARTS	•				
PREFERRED HEALTHCARE		•			
PREMARK INTL	•				
PRESLEY CO		•			
PRICE CO				•	
PRIMERICA		•			
PROCTER & GAMBLE		•			
PROGRESIVE CORP			•		
PROMUS COS	•				
PUBLIC SERV ENTER		•			
PUGET SOUND BANCORP			•		
PURITAN BENNETT				•	
PYRAMID TECH			•		
QMS INC					•
QUAKER OATS			•		
QUAKER STATE CP		•			
QUANTUM CHEMICAL		•			
QUANTUM CP					•
QUARTERDECK OFFICE	•				
QVC NETWORK INC			•		
RALSTON PURINA	•				

STOCKS	CHICAGO	AMERICAN	PHILADELPHIA	PACIFIC	NEW YORK
RAYCHEM CP				•	
RAYTHEON CO	•				
READ-RITE CP	•			•	
READERS DIGEST ASSO	•	•			
REEBOK INTL		•			
REPLIGEN CP		•			
REPUBLIC NEW YORK			•		
RESEARCH IND CP			•		
REUTERS HLDGS PLC	•	•			
REYNOLDS METALS					•
RHONE POULENCE RORER		•			
RIBI IMMUNOCHEN RSCH	•				
RITE AID			•		
RJR NABISCO	•	•	•		
ROADWAY SERVICES				•	
ROCHESTER COMMUNITY		•			
ROCKEFELLER CTR PROP		•			
ROCKWELL INTL CP	•				
ROHM & HAAS		•			
ROHR IND INC			•		
ROLLINS ENVIRON				•	
ROSS STORES				•	
ROUSE CO	•				
ROWAN COMPANIES		•			•
ROYAL DUTCH PET		•			
RPM INC	•				
RUBBERMAID INC				•	
RUSSELL CORP		•			
RYDER SYSTEM INC				•	
RYLAND CP			•		
SAATCHI & SAATCHI	•				
SAFECARD SERVICES				•	

STOCKS	CHICAGO	AMERICAN	PHILADELPHIA	PACIFIC	NEW YORK
SAFECO CP					•
SAFETY KLEEN	•	•	•		
SALOMON BROS FUND			•		
SALOMON INC			•		
SANTA FE ENERGY RES		•			
SANTA FE SO PAC		•			
SARA LEE		•			
SBARRO INC			•		
SCHERER R.P.		•			
SCHERING PLOUGH				•	
SCHLUMBERGER	•				
SCI SYSTEMS	•				
SCIENTIFIC ATLANTA				•	
SCIMED LIFE SYSTEMS	•				
SCIOS INC		•		•	
SCITEX CP LTD		•			
SCOTT PAPER CO			•		
SCOTTS CO	•				
SEAGATE TECH		•			
SEAGRAMS CO LTD				•	
SEAGULL ENERGY CP			•		
SEARS ROEBUCK	•				
SECURITY PACIFIC CP			•		
SENSORMATIC ELECT		•			
SEQUENT COMPUTER		•			
SERVICE CP INTL			•		
SERVICE MERCHANDISE			•		
SHARED MEDICAL				•	
SHAW INDUSTRIES	•				
SHAWMUT NATL		•			
SHELL TRANS & TRD	•				
SHERWIN WILLIAMS	•				

STOCKS	CHICAGO	AMERICAN	PHILADELPHIA	PACIFIC	NEW YORK
SHONEYS INC				•	
SHOPKO STORES		•			
SIGMA ALDRICH CP	•				
SIGNET BANKING CP				•	
SILICON GRAPHICS		•			
SINGER CO		•			•
SIZZLER INTL	•				
SKYLINE CP	•				
SMITH CORONA					•
SMITH INTL			•		
SMITHFIELD FOODS			•		
SMITHKLINE BEECH				•	
SNAP ON TOOLS		•			
SOCIETY CORP				•	
SOFTWARE PUBLISHING				•	•
SOLECTRON CP	•				
SONAT INC		•			
SOTHEBYS HLDGS				•	
SOTHEBYS HLDGS		•			
SOUTHERN CAL ED				•	
SOUTHERN CO	•				
SOUTHERN NEW ENG TEL					•
SOUTHTRUST CP				•	
SOUTHWEST AIRLINES	•				
SOUTHWESTERN BELL				•	
SPARTAN MOTORS				•	
SPI PHARMACEUTICALS		•			
SPRINT CP			•		
SPW CP					•
ST JUDE MEDICAL	•				
ST PAUL COS	•				
STANHOME INC		•			

STOCKS	CHICAGO	AMERICAN	PHILADELPHIA	PACIFIC	NEW YORK
STANLEY WORKS				•	
STAPLES INC			•		
STATE STREET BOSTON			•		
STEWART & STEVENSON				•	
STONE CONTAINER				•	
STORAGE TECH	•				
STRATUS COMPUTER				•	
STRIDE RITE CP				•	
STRUCTURAL DYN RES			•		
STRYKER CP			•		
STUDENT LOAN MKT	•				
SULCUS COMPUTER	•				
SUMMIT TECH				•	
SUN CO INC				•	
SUN MICROSYSTEMS				•	
SUNSTRAND CP					•
SUNTRUST BANKS				•	
SUPER VALU STRS			•		
SURGICAL CARE AFFIL					•
SURGICAL LASER TECH		•		•	
SYBASE INC				•	
SYMANTEC CP				•	
SYMBOL TECHNOLOGIES		•			
SYNERGEN INC			•	•	
SYNOPTICS COMMUN	•		•		•
SYNTEX CP	•				
SYSCO CP					•
SYSTEM SOFTWARE ASSO				•	
T CELL SCIENCES		•			
T2 MEDICAL				•	
TAMBRANDS INC					•

STOCKS	CHICAGO	AMERICAN	PHILADELPHIA	PACIFIC	NEW YORK
TANDEM COMPUTERS		•			
TANDY CP	•	•			
TCBY ENTERPRISES				•	
TEKTRONIX INC	•				
TELECOMM		•			
TELEDYNE INC	•				
TELEFONICA DE ESPANA		•			
TELEFONOS DE MEX	•	•	•	•	•
TELLABS INC				•	
TELXON CP	•				
TEMPLE INLAND		•			
TENNECO INC		•			
TERADYNE				•	
TESORO PETROLEUM			•		
TEXACO INC		•			
TEXAS INSTRS	•				
TEXAS UTILITIES				•	
TEXTRON INC		•			
THERMO ELECTRON					•
THIOKOL CP		•			
3M COMPANY				•	
TIDEWATER INC		•			•
TIFFANY & CO		•			
TIME WARNER INC		•			
TIMES MIRROR					•
TIMKEN CP					•
TJX COS INC	•				
TOKOS MEDICAL CP		•			
TOPPS CO		•			
TORCHMARK CP			•		
TOSCO CP			•		
TOYS R US	•				
TRANSAMERICA CP			•		

STOCKS	CHICAGO	AMERICAN	PHILADELPHIA	PACIFIC	NEW YORK
TRANSCO ENERGY					•
TRAVELERS CP				•	
TRI-CONTL CP			•		
TRIBUNE CO	•				
TRIMBLE NAV LTD				•	
TRINITY IND INC		•			
TRINOVA CP			•		
TRITON ENERGY	•	•	•		•
TRW INC		•			
TSENG LABS		•			
TSI CORP	•				
TUCSON ELEC PWR		•			
TYCO LABORATORIES			•		
TYCO TOYS			•		
TYSON FOODS CL A				•	
U S BANCORP		•		•	
U S BIOSCIENCE		•			
U S F & G CP			•		
U S HEALTHCARE		•			
U S SURGICAL		•			
U S WEST INC		•			
UAL CP	•				
UJB FINAN CP	•				
UNILEVER NV		•			
UNION CAMP	•				
UNION CARBIDE		•			
UNION PACIFIC CP			•		
UNION TEXAS PET			•		
UNISYS		•			
UNITED HEALTHCARE	•	•			•
UNITED STATES SHOE			•		
UNITED TECHNOLOGIES	•				
UNITRIN INC	•				

STOCKS	CHICAGO	AMERICAN	PHILADELPHIA	PACIFIC	NEW YORK
UNIVERSAL FOODS CP			•		
UNOCAL CP				•	
UNOCAL EXPLOR CP	•				
UNUM CP		•			
UPJOHN CP	•				
US AIR				•	
UST INC	•				
USC MARATHON		•			
USX US STEEL		•			
UTAH MEDICAL PROD		•			
VALERO ENERGY CP		•			
VALHI INC			•		
VALLEY NATL CP		•			
VANGUARD CELL SYS	•				
VARIAN ASSO		•			
VENTURE STORES	•				
VERIFONE INC	•				
VF CP					•
VIACOM INC			•		
VICOR CP	•				
VIDEOCART INC				•	
VLSI TECHNOLOGY	•	•			
VODAPHONE	•				
VONS COS					•
WABAN INC	•				
WACHOVIA CP				•	
WAL-MART STORES	•				
WALLACE COMPUTER			•		
WALLGREEN CO		•			
WARNER LAMBERT		•			
WASH MUTUAL SVGS BK		•			
WASTE MNGT INC			•		

STOCKS	CHICAGO	AMERICAN	PHILADELPHIA	PACIFIC	NEW YORK
WELLFLEET COMMUN	•				
WELLMAN INC					•
WELLS FARGO			•		
WENDYS INTL INC				•	
WESTERN CO N A					•
WESTINGHOUSE EL			•		
WESTMARK INTL			•		
WESTVACO CP				•	
WEYERHAEUSER CO	•				
WHEELABRATOR TECH			•		
WHIRLPOOL	•				
WHITMAN CP	•				
WILLIAMETTE IND					•
WILLIAMS COS	•				
WINN DIXIE INC	•				
WMS INDUSTRIES			•		
WOOLWORTH CP			•		
WORTHINGTON IND			•		
WRIGLEY WM JR			•		
XEROX CP	•			•	
XILINX INC	•			•	
XOMA CORP	•	•	•		•
YELLOW FREIGHT SYS	•				
ZENITH ELECTRONICS		•			
ZURN IND		•			

Table 20-2
Sample Stock Listings

INDEX OPTIONS

Chicago

S. & P. 100 (CBOE)

Option & NY Close	Strike Price	Calls-Last Oct	Calls-Last Nov	Calls-Last Dec	Puts-Last Oct	Puts-Last Nov	Puts-Last Dec
SP100	345	r	r	32½	r	1¼	2⅝
377.35	350	r	r	r	r	1 9/16	3⅛
377.35	355	20¼	r	r	r	1 15/16	3⅞
377.35	360	16½	18	r	1/16	2 9/16	4⅞
377.35	365	12¼	14½	15½	1/16	3⅜	6⅜
377.35	370	7¼	10½	13	1/16	4½	8
377.35	375	2⅜	7⅛	10	1/16	6¼	9½
377.35	380	1/16	4½	7¼	2⅝	8⅞	12
377.35	385	1/16	2 11/16	5⅛	7⅝	12	15
377.35	390	1/16	1½	3⅛	14½	16½	19⅛
377.35	395	r	13/16	2 3/16	20⅝	20⅞	r
377.35	400	r	½	1¼	26½	27	27⅞
377.35	405	r	5/16	¾	r	r	r
377.35	410	r	⅛	½	r	r	36¼
377.35	415	r	1/16	¼	r	r	r
377.35	420	r	1/16	r	r	r	45

Total Call Vol. 191,634 Call Open Int. 615,761
Total Put Vol. 228,534 Put Open Int. 562,105

S. & P. 500 (CBOE)

Option & NY Close	Strike Price	Calls-Last Oct	Calls-Last Nov	Calls-Last Dec	Puts-Last Oct	Puts-Last Nov	Puts-Last Dec
SP500	365	s	s	r	s	s	1¾
411.73	375	s	s	37½	s	s	2½
411.73	380	r	s	r	r	s	3⅝
411.73	390	r	s	r	r	s	4½
411.73	395	15⅜	s	r	r	s	6⅜
411.73	400	10	s	16⅛	1/16	s	6⅝
411.73	405	5¼	s	13⅞	1/16	s	8¼
411.73	410	1¾	s	10⅝	1/16	s	10
411.73	415	1/16	s	r	3⅛	s	r
411.73	420	r	s	5¾	10⅞	s	17
411.73	425	r	s	3¾	14¾	s	20
411.73	430	r	s	2⅝	19⅜	s	22½
411.73	435	r	s	1 9/16	r	s	26⅞
411.73	440	r	s	r	r	s	33¼

Total Call Vol. 13,561 Call Open Int. 344,898
Total Put Vol. 21,686 Put Open Int. 571,399

American

Major Market Index

Option & NY Close	Strike Price	Calls-Last Oct	Calls-Last Nov	Calls-Last Dec	Puts-Last Oct	Puts-Last Nov	Puts-Last Dec
MajMkt	300	r	r	r	r	9/16	1½
337.73	305	r	r	r	r	1	r
337.73	310	r	r	r	r	1 7/16	2 9/16
337.73	315	r	r	r	r	1 9/16	r
337.73	320	r	r	r	r	2⅛	4⅜
337.73	325	r	14	16½	r	3	5¼
337.73	330	7	r	14¾	1/16	4	6⅝
337.73	335	2 11/16	7	r	1/16	5¾	8¼
337.73	340	1/16	4⅜	6¾	2 3/16	8	11⅜
337.73	345	1/16	2⅜	4½	7⅜	10½	r
337.73	350	1/16	1¼	2⅞	12⅜	15¾	16⅞
337.73	355	1/16	13/16	1¾	r	r	r
337.73	360	r	7/16	15/16	r	r	r
337.73	370	r	⅛	⅜	33⅜	r	r
337.73	375	r	r	r	r	r	40

Total Call Vol. 8,479 Call Open Int. 77,931
Total Put Vol. 9,035 Put Open Int. 96,429

Institutional Index

Option & NY Close	Strike Price	Calls-Last Oct	Calls-Last Nov	Calls-Last Dec	Puts-Last Oct	Puts-Last Nov	Puts-Last Dec
Instldx	350	r	75⅞	r	r	⅛	r
426.89	385	r	r	r	r	⅞	r
426.89	390	r	r	r	r	1½	r
426.89	400	r	r	r	r	1 15/16	r
426.89	405	r	r	r	r	2⅜	r
426.89	410	r	r	r	r	3⅛	6¾
426.89	415	8¼	r	r	⅛	r	7¾
426.89	420	5⅝	10⅝	r	⅛	6	9¼
426.89	425	¾	7	r	1⅞	7⅜	r
426.89	430	⅜	5¼	r	5⅝	r	r
426.89	435	r	3⅛	5⅜	r	r	r
426.89	440	r	1⅞	r	r	r	r
426.89	450	r	¾	r	r	24⅝	r
426.89	455	r	⅜	r	r	r	r

Total Call Vol. 6,128 Call Open Int. 68,151
Total Put Vol. 6,671 Put Open Int. 75,936

Table 20-3
Typical Listing of Foreign Currency Options

PHILADELPHIA EXCHANGE

Option & Underlying	Strike Price	Calls—Last Oct	Nov	Dec	Puts—Last Oct	Nov	Dec
50,000 Australian Dollars-European Style.							
ADollr....	73	r	r	r	0.85	r	r
50,000 Australian Dollars-cents per unit.							
ADollr....	72	0.04	0.60	r	0.13	r	r
72.25	73	r	0.26	r	r	r	r
31,250 British Pound-German Mark cross.							
BPd-GMk	236	r	r	r	r	r	1.65
246.18	238	r	r	r	r	1.48	2.30
246.18	242	r	r	r	r	2.70	r
246.18	252	r	1.60	r	r	r	7.42
246.18	258	r	0.50	r	r	r	r
31,250 British Pounds-European Style.							
BPound..	160	4.80	r	r	r	1.65	r
169.31	165	r	4.00	r	r	2.70	r
169.31	167½	r	r	r	2.70	r	r
169.31	170	0.05	1.70	r	r	r	r
169.31	175	r	0.52	r	r	r	r
169.31	177½	r	r	0.67	r	r	r
31,250 British Pounds-cents per unit.							
BPound..	155	r	11.70	r	r	r	1.85
169.31	157½	r	r	r	r	r	2.25
169.31	160	4.82	r	r	r	1.70	2.75
169.31	162½	r	4.40	r	r	2.05	3.80
169.31	165	r	2.95	r	0.25	3.45	5.05
169.31	167½	0.04	2.05	2.90	2.35	4.80	6.60
169.31	170	r	1.55	2.00	5.00	6.55	7.80
169.31	172½	r	0.90	1.50	r	r	r
169.31	175	r	0.50	r	9.55	r	r
169.31	177½	0.03	0.35	0.68	r	r	r
169.31	180	r	r	0.50	r	r	15.30
50,000 Canadian Dollars-European Style.							
CDollar....	79½	r	r	r	r	r	1.16
50,000 Canadian Dollars-cents per unit.							
CDollr....	77	r	r	r	r	r	0.42
80.13	79	r	r	r	r	r	0.95
80.13	79½	r	r	r	0.81	r	r
80.13	80	r	0.86	1.00	0.02	1.06	r
80.13	80½	r	r	r	r	1.27	r
80.13	81	0.47	r	r	r	r	r
80.13	81½	r	0.45	r	r	r	r
80.13	82	r	r	r	1.79	r	r
80.13	82½	r	r	r	2.25	r	r
80.13	83	r	r	r	3.00	r	r
80.13	83½	r	r	r	3.23	r	r
80.13	84	r	r	r	3.75	r	r
80.13	84½	r	r	r	4.27	r	r
62,500 European Currency Units-cents per unit.							
ECU....	134	r	2.30	r	r	r	r
250,000 French Francs-10ths of a cent per unit.							
FFranc..	18¾	r	r	r	r	0.86	r
202.59	19	r	r	r	r	0.76	r
250,000 French Francs-European Style.							
FFranc..	20	0.24	r	r	r	r	r
202.59	21	r	r	r	r	12.60	r
62,500 German Marks-European Style.							
DMark....	61	6.90	6.75	r	r	r	r
68.78	64	r	r	r	r	0.15	r
68.78	64½	r	3.72	r	r	r	r
68.78	65½	r	r	r	0.44	r	r
68.78	66	r	r	r	0.01	0.70	r
68.78	67	r	1.60	2.27	0.02	r	1.32
68.78	67½	0.16	1.39	r	0.17	r	r
68.78	68	0.05	1.26	r	0.35	1.57	1.98
68.78	68½	0.21	r	r	0.89	1.86	r
68.78	69	r	r	r	1.04	r	r
68.78	70	0.03	0.44	r	2.36	3.12	r
68.78	71½	r	0.28	r	r	r	r
68.78	72½	r	0.18	r	r	r	r
62,500 German Marks-cents per unit.							
DMark....	49	r	r	0.15	r	r	r
68.78	60	r	r	r	r	r	0.15
68.78	62	r	r	r	r	r	0.30
68.78	64	r	r	4.62	r	0.32	0.46
68.78	64½	r	r	r	r	0.43	r
68.78	65	r	r	r	r	0.85	0.85
68.78	65½	2.20	r	r	r	0.41	1.15
68.78	66	r	r	r	r	0.86	1.00
68.78	67	0.65	1.58	1.80	0.02	1.15	1.70
68.78	67½	0.24	1.30	r	0.06	1.45	1.98
68.78	68	0.02	1.04	1.56	0.35	1.31	2.27
68.78	68½	0.03	0.88	1.15	0.85	r	r
68.78	69	0.05	0.70	1.01	1.37	1.73	2.36
68.78	69½	r	0.53	1.07	r	r	r
68.78	70	0.03	0.47	0.72	2.36	r	3.60
68.78	71	r	0.25	0.51	3.32	r	r
68.78	72	r	0.16	0.34	3.93	r	r
68.78	73	r	r	r	5.45	r	r
6,250,000 Japanese Yen-100ths of a cent per unit.							
JYen......	78	r	r	r	r	r	0.04
83.12	80	3.08	r	r	r	0.01	r
83.12	82	1.50	r	2.25	r	0.39	r
83.12	82½	1.01	r	1.51	r	r	r
83.12	83	0.55	1.31	1.54	0.02	r	r
83.12	83½	0.18	r	1.40	0.12	r	r
83.12	84	0.05	r	1.05	r	r	r
83.12	84½	0.03	r	0.93	r	r	r
83.12	85	r	0.43	r	r	r	r
83.12	86	r	r	0.50	r	r	r
6,250,000 Japanese Yen-European Style.							
JYen......	79½	3.50	3.54	r	r	r	r
62,500 Swiss Francs-European Style.							
SFranc....	71	r	5.62	r	r	r	r
76.94	73½	r	3.50	r	r	r	r
76.94	74	r	r	r	0.01	0.58	r
76.94	75½	r	r	r	r	1.58	r
76.94	76	r	r	r	0.40	r	r
76.94	76½	0.44	r	r	0.79	r	r
76.94	77	r	r	r	0.80	r	r
76.94	78	r	0.90	r	r	r	r
76.94	80½	r	0.34	r	r	r	r
62,500 Swiss Francs-cents per unit.							
SFranc....	59	r	s	0.32	r	r	s
76.94	73	r	r	r	r	0.39	r
76.94	75	r	r	r	0.05	1.30	r
76.94	75½	0.24	r	r	0.07	r	r
76.94	76	r	r	r	0.25	1.38	r
76.94	76½	0.10	r	r	r	r	r
76.94	77	r	r	r	0.52	r	r
76.94	77½	r	r	r	1.03	2.50	r
76.94	80	r	r	r	4.32	r	4.54
76.94	83	r	r	0.29	r	r	r
50,000 Canadian Dollars EOM-cents per unit.							
CDollr....	78½	r	r	r	r	0.21	r
80.13	79	r	r	r	r	0.32	r
80.13	80½	0.48	r	r	r	r	r
80.13	81	0.23	r	r	r	r	r
62,500 German Marks EOM-cents per unit.							
DMark....	65	r	r	r	r	0.27	r
68.78	66	r	r	r	r	0.30	r
68.78	67	r	r	r	r	0.65	r
68.78	68	1.14	r	r	r	1.00	r
68.78	70	0.22	r	r	r	r	r
68.78	68½	0.80	r	r	r	1.06	r
68.78	71½	0.12	r	r	r	r	r
6,250,000 Japanese Yen EOM-100ths of a cent per unit.							
JYen	84	0.28	r	r	r	r	r
62,500 Swiss Franc EOM-cents per unit.							
SFranc....	74	r	r	r	0.33	r	r

Total Call Vol 38,270 Call Open int 658,149
Total Put Vol 47,501 Put Open int 726,929

Glossary

Advance-decline indicator—A technical indicator used in conjunction with the Dow Jones Industrial Average to help determine market trends. As theory has it, if the advance-decline indicator and the Dow Jones Industrial Average move in unison, then whatever the trend is should continue. If the indicator peaks but the averages continue to go up, the the market is expected to be near its top. If the indicator bottoms but the averages continue to fall, then the market is approaching its low.

Asking price—The lowest price at which a stockholder is willing to unload his shares.

All-or-none—This is an order to a broker which specifies that the entire order must be filled, or it is not to be placed. This is a very important condition for the placement of orders but often options traders fail to specify it and wind up paying much more in commissions than they may have anticipated. Consider the covered call writer who wants to write 10 calls on a stock for $¼. Now suppose that she fails to specificy "all or none" and when her order is on the floor, only ¹⁄₁₀ of the order can be filled. The result is that she will sell one call for $25 but then get hit with a $35 commission charge. The result is a $10 loss. Shouldn't the broker know better? Yes, and safeguards should be set up to assure that this does not happen, but at the present time there are no such safeguards from such foolish execution of an order other than to specify "all or none."

Assets—Assets represent intangible rights and physical property, including cash and investment holdings, that have market value. From an accounting perspective, assets are usually divided into two broad groups—current or noncurrent. Current assets are those which are either cash or something which can be readily turned into cash. Noncurrent assets are those which cannot be converted into cash over the short term (less than a year) and include such items as land, buildings, equipment, and certain long-term investments. Not all assets are so tangible as those listed above. Sometimes rights or privileges, as may be represented by copyrights, patents, trademarkes and sometimes goodwill, also qualify as a company's assets.

At-the-money—When options have a striking price equal to the price at which a stock is selling, they are said to be at-the-money. Options in this money position usually have higher premiums than those which may be out-of-the-money and have the same expiration date.

Stock Price	Striking Price	Money Position
$25	$25	At-the-money
$30	$30	At-the-money

Bankers' acceptance rate—These are short-term negotiable discount time drafts usually offering rates comparable with commercial paper rates.

Bear—This term refers to an investor who anticipates a declining market in general, or a decline for a specific security. Thus, someone may be bullish on the market in general and bearish on a particular stock, or vice versa. But while the bear may be anticipating a decline in a stock, stock group, or the market in general, this does not mean that she is feeling negative about her chances of making money as a result of the anticipated decline. There are a number of ways in which a bear may position herself to profit from market declines: she may sell stock short, buy puts or sell calls.

Bear market—A market for short sellers, call writers and put buyers. Bear markets may occur at anytime and extend for years. They may also occur as temporary technical corrections in a bull market. Often when the market advances too quickly or steadily over a long period of time, there are bear phases which occur as investors begin their profit taking. In times of economic contractions, bear markets—with occasional bullish corrections—drive the stock markets lower and lower for extended periods. When the markets drop, they usually drop much quicker than they advance. Even in periods of extended rises in stock prices, it is well to "insure" one's portfolio by buying puts or selling covered calls. In this way, an investor can benefit by those temporary drops in market prices which, though short-lived, may be very extensive.

Bear pools—Now outlawed, these were funds specifically organized for the purpose of putting downward pressure on stock prices.

Big Board—Another name for the New York Stock Exchange.

Book value—Not to be confused with either the liquidating or par value of a stock, the book value is simply the difference between a corporation's assets and its liabilities. From a theoretical point of view, book market and liquidating value should be the same, but this is rarely the case. Liquidating value is simply an accountant's guess on the value of a corporation's assets, and these assets rarely command the type of figure the accountants estimate. Book value is an important factor in determing which underlying stock should be purchased for call writing. A stock should generally be selling at or near book value or projected book value according to the most conservative analysts. Any higher price makes the stock much less valuable as an investment, and any lower price makes it much more attractive.

Bull—Anyone who expects the market to go up and has a generally optimistic attitude about the future. The bull is usually long on stocks, and/or buying calls or writing puts.

Buying long—Making the usual trade, wherein the stock is purchased with the hope of selling it at a later date at a higher price. Investors who buy long will often try to increase the yield from their portfolio by selling covered calls.

Call money rate—The special rate available to brokers.

Capital gains—The profit made from the buying and selling of stocks, options, or other securities. For instance, if you buy a stock at $10 and sell it for $12, your capital gain is $2. If you buy an option for $5 and sell it for $10, your capital gain is $5.

Commercial paper rate—The rate available on high-grade corporate promissary discount notes that are dealer placed.

Current ratio—A ratio that reveals just how liquid a corporation is. It is determined by dividing current assets by current liabilities.

Closing transaction—The second position which an options trader takes in an option he has already bought or sold.

Contingency (conditional) order—An order placed with the understanding that certain things must happen before the order may be executed. Contingency orders are an important tool for the options investor because writers and buyers are always playing two markets at the same time—stock and options markets. Thus, it is necessary to an option trader's success to specify not only the price for which he wants to buy or sell an option, but also the price at which he wants the stock to be at the time of purchase.

Curb Exchange—The name of the American Stock Exchange from 1929 until 1953. Brokers on the exchange are still sometimes referred to as "curb brokers" but the name is gradually losing popularity as new generations begin to take over Wall Street.

Current price—The price at which the last trade in a stock took place.

Current ratio—The relationship between a corporation's assets and its liabilities. Thus, if a company's assets are $2 million and its liabilities are $1 million, its current ratio is 2 to 1.

Day orders—A type of order which specifies that it is to be cancelled if it cannot be executed on the day it is placed. Normally, all orders are accepted as being day orders unless the investor gives different instructions.

Discount rate—The rate which the Federal Reserve charges depository institutions.

Dow Theory—A method of analyzing stock market activity. It was originally developed by one of the founders of the *Wall Street Journal*, the late Charles H. Dow, and later perfected by William P. Handon. Basically the theory says that if there is coincidence between the Industrial and Transportation Averages during periods of heavy volume, the market is bullish for the near and intermediate terms. If they fall in coincidence, however, they point to a coming bear market.

Equity margin—The amount of cash or marketable securities brokers require for maintaining an account. When an investor is unable to meet the equity margin requirements, the broker has the right, given to him by signed agreement at the time of application, to sell the necessary securities from the account to make up the difference.

Exchange floor—The place where brokers and dealers conduct their business.

Execute—This term refers to the completion of a buy or sell order.

Expiration date—The date on which puts, calls and other special subscription rights become worthless.

Federal fund rate—The rate charged on overnight interbank loans. It serves as the basis for money market rates.

Fill-or-kill—A type of order that specifies it must be executed as soon as the floor broker receives it, or else it is to be cancelled. "All-or-none" is inherent in fill-or-kill orders.

Fundamental analysis—Analyzing a stock in terms of its current and future financial, managerial, and marketing strength.

Immediate-or-cancel—A type of order that specifies it must be executed as soon as it is received on the exchange floor. Unlike the fill-or-kill order, this order need not be executed in its entirety.

Inflation—A continuous upward movement in the general price level, resulting eventually in the declining value of the dollar.

Initial margin—The amount of cash which an investor may borrow from his broker to purchase stock.

In-the-money—A term specifying the money position of an option, in terms of an underlying security's relationship to the striking price at which the option may be exercised. For a call to be in-the-money, the underlying stock must be above the striking price; for a put to be in-the-money, the underlying stock must be under the striking price.

Stock Price	Striking Price	Put	Call
$25	$30	in-the-money	out-of-the-money
$30	$25	out-of-the-money	in-the-money

Liabilities—The entire debt of a corporation. Liabilities include outstanding loans, accounts payable, income taxes, nondeferred tax credits, salaries and wages, and deferred revenues.

Limit orders—These orders establish a specific price at which they must be placed.

Market orders—These orders are executed as soon as they reach the trading floor. Market orders are never recommended for options traders.

Month (of expiration)—The month in which an option expires. The specific day is the Saturday following the third Friday of the month. Expiration cycles generally include four months, but trading is generally limited to the first three months in each cycle, though these months may not necessarily be successive months on the calendar. That is, expiration months for a given option may be September, October and January.

NASD—This is the National Association of Securities Dealers, an association made up of brokers and dealers who specialize in trading those securities that make up the over-the-counter market. NASD has its own computer-based quotation system, referred to as NASDAQ, but only a percentage of OTC stocks which meet certain financial and marketing requirements are part of this computer trading system. Stocks which do fall into this computer-based system are listed in the financial dailies under the headings of "National Issues" or "NASDAQ National Market Issues." Other OTC stocks are listed under "OTC" headings or as "NASDAQ Bid-and-Asked Quotations," or "Other OTC Stocks."

Opening position—The first position an option trader takes as either a buyer or a seller of a contract. Any trader may be the buyer or seller of an option. See also "closing transaction."

Option & close—Heading in options listings which gives the underlying stock for an option contract and the price at which the underlying stock closed.

Out-of-the-money—A term specifying the money position of an option, in terms of the relationship of the price of the underlying stock to the striking price. For a call to be out-of-the-money, the price of the underlying stock must be less than the striking price; for a put to be out-of-the-money, the price of the underlying stock must be higher than the striking price.

Stock Price	Striking Price	Put	Call
$25	$30	in-the-money	out-of-the-money
$30	$25	out-of-the-money	in-the-money

Over-the-Counter (OTC) Market—The market for stocks which generally do not have the financial or marketing muscle to qualify for listing on the major exchanges. Nevertheless, many of these OTC stocks often outperform those on the major exchanges. OTC trading is generally handled by an association of brokers which function in some ways similar to how an exchange might. Some OTC stocks are listed under the heading of "National OTC" or "NASDAQ National Markets." See also "NASD" in this glossary.

P/E ratio—The relationship between a stock's price and its earnings. Thus, if a stock is earning $10 per share and selling for $50, its P/E ratio is five. P/E ratios alone should not be a signal to buy or sell. Different stocks in industry groups and certain stocks within those industry groups will have their own range of P/E ratios at which they normally sell.

Premium—The price of an option. It is the premium which excites the options markets. If the premiums are not high enough, writers are not willing to take chances. On the other hand, if they are too high, no one is going to be much interested in buying. Option writers are looking for the income the premium affords, whereas option buyers are hoping the premiums will increase at a later date and they can, therefore, sell their options for a profit.

Prime rate—The rate charged by banks to those customers having excellent credit ratings.

Psychological analysis—Analyzing a stock in terms of mass opinion and going bearish or bullish in opposition to the general sentiment. When the market is strong and opinion favors continued advances, then this would be a sign to buy puts, sell calls, or sell short. On the other hand, if the market is falling and sentiment is negative, then this is the time to buy stocks, buy calls or sell puts.

Put—An option which gives the buyer the right to sell an underlying security at a fixed price during a specific time period. The put buyer hopes to benefit from the increase in price of put. The put, generally, should increase as the stock goes down in price, depending on its time value. If the stock goes up in price, however, the put will lose value unless it's far out-of-the-money.

Reverse split—An accounting method which decreases the amount of shares outstanding and increases the value of the shares. For example, if a corporation has 50 million shares outstanding and these are valued at $10 per share, after a two-for-one reverse split, the corporation will have 25 million shares outstanding, each share now valued at $20 per share. Dividends will also be adjusted. As you can see, the par value of the stock has doubled, but the stockholder has half as many shares, so his proportionate ownership in the corporation remains the same. Reverse splits are very uncommon these days, as most boards of directors believe that they signal financial trouble to the community, and that the reverse split is designed to simply prop up the price of the underlying stock. Still, some companies, such as Storage Technology, have found them highly effective.

Selling short—A method of investing designed to make money when prices are falling. This necessitates selling a stock or option before you own it. Profit or loss is determined in the usual way—by the difference between the buying and selling prices, but in this case the sale takes place first.

Short interest—The total amount of short sales which are outstanding. Short interest statistics are usually published weekly.

Short stock—Stock that has been sold by someone who does not own it. The seller, however, has made the opening transaction by informing his broker that he does indeed plan to buy it back at a later date, and therefore is not selling a stock already in his account.

Speculator—An investor who is willing to take great risks in order to realize unusual capital gains or income, and who will trade his securities quite frequently, sometimes within minutes after purchasing them. Naked option writers may be classified as speculators because their risks are great and they must necessarily trade quite frequently. Covered call writers, however, are not considered speculators.

Spread—An options strategy which takes advantage of the relationship in price between two or more options. Here the options trader is interested only in the present and future relationship between the options and not the movement of one independent of the other. There are many types of spreads—bull spreads, bear spreads, butterfly spreads, and calendar spreads. See "Complex Strategies" in Chapter 3.

Stock markets (U. S.)—These are organized markets providing a convenient means for stock and sometimes options trading. Stock exchanges provide the major markets, and have been around for hundreds of years. Not all offer index or equity options markets. One exchange, the Chicago Board Options Exchange, offers only index and equity options but is included in the list below because it is registered as an exchange with the S.E.C. NASDAQ (National Association of Securities Dealers) is not actually an exchange but rather an association of dealers which create an orderly market in OTC stocks.

Market	Location	Index Options	Equity Options	Stock
American	New York	Yes	Yes	Yes
Boston Stock	Boston	No	No	Yes
Chicago Board Options	Chicago	Yes	Yes	No
Cincinnati	Cincinnati	No	No	Yes
Intermountain	Salt Lake	No	No	No
Midwest	Chicago	No	No	Yes
NASDAQ	D.C.	No	Yes	Yes
Pacific	San Francisco	Yes	Yes	Yes
Philadelphia	Philadelphia	Yes	Yes	Yes
Spokane	Spokane	No	No	Yes

Stock rights—These are privileges to buy additional shares of stock. They must not be confused with warrants. Stock rights most often carry an exercise price below the current market value of the underlying security, thus giving them immediate value, whereas warrants are issued at exercise prices above the current market value of the underlying security.

Stock split—This is the division of a corporation's stock into a greater number of shares; but each of these shares will now have their value reduced accordingly. For instance, if a corporation has 50 million shares of stock worth $20 per share before a two-for-one split, after the split it will have 100 million shares worth $10 per share. Dividends on each share are generally reduced in the same proportion as the split, though sometimes the dividend is kept at its original amount, or only partially reduced. Though each stockholder now has twice as many shares, they are worth half as much so her proportionate ownership in the company remains the same. The main purpose of the stock split is to make the price more attractive to the investment community. Increasing demand for the stock may put additional upward pressure on the price, and now with two shares for every one they used to have, the stockholders can see their profits double with each increase in market price.

Straddle—An option trade that is actually a combination of put and call contracts.

Street name—This term describes a situation in which purchased stock is not registered in the purchaser's name but is rather kept on account with the broker. Frequent traders must necessarily have their stock in their brokerage accounts, in which case the stock is registered in street name.

Strike price—This is the price at which the buyer has the legal right to purchase the underlying stock that served as the basis for an option contract.

Subscription right—Opportunity to shareholders to buy additional stock at a price lower than that at which it is currently available on the open market. Stockholders need not exercise these rights but may trade them in the open market just as they might trade other options.

Technical factors—These are trading trends or characteristics which are believed to be strong indicators of the geneal direction of market prices. Technical analysis of individual stocks include noting volume, new highs and lows, margin purchases, etc.

Ticker symbol—An abbreviation by which a stock or option is recognized. In many cases, the abbreviation has no direct relationship to the initials in a stock's name. In the case of OTC stocks, there are two separate ticker symbols for stocks, necessitated because NASDAQ ticker symbols used to access stock information containing more than three alpha characters, and option ticker symbols are programmed for three alpha characters. Following are stock and option ticker symbols for some of the more popular OTC options.

Stock	Stock Ticker Symbol	Option Ticker Symbol
Alexander & Baldwin	ALEX	ALQ
American Greetings	AGREA	AGQ
Apple Computer	AAPL	AAQ
Cetus Corp.	CTUS	CTQ
Intel Corp.	INTC	INQ
LIN Broadcasting	LINB	LNQ
Liz Claiborne	LIZC	LIQ
Lotus Development Corp.	LOTS	LDQ
NIKE	NIKE	NIQ
SAFECO	SAFC	SAQ
Subaru of America	SBRU	SBQ
Sun Microsystems	SUNW	SUQ
Tyson Foods	TYSNA	TYQ

Treasury bill rate—The rate available to holders of discounted short-term government securities.

Warrant—A certificate which entitles the owner to buy securities at a discount. There are basically two types of warrants, subscription warrants and stock purchase warrants. Subscription warrants are tied to new stock issues and offer first subscription privileges. Stock purchase warrants are equity privileges and are usually only offered to holders of specific corporate securities. Corporations find warrants a relatively safe way to raise additional money over a short period of time. When warrants are exercised, however, shareholders' equity is reduced.

Yield—This refers to an investor's return on investment. For instance, assume that you invest $10,000 in a stock. Over a period of a year, you receive $200 in dividends and $1,800 in premiums from writing calls. Additionally, when you sell the stock at the end of that year, you realize a profit of $2,000. In this case, your total yield from this investment is $4,000 or 40 percent.

Index

For Further Reading ....

The Art of Short Selling
Kathryn Staley $49.95 Item #2006

> "Kathryn Staley is the short seller's #1 analyst. Her book is a 'must read' for all equity investors." - **Harvard University Business School**

Finally, a book showing serious investors how to cash in on the latest lucrative investment trend: Short Selling. Industry expert Staley explains what it is, how it works, best type of companies to short, and never before released strategies of the top short sellers. Even in a raging bull market, millions are made by investors who short stocks - many of which are in your own portfolio. So position yourself to profit from any stock selloff, by learning to spot the best shorting candidates with this best-selling new book.

The Bear Book
Survive and Profit in Ferocious Markets
John Rothchild $24.95 Item #8449

Despite new record highs in the market, many recall the crash of Oct. 28, 1997 vividly - and don't wish to relive those painful moments! And it will happen again - it's inevitable. But this new book tells not only how to survive when a bear emerges from hibernation, but how to profit in all financial seasons. Coauthor of Peter Lynch's *One Up on Wall Street*, he includes interviews and profiles of top bearish investors.

Stocks for the Long Run, 2nd edition
A Guide to Selecting Markets for Long-Term Growth
Jeremy Siegel $29.95 Item #6021

"A simply great book," raves *Forbes*. "Belongs on every investor's shelf," says *Business Week* about this newly revised bestseller that teaches how to pinpoint opportunities that'll add to returns year after year. No "get rich quick" schemes here, just solid, balanced guidance for profiting in any market environment, based on decades of proven analysis.

Selling Short
Risks, Rewards and Strategies for Short Selling Stocks, Options & Futures
J. Walker $49.95 Item #2003

This comprehensive guide fully explain all aspects of selling short froma trader's perspective. Covers strategies for futures, options and stockshorting along with in-depth risk analysis.

Secrets for Profiting in Bull & Bear Markets
Stan Weinstein $18.95 Item #2055

Easy-to-understand, concise and hands-on methods for technical market analysis. Here are the same techniques that have made Weinstein's own market moves successful in bull and bear markets.

Short Sales and the Manipulation of Securities
Bernard Baruch $19.95 **NOW $15.00** Item #2550

Out of print for over 50 years, this privately published classic offers a well-reasoned defense of short-selling and its benefits to worldwide markets. Many investors who survived the Crash of '29 may have used information in this booklet to profit from the crash - just as it could help you in the next major market correction.